The Bicycle Touring Book

The Bicycle Touring Book

The Complete Guide to Bicycle Recreation

by Tim & Glenda Wilhelm

 Rodale Press, Emmaus, Pa.

Book design by Barbara Field
Copy edited by Susan Weiner
Cartoons by Gene Mater
Illustrations by David Bullock

Printed in the United States of America on recycled paper, containing a high percentage of de-inked fiber.

Library of Congress Cataloging in Publication Data

Wilhelm, Tim.
    The bicycle touring book.
    Bibliography: p.
    Includes index.
    1. Bicycle touring.   I. Wilhelm, Glenda, joint author. II. Title.
GV1044.W54   796.6   80–11506
ISBN 0-87857-295-3 hardcover
ISBN 0-87857-307-0 paperback

2 4 6 8 10 9 7 5 3 1 hardcover
2 4 6 8 10 9 7 5 3 1 paperback

To Kirsten and Erik,
May your roads reach.

There is more to life than increasing its speed.
Gandhi

Contents

Contents

Contents

Contents

Contents

Price Warning

The prices quoted in this book are those that were commonly applicable in 1979. We do not expect them to remain in effect for long. Please use quoted prices only as a guide for comparison of similar products.

Chapter One
What Is Bicycle Touring?

It had been a spectacular day of sunshine sprinkled with thunderstorms as only the Colorado Rocky Mountains can provide. With our nine-year-old daughter Kirsten and our two-year-old son Erik we were three weeks into what was to become a bicycle tour across America in midsummer of our nation's 200th year. But all we knew at the time was that we were well over a mile high in the middle of a range of mountains that had historically been a barrier to westward movement. We were heading east and the Rockies were proving to be a challenge.

The day delighted us as we climbed the last summit onto what seemed the top of the world. We saw a huge high basin filled with Blue Mesa Reservoir, the largest body of water in Colorado, which promised us almost level miles and no summits for the rest of the day.

Along the way people told us the pedaling would be fairly easy to Gunnison and beyond to the foot of Monarch Pass, the high point of our tour at 11,312 feet.

Kirsten pedaled her small bike ahead of us, dropping back occasionally to work with Erik who was trying to learn the alphabet from his backward view of the world in the trailer behind Glenda's bike. Kirsten had mastered the mountains up to that point and was feeling pretty good about herself and her world that summer. She was also falling in love with Colorado. None of us knew it at the time but Colorado was to be our home some four years down the road.

That night in Gunnison we enjoyed the companionship of other campers and some bicyclists in a spot somewhere on a staircase to the stars. We sat around the campfire — something we

1

The Many Faces of Bicycle Touring

Bicycle touring is a shared social experience, requiring cooperation and mutual give-and-take. These members of the Pensacola Freewheelers ride in "tandem" in the Pensacola Beach area (above). One of the real attractions of bicycle touring is that everyone can do it — together. Here a Rhode Island family takes time out for equipment adjustment during a group ride across Iowa (upper right). Bicycle camping is just another dimension of bicycle touring in which cyclists like these Pensacola Freewheelers can relax and enjoy each other's company after a hard day's ride (lower right).

Bicycle touring can be a collective celebration, as it is in the annual across-Iowa bike ride where the social dimension of the ride is as important as anything (left). Bicycle touring is travel, liberation, and freedom. It is an opportunity to explore, as in the case of these tourists cycling the TransAmerica Trail outside Breckenridge, Colorado (below).

didn't get to enjoy very often — talking, laughing, doing what strangers do when drawn together around that primitive pivot point at the end of a satisfying day.

Some of our visitors talked with the children, questioning them about the trip and how they were getting along. At one point a lady looked down at little Erik, only a few blinks away from sleep, and asked him somewhat sadly, "I'll bet you would rather be at home in your own bed right now, wouldn't you? Where is your home, honey?"

Erik's eyes didn't waver at all as he looked up at her and said, "Right here."

o o o o o o o

Being at home on your wheels wherever you happen to be is what bicycle touring is all about. It is traveling not just to go somewhere but to be completely involved in the going itself. We think of bicycle touring as more than a sport; it is a way of life that is at once simple yet sophisticated, easy yet demanding, with just the right combination of mental freedom and physical challenge — whether that is in climbing a mountain or patching a tire.

Bicycling long distances for the fun of it is an idea that is just now finding its way through the blur that is most of our lives. There have been more bicycles sold in the United States since 1970 than automobiles, which is amazing in a nation considered to be the most motorized in the world. With almost 100 million bicycles in our garages and on the roads, bicycling is the most popular participation sport in the country, more popular than fishing or camping. Yet the majority of bicycle owners are shocked at the idea of riding more than a few miles.

Many of us got our first bicycle under the Christmas tree with all the other toys, and were then turned loose at an early age, before we knew the rules of the road. Is that partly why we doubt that the bicycle could seriously compare with the automobile when it comes to getting around?

The bicycle is the most efficient means of movement known — more efficient even than a dolphin sliding through the ocean — yet we continually use two tons of nonrenewable energy-consuming metal to move ourselves — 80 percent of the time — less than eight miles from home. Of course, time is the real factor. "Lack" of it, a desire to "save" it, not wanting to "waste" it; all of those ideas keep us locked in our inefficient, expensive, smelly gas-consuming cars. To "save" time the average American devotes almost four hours a day to the automobile: driving in it, parking it, searching for it, working to pay for it and gas, insurance, taxes, tickets and cleaning. We join health spas and clubs, buy exercise machines and stress our systems with rigid diets to lose the excess weight we otherwise could simply by regularly using our bicycles as a means of transportation.

But more than saving energy, resources, time and money, bicycling offers a whole new way of looking at the world. You see, hear, smell and feel things on a bicycle that we sometimes think are far gone in this complex, industrial fast-action world of ours. The bicycle is a means of gaining control over the speed of your life, of slowing it down a little. The gas crisis is irrelevant to the bicycle tourer and commuter. We dream of being free of the hectic pace in our lives, free of much that civilization has come to mean. The bicycle offers an exciting alternative if we just see it for what it is; an inexpensive, unencumbered, exciting alternative with unlimited travel potential.

Bicycle touring extends beyond the quick ride to the grocery store or the daily ride to work and back. It is using the bicycle to travel many miles for recreation. If we master the idea of daily, consistent use of the bicycle, it is only a step further to using it for weekend and vacation travel. Accustomed to postponing recreational fun until we arrive somewhere else, the bicycle vacation begins the minute you mount up and leave home. Its range is unlimited and just about anyone can ride. Don't we mean anyone "young enough"? No, anyone physically able to can and should ride a bike since it also improves physical conditioning and health. People in their seventies regularly tour on bicycles; so do children big enough to reach the pedals (and others who aren't but go along for the ride). Many middle-aged people discover a whole new life while bicycle touring, proving that life

begins on two wheels if not at 40.

Bicycle touring can be as simple or as complicated as you wish to make it. You can begin by cleaning, oiling and pumping up that single- or 3-speed in your garage or you can go down to the local bike shop and invest from $200 to $1,000 to get started. You can stay in the very best hotels or in budget motels, or you can camp out; you can fly first-class with your bike to a touring place or you can leave from your front yard and perhaps for the first time really see the region where you live. You can travel alone, sign up on a tour with like-minded strangers or take your family along for anywhere from one day to all year.

Jack and Alice Winner use their bicycles in a variety of ways. Jack commutes 10 miles a day to work and Alice rides to the local school district office where she is a nurse. They, with their two children, join a local bicycle club for weekend rides of up to 50 miles on Saturdays with an occasional camp-out at a distant beachside park. They travel with the children two weeks each summer during their vacation. Last year they toured Yellowstone National Park and the Grand Tetons; the year before they traveled back East to visit grandparents and tour the Pennsylvania covered-bridge country and Philadelphia. Next year in autumn they plan to leave the children with grandma while they vacation with a bicycle-tour group among the inns of Vermont.

Then there is Ian Hibell. When last

5

seen he was biking across the Amazon basin. In 16 years he has toured over 100 thousand miles. (Read about him in *Bicycling* magazine; November 1973, September 1974 and December 1976.) He was the first to travel by bicycle from the tip of South America up to Alaska, the first and only one to bicycle from the Arctic Circle in Norway to the southernmost tip of Africa. At 44 he is going strong.

Dervla Murphy, a middle-aged nurse from Ireland, decided to do something different for awhile and set out alone on a single-speed bicycle to ride across Europe in the blizzard of 1964 through Afghanistan and on to India. You can read about her experiences in her book, *Full Tilt.*

This book isn't about long-distance bicycle tourers, nor is it about average people who regularly spend days and weeks touring their neighborhoods and the country on bicycles. This book is about you and your first bicycle tour, the most exciting one of all. We wrote it to encourage and help you to use your bicycle for days at a time to take you farther and farther from your home into the fascinating world of bicycle touring. If you are already riding and touring, we think you will find in these pages considerable help in filling gaps, answering questions and getting ideas to help you enjoy touring even more.

We use a step-by-step approach based on our own touring experiences, teaching bicycling safety and leading tours. As much as we would like to talk only about the aesthetics of touring itself, we must spend a seemingly disproportionate amount of space on things like frame dimensions, cadence and derailleur maintenance. If we didn't, you would not need this book at all; it is the mundane subjects such as choosing gears, getting a proper fit on your bike, and learning how to care for it that will not only get you out to where you can find your own aesthetics but will keep you there long enough to enjoy them.

In the following chapters we take you from choosing a touring bicycle through fitting it properly and learning to ride efficiently and smoothly, to choosing the best auxiliary equipment for your needs. We discuss clothing best suited to touring and how to carry everything on the bicycle safely. We talk about things you need to know for planning your tours and about camping by bicycle as an option we hope you will try, to extend your range and enjoyment. We take you through a typical touring day and discuss group touring, a subject of interest to many. The last chapters on physical conditioning, food and maintenance are essential to everyone for successful touring.

As with any subject worth learning, it is worth learning well. Throughout the book we stress the need for hands-on experience; read with your bicycle nearby so you can see what we are talking about. Perform the various procedures, practice things at home, learn the terminology and you will enhance the hours you spend on the road.

This approach to bicycle touring is one way, our way, but it is not the only way. You will meet, talk with and read others who do not see things as we do, who have opposing ideas about equipment, technique, even touring itself. Bicycling is a strong opinion-producing sport, perhaps because the people who do it care about it very much. We would have it no other way. We present to you our ideas, knowledge, experience and reasoning; it is up to you to take what meets your needs and make it part of your own set of values and knowledge.

The most important factor in any tour had to be omitted from this book because we know nothing about it — that is your own mental attitude. It will make or break a tour quicker than any amount of mechanical difficulties or bad weather. If you are the proverbial pessimist who sees a half-full glass of water as half-empty, it might be good to consider packing an optimist along on your tour. But you must be used to seeing the world that way so maybe it works for you. Tim tends toward the pessimistic direction while Glenda pulls hard the other way; we seem to manage well somewhere between the two extremes on tour.

But something you really can't do well without is flexibility. Being able to adapt to whatever comes along is partly the result of preparation and skill development, but for some it is just a way of life. Adaptability will see you farther down the road than anything else you can pack in your panniers. The rest of what lies between the covers of this book will only add to your preparation, strengthen your skills and we hope inspire you to begin.

Use this book as a guide in learning about and planning for touring. It should help you to think about things you would otherwise have forgotten, to avoid some problems you would otherwise have encountered and to gain more fun out of your touring life than if you had not read it. Most of all we hope it gets you out on your bicycle seeing what there is to see with the least possible amount of trouble and a maximum of joy.

Chapter Two
Choosing a Touring Bicycle

In order to choose a good touring bicycle, you must first understand exactly what a touring bicycle is and how it differs from other bikes. Some say it is any bicycle not meant for serious racing. Others see it as a bicycle specifically designed for use on long-distance, cross-country or around-the-world adventures, and say it is as rare as a clean bike chain. We see the touring bicycle as one suitable for journeys of more than 50 miles a day and, most important, one that can be ridden day after day with the greatest safety, comfort and efficiency possible.

There is no single "best" touring bicycle, rather a continuum along which some meet the needs of touring cyclists better than others. Final selection is usually a blend of knowledge, experience, prejudice, capital availability, peer pressure and vague gut feelings.

We hope the knowledge you gain here will lead you to the touring bike that is best for you.

How Many Speeds?

The 1-speed bicycle with its single front chainwheel (see Figure 1) and single rear cog cannot be shifted as the terrain varies to allow the cyclist to maintain a regular cadence or pedaling rhythm. This, along with the substantial weight of the 1-speed, eliminates it from our discussion of touring machines although 1-speeds have been ridden across country and even around the world.

The 3-speed bicycle has some touring possibilities. It has a well-designed, rugged, multi-speed gear selection mechanism in the rear hub, which is

Choosing a Touring Bicycle

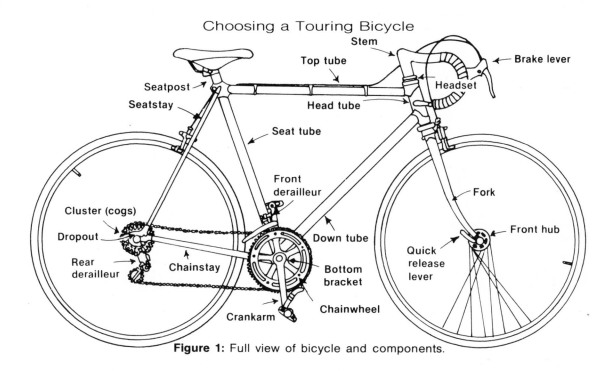

Figure 1: Full view of bicycle and components.

controlled with a narrow cable moved by a shifting lever that is usually mounted on the handlebar. Three-speed advantages are simplicity of operation, rugged construction, completely enclosed mechanism, minimal maintenance, ease of gear selection and a relatively low cost. However, you are strictly limited to a few gears. The rear cog and front chainwheel can be changed or close- or wide-ratio hubs installed, but you still end up with only three specific gear choices. That may be fine in a basically flat, sort-of-uphill, sort-of-downhill world, but in tough terrain and wind conditions 3-speeds are restrictive. The 4-speed or 5-speed internal rear hub is better than 3, but still is less adaptable to the individual rider than 10-speeds.

A final negative aspect of the 3-speed is that the basic bicycle is usually heavy, cheap and poorly designed. With inclination and cash you can produce a very acceptable 3-speed from quality parts or convert a 10-speed, but be prepared to pay the tariff.

For an individual wanting only to tour relatively short distances over mild terrain, such a 3-speed would make a lot of sense.

The majority of moderate-distance tourers would be better off on simple, trusty 3-speeds but we know of no high-quality, lightweight (under 30 pounds with alloy wheels) 3-speed available on today's market. Hopefully, some are on the drawing boards. Tim built his own 3-speed for commuting and around-town riding. It is a joy to ride but cost well

Three-speed hub mechanism.

Rear derailleur/cog interrelationship.

Cluster/freewheel.

quality 3-speed or 5-speed bicycle for the American market; it is overdue.

Most people automatically think of a derailleur-activated multi-speed bicycle when shopping for a bike. Such bicycles have either a single, double or triple chainwheel in combination with five or six rear cogs (cluster). The cluster is attached to a freewheel, which allows the chain to be driven at various speeds regardless of the wheel speed itself. The rear derailleur moves the chain over the rear cogs to change the drive ratio according to which cogs are engaged. The front derailleur moves the chain from one chainwheel to another.

A 5-speed bicycle has five rear cogs with a single front chainwheel. A 10-speed has two front chainwheels with five rear cogs giving 10 combina-

over $200 and took more time than Glenda likes to talk about. Perhaps some manufacturer will produce a high-

Arrow points to front derailleur attached to seat tube, positioned over chainwheel.

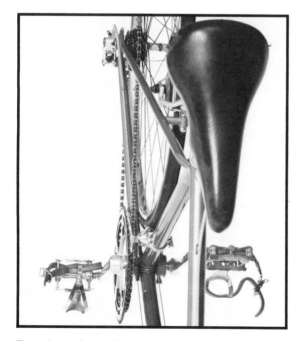

Top view of two front chainwheels and five rear cogs.

tions (gears). The 15-speed is like the 5-speed and 10-speed but with three chainwheels making 15 gear possibilities. Some bicycles have rear clusters of six or even seven cogs to produce 12-speeds, 14-speeds, and 18-speeds. Because manufacturers are always bringing out new products, a variety of gearing systems is inevitable with the newest usually promoted as the best.

Since multi-speed derailleur bicycles dominate the adult market in the United States and lend themselves well to the needs of the bicycle tourer, most cyclists choose their touring bikes from among them. But how many speeds are enough? Since the passing of the English racer 3-speed with upright handlebars, the American public has been bombarded with advertising and peer pressures implying that a "serious" cyclist must have a 10-speed bicycle. Although true for the cycle tourist riding more than 25 miles in hills and with baggage, 10-speeds are really unnecessary for most short-distance recreational riders and commuters.

At first glance the 5-speed seems to offer just enough speeds with only one derailleur. Beginning riders easily master a single rear derailleur with its five gear choices, but the additional front chainwheel and derailleur on a 10-speed seem just too much at first. However once the concept is mastered, the 5-speed too frequently becomes an expensive experiment on the way to a 10-speed. There are not many quality 5-speeds around; they are at the lower end of most bicycle lines and consequently have a lower resale value. If you really can't fathom 10-speeds or are a beginning rider, it is better to convert a good 10-speed into a 5-speed by doing away with one chainwheel or simply not using the front derailleur at all. You can either use your rear cluster as is or regear it in a suitable 5-speed range. You will still have a quality 10-speed with the option of returning it to its original gearing, yet you will be suiting your own riding needs rather than accepting a Madison Avenue version of what your needs are.

OK. If a 10-speed is good, isn't a 15-speed better? Unfortunately, that extra chainwheel adds more than its share of trouble. Both front and rear derailleurs must be of special design to accommodate the extra chain length and greater range between the largest and smallest chainwheels. Adjustment and operation require special care to insure trouble-free shifting. Both chainstay and axle length are critical for correct operation. Finally, unless you fully understand the functioning of the various gear combinations, much of the advantage of those extra gears will be lost in sloppy shifting by the rider. More is not necessarily better when it comes to multi-speed bicycles unless you live in mountainous terrain or have considerable experience backed by personal preference.

Does adding a sixth cog (as in a 12-speed) increase gearing capacity without the hassles of that extra chainwheel? Well, nothing is free. To accommodate the extra width of the sixth cog, the dish (offsetting of the rear hub to make room for the freewheel while allowing the tire to run centered in the frame) must be increased in most instances. This makes the angle at which the spokes run to the rim more severe, producing a less laterally stable wheel. In other words, for two extra gears you sacrific some rear wheel strength, which is critical in touring bicycles.

Some manufacturers have introduced 12-speeds with thinner spacers between the cogs so six fit in the space normally used by five. This maintains wheel strength but a thinner chain is needed. How that thinner chain holds up under stress is an open question. What happens when a chain or cluster needs replacing but the local bike shop on your tour doesn't stock that "exotic" gear? Simplicity is of major importance in our personal touring philosophy so we suggest careful consideration of the advantages over the disadvantages of the 12-speed system on a long-distance touring bicycle. Innovations are always being made, but make sure they are substantial improvements, not just changes.

One innovation worth looking at is the Shimano EX Freehub, an integral hub-and-freewheel combination that offers many advantages over the standard hub-and-freewheel system. There is a reduction in the spoke dish required on both 5- and 6-speed assemblies, which makes for stronger wheels.

Right now cog selection is somewhat limited, extending to only 28 teeth. This might be the trend of the future, but for now we are sticking to our reliable five-cog freewheel with easy-to-find-and-service parts. When touring, stick to the proven and reliable; leave innovations and "ultimate" components to the weekend rider who can always walk home or call for help. When new equipment is proven and commonly available, then is the time to change if it is truly something better, not to change for the sake of change alone.

Frames

The frame is the largest, most expensive, and most important single component of your touring machine. Just about everything else can be changed but once you choose a specific bike you are pretty well stuck with that particular frame. Frames differ in material, construction and design.

Material

Most standard frames today are produced from steel alloy tubing. This varies in specific strength and properties depending on its purity, materials used, and the percentage of various additives, specifically carbon, chrome-molybdenum and manganese-molybdenum. At the very least, the frame on a touring bike should be high carbon or high tensile; chrome-molybdenum or manganese-molybdenum (Reynolds 531) is an even better choice. Better material means greater strength, which in turn allows for thinner, more resilient walls with a higher yield strength (the point at which a bent tube will not return to its original shape). Resilience and strength translate into a more comfortable ride on a touring bicycle; the tubing flexes and springs back quickly and can take greater stress without becoming deformed. You will appreciate this most as you put on many miles over rough roads with a loaded bicycle.

Most inexpensive bike frames have plain-gauge, pipelike tubing with the same wall thickness throughout. The structural strength of the material used determines the thickness of the walls and the purpose for which it is used. Most of the force exerted on the diamond-shaped bicycle frame occurs where the tubes are joined. The tubing must be thick enough to withstand force at these major junctions as well as the heat that is applied during the actual brazing process.

Another type of tubing is "double butted." Generally found on specific tubes on better bicycles ($200 and up), this tubing is thicker at both ends and thinner through the center of the tube. This gives adequate strength at highly stressed joints yet it is lighter and lets the tube flex in the center for a more comfortable ride. Not all tubes used in a cycle frame are double butted. Even on the highest quality frames, double-butted tubes are usually used only for the top and down tubes (see Figure 1).

13

The seat tube, generally, is single butted (thicker at one end only), as is the steerer tube, which attaches the fork to the main frame body through the head tube. The fork blades are taper gauge (thicker walls at the top tapering toward the dropout) on Reynolds and a few other brands of butted tubing. The head tube, chainstays, and seatstays are all plain-gauge tubing. If you doubt these facts or talk with bicycle shop personnel who contradict them, refer to Table 3.2 on pages 44-45 in *DeLong's Guide to Bicycles & Bicycling*.

Manufacturers seem content to keep consumers guessing by not using specific decals stating exact information on materials and construction in the various tubes on a single frame. Most gloss over the information or even mislead through generalizations. You cannot see the inside of most tubes so you must rely on manufacturers' decals. Carefully read specifications to make sure you are actually getting what you think you are getting and are paying for in frame tubing.

Butted tubing comes in various weights (wall thicknesses), depending on intended use. The earliest manufacturer, Reynolds of England, is still the most prestigious name in tubing for touring bikes. Reynolds 531 is probably the most commonly used material in top-quality bicycles in the world. Many other companies produce top-quality double-butted tubes, including Vitus (France), Columbus (Italy), Champion (Japan), and Ishiwata (Japan). All make excellent tubing but the relative merits of each are matters for conjecture.

Some manufacturers have specific design features that better suit their product to different riding needs. On the whole, however, we are not so sure that the difference in various brands of similar-weight tubing can be detected by a rider on a fully loaded touring bike. More important, given good-quality tubing, are the actual fitting together of the tubes, workmanship, and the design of angles and lengths of the tubes themselves.

Construction

Workmanship is a difficult factor to determine unless you can actually witness the factory procedure. In lieu of that, you must rely on the manufacturer's reputation and guarantee and dealer recommendations. Frame failure on moderate- and higher-priced bicycles is infrequent and most manufacturers stand solidly behind their products. Still, in this buyer-beware world there are some surface checks you can make to reassure yourself and reinforce the manufacturer's claims. But first you must understand the process by which tubes are joined to make a frame.

The two most common joining methods on higher-priced bicycles are "lugged" and "lugless." Lugless hand-brazed joints are seldom found on production-line bikes — Viscount is an exception. In lugless types each tube is cut to fit the adjoining tube perfectly (mitered), then a bronze bead (fillet) is

Lugless frame joints.

Lugged frame joints.

brazed completely around the joint. These high-quality bike frames are not welded, a process that can make the tubing brittle. Instead they are brazed, using lower temperatures and relying on the bronze or other material to make the actual bond.

Lugged construction is more commonly used than lugless. Some manufacturers use an internal lug that is not visible from the outside and produces a frame that may be mistaken for a lugless frame; some Schwinn models are an example. Lugs are malleable steel sleeves made at specific angles, which fit over two mitered connecting tubes at the point where they join. They are brazed into place by filling the space between the lug and the tube with molten brazing material, usually a bronze alloy. In some cases lugs are silver-brazed into place. Silver brazing is stronger and can be applied at lower temperatures, which

makes for an extremely strong joint.

Once the lugs are in place they are finished by filing the area around the joint to remove any sign of the brazing material. Here is your best clue to the quality of workmanship that has gone into a single frame. Is the lugwork smooth and clean looking? Are there bits of brazing material or little pin holes around the joint? You can't determine the tolerances in the mitering process or whether the lug has been completely filled with brazing material, but you can see if care was used to finish and paint it. Check several bikes of the same make and model to determine if they show the same quality control. If workmanship varies a great deal between the bikes, look at a different manufacturer's line. Don't assume any manufacturer produces only top-quality frames; even the best have their lemons.

The comparative strength of lugged versus lugless construction is debatable. Most high-quality bicycle frames are made with lugs, but many tandems and custom frames are lugless. Workmanship, rather than method of construction, is a better test of frames from the consumer's viewpoint.

Design

Design here refers to the length and angles of tubes on the frame itself. This really differentiates the touring frame from the racing or recreational frame and is easily detected by the discerning buyer. When you go shopping for your touring bicycle, take a tape measure and read the specification booklets carefully to make sure you are looking at a touring frame instead of one designed for racing. A touring frame will give you a more comfortable ride, because of its longer, lower construction.

The seat tube angle is measured between the top tube and the seat tube where they join under the seat (see Figure 2). This angle has varied over the years but generally a seat tube angle of 72 or 73 degrees is standard on touring bikes, whereas a larger angle (more vertical seat tube) of 74 or more degrees shows that the frame was designed for racing.

Another important measurement is the length of the chainstay. This largely determines the bicycle's adaptability to

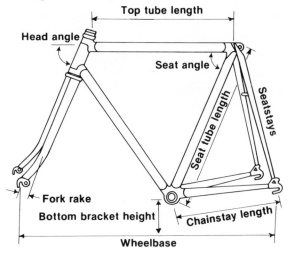

Figure 2: Basic frame angles and dimensions.

wider range, especially 15-speed gearing. Without a long-enough chainstay the angle of the chain (viewed from above) as it moves over the chainwheels in relation to the rear cogs is greater, putting more stress on the chain and causing more difficult shifting. The longer the chainstay, the smaller the angle between shifting extremes, hence the easier and less wearing the shifting process. Short chainstays also make removing the rear wheel difficult if fenders (mudguards) are attached, and can mean inadequate heel clearance for rear panniers. We consider 17¼ inches the absolute minimum length for touring chainstays, with 17½ or 17¾ inches being a much better choice.

Fork rake is important to the riding comfort and handling of a touring bike. The greater the rake, the more forgiving the steering and the smoother the ride.

Fork rake is the amount of bend a manufactuer puts into the front forks of the frameset. Most touring bikes have a rake in excess of two inches, measured between the straight line of the fork and the center of the front wheel axle (see Figure 2).

These three design features — seat tube angle, chainstay length and fork rake — tell you what the builder had in mind in producing a specific frameset. They are the components of one single measurement, "wheelbase," which is frequently used alone to determine the suitability of a touring frame. Wheelbase is the overall length from the center of the front axle to the center of the rear axle. Generally, 40½ inches is the absolute minimum for an acceptable wheelbase (23-inch frame) in a double-butted touring bicycle. Don't settle for less. This measurement varies with different frame sizes; larger bikes have longer wheelbases and smaller bikes have proportionately shorter ones. The separate measurements of seat tube angle, chainstay length and fork rake give you a more accurate picture of your bike frame's suitability for touring.

You will probably hear references to frame "stiffness" somewhere along the line. It means different things to different riders, but generally it refers to a frame's ability to transfer power from the rider directly to the rear wheel without loss through frame flex. A stiff frame can mean a stiff ride, but not necessarily. It is possible to design a bike to be stiff laterally (maximum power is exerted

to the rear wheels with minimum whip or fishtailing), yet maintain a comfortable ride. Good frame angles, a long chainstay, deeper fork rake, resilient material and clean workmanship not only make the touring bicycle comfortable mile after mile, but also make it efficient in transferring rider power to the rear triangle. Your best bet is to ride as many different bikes as possible to determine for yourself which frame feels best for you.

Cranksets

The crankset consists of two crankarms (which hold the pedals), chainwheels (which engage the chain and determine the gear), and the bottom bracket assembly with its axle, fixed and adjustable cups, lockring and bearings to hook it all to the frame.

On most less-expensive machines the crankset is one piece, and is called an Ashtabula after one of the manufacturers. This type of crankset consists of a solid steel, one-piece crankarm/axle arrangement onto which the chainwheels are attached. Although extremely strong, inexpensive and easy to service, it is not found on touring bicycles because it is heavy and makes it difficult to replace worn chainwheels or to change gear combinations.

Another crankset is the cottered three-piece type. The crankarms are held on the axle by tapered cotters that wedge against the axle. This allows for

Parts of crankset (top to bottom) — chainwheel and crankarms, crankarm, lockrings, cups, bearings, and axle.

One-piece Ashtabula crankset.

Cottered crankset.

a variety of axle and crank lengths and can be fitted (on most models) with a wide selection of chainwheels. It is lighter than the one-piece crank and is available in aluminum alloy. However, the cotters tend to work loose or malfunction. On the majority of better touring bicycles, three-piece cottered cranks are being replaced with cotterless cranksets.

The cotterless crankset, made of aluminum alloy, is held in place with steel bolts or nuts that force the crankarms onto the tapered axle. Removal takes a special tool set but is relatively simple. Cotterless cranksets range in price from $30 to over $100. You usually get what you pay for in design and quality of materials. On cheaper sets be sure

Cotterless crankset.

Brakes

There are three main braking systems — sidepull, centerpull and cantilever. Most factory production bicycles come with one of the first two. All are caliper systems.

Sidepulls are "in" on most moderately priced bicycles. Their popularity is partially due to the variety of models available and to their high grade of finishing. They are lighter than centerpulls since their simple design requires less material. The cable and housing run directly to the brake without the need for specific attachments for hanging gear. Easier installation and cleaner looks, along with firm action, add to their popularity with racers. All of these factors are important to the competitive cyclist but we question how important they are to the tourer. However, several of the past Tour de France bicycle races have been won by riders using centerpull brakes so maybe the pendulum will swing away from sidepulls.

Sidepulls are popular for all the wrong reasons. They are difficult to keep centered on the rim (especially in cheaper models), which makes for inefficient braking. More important, it generally takes more hand pressure on the lever to put a braking force on the rim equal to centerpulls, especially with the cheaper sidepulls. There seems to be a direct relationship between the amount paid for sidepulls and stopping power. It is a bad situation when price is usually

you can change both chainwheels if you want. On some the right crankarm is permanently attached to the outer chainwheel, making replacement of that chainwheel alone impossible.

You may be happy with the stock gear range on a particular crankset, but check the manufacturer's range of chainwheel sizes available in stock. Some chainwheels are not available in the smaller sizes. There are only a few models of the triple chainwheels necessary for 15-speeds. The TA Cyclotouriste is the most versatile, having chainwheels available with 26-68 teeth on both double and triple sets. The TA is seldom found on production bikes so it must be substituted or be put on a custom bike. If the frame you select has a crankset you don't like, the TA is worth considering.

Sidepull brakes.

Centerpull brakes.

the main criterion for production components.

A touring bike requires brakes with a longer reach to handle the built-in allowance for fenders and larger tires. Reach is the length of brake arm between the mounting bolt and the brake pad. As the reach becomes greater, the brake is more flexible but more inefficient unless constructed of sufficiently heavy material. Most sidepulls are not so constructed; even some higher-quality ones have such a short reach that they won't fit on a touring fork and frame.

Centerpulls are less common on production models, perhaps due to their cost as well as the fact that sidepulls are generally better finished. Centerpulls have more parts, are thicker and heavier than sidepulls. This is a plus factor for the touring bike as heavier construction means less flex in the yoke arms on brakes with the long reach necessary for touring frame dimensions. Because centerpulls pivot on either side of the yoke arm at a point closer to the rim than on sidepulls, there is considerably less flex and a more positive, efficient action. The centerpull design requires less hand power to achieve good leverage on the rims and the pads are more prone to stay centered. Finally, a high-quality centerpull costs less than a high-quality sidepull.

Are centerpulls all positive? Hardly. They require special attachments where the brake cable leaves the brake housing, and they are definitely not as clean and simple looking as the sidepull. Some dislike their spongier, less responsive feeling due to the extra material and design geometry. You will have to decide for yourself which is best for your bike.

No matter which brake you use, stay away from so-called "safety levers," which extend from the normal brake levers and are parallel to the top portion of the handlebar. In an emergency-stop situation, especially if the brakes are even slightly out of adjustment, safety levers will not give you the stopping power needed because of their faulty design and limited lever ac-

tion. If your bike has them, remove them or ask that they be removed before you develop the bad habit of relying on them. Removal is a simple operation and should not involve extra cost.

The third type of brake on the market is the cantilever. This brake requires a braze-on fitting (boss) on the front forks and seatstays so it can be mounted directly onto the frame. Unusually large brake pads increase the cantilever's stopping ability. This brake is very rigid with a simple, powerful stopping action. Usually found on tandems and occasionally on custom touring frames, it is rarely stock on production bicycles.

Brakes are a highly controversial subject among avid bicyclists. Feelings and opinions run strong so it is best to

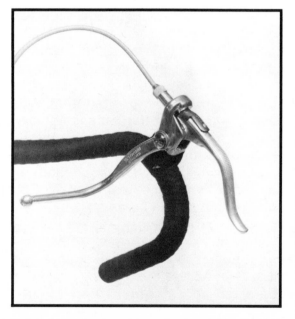

Safety lever (appears here horizontal to the top of the handlebar). For better braking performance, we recommend removal of these levers.

Cantilever brakes.

listen to various knowledgeable touring cyclists, then decide for yourself on the basis of your own experience and the importance you place on the differing opinions. The brake pad itself is usually ignored in discussions of leverage, design and reputation. The type, condition and fit of the pad are extremely important, as are brake cable and housing quality. Most important overall is the attention given to maintaining close tolerances between the brake pad and the rim; that is the job of the cyclist (see chapter fourteen).

Upright handlebars (all rounders).

Handlebars

Handlebars are as critical to riding comfort as brakes are to operation. The three types of handlebars are upright, racing and randonneur.

Upright bars allow the rider to sit in a relatively upright position and are usually found on lower-priced and mixte-style (straight-bar women's frame) bikes. They give short-ride comfort and easier visibility on commuter and around-town bicycles, although "serious" cyclists tend to look down on them. They are excellent for those who use their bikes only occasionally, for those who may have trouble balancing or are just getting used to riding a bike again after many years, and for those who spend most of their time riding in heavy traffic. For these situations, the upright "all rounder" is an especially good choice.

Upright bars are not best for long-distance touring because the body is not nearly as efficient at pedaling while sitting upright as in the drop position. Power is lost on the seat rather than distributed through arms and legs for more powerful strokes. The vertebrae are compressed against one another with each bump so that the back is actually more comfortable stretched out in the drop position. Wind resistance is greater in the upright position and, finally, the hands are restricted to just one position on the bars.

Most production 10-speeds have the racing (*maes* or drop-style) handlebar. It comes in a variety of shapes but all are flat across the top and have the characteristic ram's-horn drop or curl. This style does away with most negative aspects of the upright ride and is used successfully by many cycle tourists. It

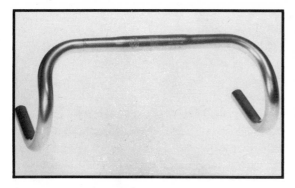

Drop racing handlebars.

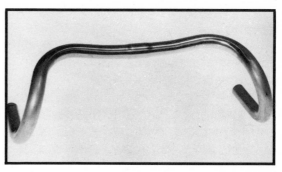

Randonneur handlebars (compare with the drop handlebars photograph at left).

does not, however, offer the refinements of the randonneur, specialized touring bar.

The randonneur is shaped basically like the racing bar but its drop is not as deep. The rider is able to use the drop position with less discomfort for the neck and upper back. The bar bends slightly upward and forward across the top to give the rider more comfortable hand positioning when riding on the top of the bars. A variety of hand positions helps prevent or alleviate pinching of the ulnar nerve in the hand, which can be permanently damaged when pinched for a long length of time while riding with your hands in the same position.

Randonneur bars in combination with padded riding gloves and handlebar tape help alleviate this condition if the rider uses a variety of hand positions on the bars. You can change from racing to randonneur bars anytime or you can have the dealer do it for you (for a small fee) before you take home your new bike. We highly recommend them for those contemplating lengthy touring or rides of more than a few hours a day.

Shifters

Shifters move the derailleurs that in turn move the chain over the cogs and chainwheels. There are three types, differentiated mainly by their location.

The stem shifter is located on the handlebar stem (gooseneck). Common on machines in the lower to moderate price range, it is usually found in combination with safety levers to allow braking and shifting while the rider is in the upright position. This is a popular arrangement, although we wonder why bother with drop bars at all if everything is done while upright? In order to shift stem shifters, you must move your hand inward. For some this is an unstable and awkward maneuver. Some stem shifters extend ominously above the handlebars of the bike. If ever you take that infa-

Stem-mounted shifters.

Down-tube shifters.

mous trip over the handlebars, or even get thrown against them, you will gain a better understanding of this negative aspect of stem shifters.

Another shifter is located on the down tube, and is favored on most moderate- and higher-priced bikes. Situated about three to six inches back from the head tube, it is simple, reliable and out of harm's way. It is the most positive and quick acting of the shifting mechanisms because it requires the shortest amount of cable to reach each of the derailleurs. But with it down there, somewhere, it can be awkward to reach, especially if you are not riding in a down position when you want or need to shift. Your hand must leave the handlebar completely while reaching down to a position somewhere behind your spin-

ning front wheel. Once you are used to this, it is not nearly as disconcerting as it sounds, but don't practice in heavy traffic or while coasting downhill. Some riders report uneasiness at having to spread the legs somewhat to make the shift. This is especially bothersome when pushing up a steep hill on a heavily loaded bike as you lose power and cadence during the maneuver. However, many experienced touring cyclists are happy with and defensive about their down-tube shifters.

A growing number of riders are turning to bar-end (fingertip) shifters. Located at the extreme tip of the drop handlebar, the cable housing runs underneath the handlebar tape to just before the brake lever where it emerges and travels to the derailleurs. Because

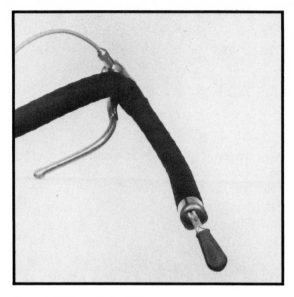

Bar-end (fingertip) shifters.

of the extra cable, bar-end shifters have a less-positive shift but their added convenience somewhat balances out that drawback. You don't have to remove your hand from the handlebar in order to shift — the primary advantage — and this is great when negotiating heavy traffic, high winds or steep grades. With practice you can shift with the palm and two small fingers while maintaining complete control of the bicycle.

If you decide you want bar-end shifters, have them installed before you take your new bike home. They should cost under $20 and the trade-in value of the stock shifter helps defray the installation fee. If you aren't sure about bar ends, borrow a bike that has them from a friend and ride it long enough to be-

come comfortable with the shifting process. Don't switch if you are happy with what you have.

Wheels

All of the components covered so far are critically important to the basic structure and performance of your touring bicycle. If chosen wisely in the beginning, they won't require much time or thought while you are out on tour. Not so with your wheels. Wheels, made up of hubs, spokes, rims and tires, are the bike's single, most important feature in daily performance, reliability and safety. The spokes and tires are usually first to fail on a tour and will to a certain extent determine the amount of time you spend enjoying your tour as opposed to the time you spend sitting along the roadside making repairs or looking for someone to make repairs for you. If you must cut corners when buying a new bike or refitting a used one, look for savings in some component other than wheels.

Hubs

The two hub types found on production bicycles are high flange and low flange. The flange is where the spokes attach to the hub; high or low refers to the distance from the center of the axle. High-flange hubs are heavier due to their extra material, require

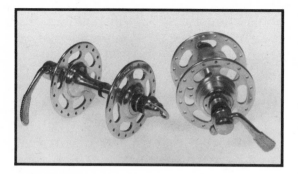

High-flange hubs.

Low-flange hubs.

require no specialized tools, have easily obtainable spare parts, but require periodic maintenance. The choice is whether you prefer to do your own maintenance (or remember to have it done) or whether you like to simply forget about it until the sealed unit needs replacement.

Be aware of hub prices. The quality difference between a $15 hub set and one for $50 is tremendous. When buying a production bike, ask to see the same brand and model of hub alone. Compare it to hubs on other more-expensive and less-expensive bikes and ask the price of the hub by itself. A quality hub is worth a lot on a touring bicycle; unless you have experience or someone to guide you, price is your best indication as to quality.

Spokes

Spokes attach the rest of the wheel to the hub and come in different lengths, thicknesses, shapes and materials. Most bikes have galvanized-steel spokes; the better types are the most reliable spokes on the market. They don't rust but will turn a flat gray with exposure to the elements. Some bikes have chrome-plated spokes. They look great for awhile, but will eventually rust through. There is a trend now toward stainless-steel spokes. These hold their shine indefinitely but cheaper grades are brittle and more prone to breakage than the best galvanized spokes. If you

slightly shorter spokes, and make for a stronger wheel but a harsher ride. Lighter, low-flange hubs use longer spokes, which weaken the wheel laterally somewhat but soften the ride. The choice is yours and most cyclists have strong opinions about flanges.

Hubs come with sealed bearings or with the traditional, nonsealed cones and bearings found on most production bicycles. Sealed bearing hubs need no maintenance for the life of the bearings but sometimes require special tools and parts for complete replacement when they wear out. Nonsealed bearing hubs, on the other hand, are easy to adjust,

Double-butted spokes. Note thickening at nipple end.

Three-cross (3X) spoke pattern (crosses marked with pointers).

prefer stainless steel, DT (Swiss made) spokes are your best choice with actual strength properties superior to galvanized-steel spokes.

Spokes are either straight (plain gauge) or double butted. Double-butted spokes are thinner through the center portion of the spoke and thicker at each end. Since most spoke breakage occurs at the end around the curved head, strength is not sacrificed for the slight savings in weight.

Spoke thickness (gauge) differs with intended use. Most spokes for 10-speeds are 14-16 gauge (the higher the gauge, the thinner the spoke). For a touring bicycle meant to carry packs and panniers, straight 14-gauge spokes are a good choice. Double-butted spokes should be $^{14}/_{16}$ or $^{14}/_{15}$ gauge.

Spoke length is determined by whether it is a high- or low-flange hub,

the make of the rim, and the number of times the individual spoke crosses neighboring spokes from hub to rim. The greater the number of crossings the more flex there is in the wheel and the smoother the ride. All touring bikes have either a three- or four-cross (3X or 4X) pattern.

What spoke pattern to use is determined by the type of ride anticipated, the load to be carried by the bicycle (both rider and baggage), the type of hub (high or low flange) and the individual preference of the rider. Endless discussions and heated arguments occur over wheel patterns. For the sake of simplicity (or oversimplification, as some will say), Tim's suggestions for wheel configuration, assuming 14 straight-gauge or $^{14}/_{15}$ double-butted spokes, are as follows: for those who want a rigid, solid-feeling pair of wheels, use high-flange hubs with three-cross (3X) spoking; for those wanting a resilient, smooth-riding pair of wheels, use low-flange hubs with four-cross (4X) spoking. He recommends Robergel Sport $^{14}/_{15}$ galvanized or DT 14-gauge stainless spokes.

The ultimate quality of the wheel depends on the skill and patience of the individual who builds it. Wheel building is not learned overnight. It takes experience and a definite feel for the job, so look around carefully before selecting a wheel builder.

Rims

Rims are made of chrome-plated steel on most lower-priced general-purpose bicycles. They are good looking, strong and heavy. They stand up to considerable abuse but add appreciably to the weight of the wheel and consequently to the amount of energy needed to get the bicycle moving or to stop it in wet conditions. Because the weight of the wheels is, within limits, the most important factor in determining responsiveness in a bicycle, steel rims have no place on a long-distance touring bicycle.

Aluminum-alloy rims are standard on most moderately priced bicycles (over $200). If properly built and not abused, good-quality alloy rims give excellent service; the better grades provide nearly the strength of the best grade of steel. Some of the better brands of box-type construction rims are Super Champion, Mavic, Weinmann and Rigida.

Tires

Tires are of two types, tubulars (sew ups) and clinchers (wired ons). A tubular casing is made of silk, cotton or nylon material with a thin tube actually stitched inside. Tubulars are very light and thin, weighing only 150-330 grams (5-12 oz.). Tubulars are held on a special rim with a coating of cement or double-faced tape. Advantages are obvious: both tire and rim are very light; they have minimal rolling resistance; they are easy to remove when necessary; and they are highly resilient due to almost complete surface exposure outside the rim. This latter point needs some explanation. Resiliency is the ability of a tire to spring back to its original shape after being compressed by an object on the road. It gives the wheel that lively quality associated with responsive bicycles. If all other factors are equal, the more tire area outside the rim, the more resilient the ride.

Tubulars have many disadvantages. They cost $10-$40 each although that wouldn't be so bad if they lasted longer; but they are fragile and prone to flats, especially the cheaper ones. Tubulars are difficult to patch as they must be opened up once off the rim to expose

Tubular tire, unmounted. (Tube is completely enclosed in tire.)

Clincher tire, unmounted (no tube).

the tube, then must be resewn after the tube is patched. (Most riders using tubular tires carry spares and save patching for later.) Tubulars and their special 700-millimeter rims are not generally available in nonspecialized bike shops. Except for excellent road conditions and with light loads, we don't recommend tubulars for touring bicyclists.

Clincher tires, more correctly known as wired ons, are found on virtually all production-line touring bicycles. Usually made with nylon casings, they have a wire, nylon or fiberglass bead extending around the inner portion of the tire on both sides. When a tube is

placed in the tire on the rim and inflated, it pushes the bead against the rim to hold the tire on.

Clinchers are heavier than tubulars, weighing 200-520 grams (7-19 oz.), and the lower-quality models have greater rolling resistance. They are harder to remove from the rims and are less resilient since more of the tire is enclosed by the rim. However, they are less expensive ($4-$10) than tubulars, easier to patch, safer in that they are more securely held on the rim, more readily available, less prone to puncture, and more durable. Better brands stand up to thousands of miles of wear.

Schrader valve.

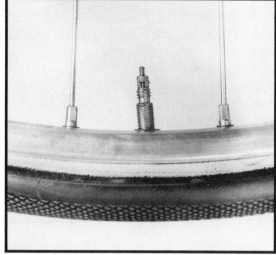

Presta valve.

Tubes for clincher tires come with two types of valves. The Schrader valve is more common in the United States. Since it is the same as the valve on automobile tires, it can be filled by any gas station or bicycle air pump. The other type is the Presta, or European style. It is narrower than the Schrader 'with a small, nutlike fitting that must be opened before filling with air. Presta valves need either a specialized pump head or an adapter in order to be filled with a pump having a Schrader valve fitting. Tubes with Presta valves are difficult to find while Schrader valve tubes are available everywhere in North America. Stick with Schrader valves unless you are planning a trip to Europe. Tubular tire tubes come with Presta-type valves.

Unless you can work out an ami-able exchange with the dealer when your bike is new, it is best to use up the poorer-quality stock tires, then switch to high-quality replacements. Some of the better heavy-duty tires (27 × 1¼ inch) suitable for long-distance touring are Schwinn Le Tours, Michelin High Speeds and Michelin Sports for heavy-duty use and poor or gravel roads, and Specialized Bicycle Imports Touring Tire for lighter duty on good paved roads. Michelin Fifties also are good for the latter.

The cycling world is undergoing a revolution in rim and tire size. For several years there has been a movement away from the standard 27 × 1¼-inch tire toward a narrower width. First came the 27 × 1⅛-inch tire; now many bikes are coming off the line with 27 × 1-inch tires. There is also considerable interest by some cyclists in converting their 27-inch tires over to the European equivalent 700C. The 700C tire, although close, is not interchangeable; it requires a special 700C rim. Once again, unless you are planning an extended tour in Europe, you are better off with the more readily available 27-inch tire and rim.

The movement toward thinner tires on production bicycles is probably a result of amateur racers' expressed desires to move away from the expensive, fragile tubular tire to narrower and

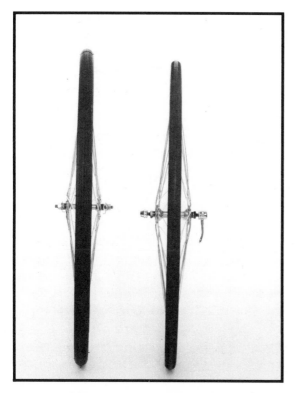

Frontal view of a 27 × 1¼-inch tire and a 27 × 1-inch tire, mounted. Note different thicknesses in tire profiles.

tougher clinchers for training purposes. Since bicycle innovations have historically come from the racing element, manufacturers have begun to stock thinner wheels on most of their moderate- to higher-priced bicycles even though some of those are designated and designed for touring, not racing. This makes us wonder what the manufacturing concept is of a touring bicycle or perhaps they are concerned only wih following the latest fads to maintain sales. Whatever the business reason for thinner tires on touring bicycles, touring cyclists are making a serious mistake if they purchase a touring bicycle with one-inch tires and rims.

Manufacturers and dealers will say that the thinner wheels are better for touring because they are lighter. For the racer, fine; for the tourer, no. Narrower tires are not as resilient as 1¼-inch tires because a larger percentage of the tire and air is enclosed in the rim. This gives a harsher, more fatiguing ride. Rolling resistance should improve with narrower tires, but that might not actually be the case. The road surface over which a tire passes is not perfectly smooth, but is filled with irregularities. The narrow tire is more apt to be deflected by holes and loose material whereas a wider tire will simply run over smaller impediments. The safety aspect is obvious. Narrow tire deflection actually slows progress and makes the ride more unforgiving and dangerous. Wider tire stability is apparent when the two types are comparison tested.

The narrower tire is more prone to damage when the wheel bottoms out in potholes or on other uneven road surfaces. On the whole, the narrower tire is less durable and more liable to flats, sidewall damage, casing rupture and faster reduction in tread life. Most important, it does not have the stability and surefootedness necessary for a loaded touring bike. Finally, in a pinch you can always get a $27 \times 1\frac{1}{4}$-inch tire at Western Auto, K-Mart or even in a large supermarket. Not so with the narrower models. This may change as they become more popular; for the sake of the touring cyclist, we hope not.

A word about interchanging tires. When the new $27 \times 1\frac{1}{8}$-inch tires came out they could be placed on rims that would also accept the more common $1\frac{1}{4}$-inch tire; this is not so with the narrower 1-inch tires. The standard rim is about 22 millimeters wide whereas the new 1-inch or $\frac{3}{4}$-inch tire requires a rim with an outside width of about 19 millimeters. We have seen wider tires mounted on the narrower rim, but would be very cautious about doing it and would never recommend it. Since many moderately priced, production touring bicycles now come with the narrower rims and tires, we suggest you trade in the narrow stock wheels for a pair of wider touring wheels with high-quality components. Deal with a shop that is experienced and willing to build or otherwise get such wheels for you. An option is to keep the narrow stock wheels for day rides when not carrying

a load so the added responsiveness can be appreciated. Then for longer trips use a pair of custom touring wheels from a recognized builder who specializes in touring gear. Remember, wheels are not the place to cut corners on your touring bike.

Air pressure affects your wheel's life. The present trend in tires is for manufacturers to keep raising recommended pressure. High pressure is equated with better quality in some persons' minds. Actually the higher the pressure the harsher the ride and the smaller the imprint of the tire on the road. Both qualities are undesirable on fully loaded touring bikes. Choose tires for their durability, design and handling qualities and don't get caught up in exaggerated high-pressure claims. Schwinn Le Tours work great at their rated 85 pounds, but if you want to soften the ride drop them down to 75 or 80 pounds. The same goes for other tires. Fill them to the right pressure for the type of riding you do, the load you are carrying and the road conditions. On rough paved and gravel roads we have been satisfied with Michelin Sports at 70 pounds; a very low pressure by most standards, but satisfactory and safe for that type of touring with a load.

Saddles

The saddle is too often a major sore point for long-distance riders. Saddles on most production bikes are of mediocre quality at best. When modifying a new or used bike for serious touring, there is little question as to whether to change the saddle; the only question is which one to replace it with. The length of time you can sit on the saddle is the main determinant of the daily distance you cover on tour — even more so than your strength and stamina. The highest-quality custom touring bike is no better than a department store special if you can't sit on the seat for more than a few hours a day.

Some saddles are designed for recreational touring but most are cheap copies of saddles designed for racing. They are very narrow with a stiff, unforgiving base. These are good features for racing where light weight, minimum width (less leg interference) and stiffness are needed so no power is lost through the saddle. Their lack of suitability for touring is quickly brought

Wide, spring-loaded vinyl saddle.

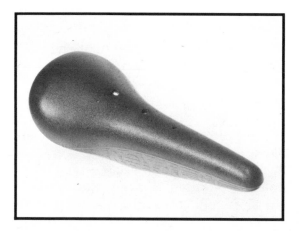

The pseudo-racing vinyl saddle is standard equipment.

home when you try to sit upright for any length of time on a racing saddle.

Wide, spring-loaded saddles are no better for touring. They are too wide for comfortable leg movement, especially in the forward leaning position that provides the most powerful stroke. Too springy for efficient cycling (power is absorbed by the springs rather than the crankset), they are also too hot with their large, vinyl-covered surface becoming a minisauna in anything but arctic conditions.

Hang in there. There are a variety of solid-leather or leather-covered saddles designed for touring efficiency and comfort. For many years top-quality leather touring saddles have come from either Brooks of England or Ideale of France. Each has a full line of leather

33

saddles ranging from the not-so-good to the top-of-the-line "professional" models. Most are solid leather that needs conditioning and breaking in, but some are preconditioned to more quickly conform to the rider.

Unless you have a preconditioned leather saddle, take the time and effort to break in a solid-leather model. The more time you spend breaking in your saddle off your bike, the more comfortable will be your miles on your bike. First, place the saddle either directly in the hot sun or near a 100-watt light bulb. Do not put it where your hand is not comfortable with the heat. Turn it over after about half an hour. When the leather is as warm and soft as it is going to get, tighten the nut under the front of the saddle. On some saddles it is necessary to hold the bolt that the nut tightens onto with a pair of pliers. Tighten the nut to the point where the saddle is drum tight, but don't overdo it and tear the saddle from the rivets.

Next, while the saddle is still warm, apply some type of leather oil (Neat's-foot, mink, Brooks Special Saddle Dressing, Huberd's Shoe Grease) to both sides of the saddle. Keep the saddle warm and apply oil until the leather won't absorb any more. If the leather loosens, tighten the saddle's adjusting nut again to keep it taut.

Once the saddle is saturated, keep it in a warm place for 10 to 12 hours — in the sun or under a warm light. Now, find a comfortable place to sit and beat on the top of the saddle with a 12-ounce to 16-ounce ball peen hammer. Use the round ball end. If you don't have a ball peen, use a rolling pin, section of pipe or any smooth rounded object. Beat on the entire upper surface but concentrate on the rear portion and along the top edge of the saddle where it folds over. Let the hammer do the work; you don't have to pound hard, just continuously. How long? How soft do you want your saddle? The more you beat, the softer the saddle becomes.

If the saddle loosens up a lot, tighten the adjusting nut again. This process takes a few days to complete because your arm gets too tired. Do it while you watch TV or walk around the block — that will give the neighbors something to talk about. When you don't want to beat anymore, wipe the saddle well with a dry cloth. The oil you put into the leather will take years to work itself out so be sure you ride in dark-colored shorts.

Now, test the saddle for flexibility. Most tourists like their saddles to flex a little; loosen the adjusting nut to accomplish this. You don't want it so loose that the nut and bolt squeak, but you don't want it drum tight either. Your saddle is now ready to ride.

Try to keep a fine, solid-leather saddle dry at all times (saddle covers are available for $2); don't ride on it if it becomes saturated. If your bike doesn't have fenders, be especially careful to keep the underside dry and clean. When you clean your bike take a damp cloth and wipe down your saddle too.

Depending on how much you ride, periodically give the saddle a light coat of oil to keep it in good shape. With care it should last your lifetime and feel more like home the longer you ride on it. If ever our bikes are stolen, we hope the thief at least has the decency to leave the saddles behind.

There are now a number of leather-covered saddles with foam padding over a semiflexible plastic or nylon base. When deciding between a solid-leather or padded leather saddle, keep some of the following points in mind. A high-quality solid-leather saddle, properly cared for, represents an almost lifetime investment. The longer you have it, the better it will fit and feel. Solid-leather saddles can be returned to proper tension as they loosen up by adjusting the nut under the nose of the saddle. This type of saddle has the important ability to breathe, allowing sweat and heat to pass through the pores of the leather away from the rider. Finally, a solid-leather saddle is fairly impervious to serious injury. Scratches and accidents detract from its appearance but not its effectiveness.

On the other hand, leather-covered cushioned saddles can be seriously harmed or even ruined when cut or otherwise damaged. Since there is no need to break them in, they feel pretty much for the first 50 miles as they will thousands of miles later. Remember that when you first sit on one; it will not feel much different as it wears.

Leather-covered saddles do not breathe as well as solid-leather saddles due to the closed-cell foam padding and the nylon or plastic core. They tend to trap sweat and heat, although not as much as the all-vinyl saddles. Some covered saddles have suede leather tops, said to be more resistant to abrasion; but the extra friction adds heat where it is least desired.

The better models of solid-leather saddles are Brooks Professional, the B17, and the B15. The latter is wider, of slightly poorer leather and costs a little less. Also good are the Ideale 90 and the slightly lesser quality Ideale 80.

What about women's saddles? The Brooks B72 is wider where it needs to be and has double shock-absorbing rails; Glenda prefers it to all others. The B15 is suitable for small or thin women and the Ideale 6 is a unique attempt to meet women's special needs. These wider saddles are suitable for men who need more support or ride with upright

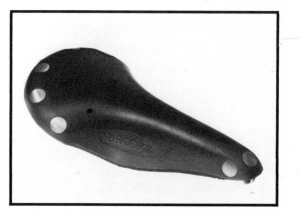

Brooks Professional leather saddle.

handlebars. Tim uses an Ideale 6 on his upright, 3-speed commuter bike and is very happy with it.

The Avocet line has pretty much captured the market in leather-covered padded touring saddles. Be careful though as the difference between the Avocet Touring I and the Touring II models is minimal. You end up paying $10 more for basically the same saddle. Insist on seeing and feeling both models before you buy. Avocet also makes a women's touring saddle of excellent design and quality.

Except for the Ideale 6 and the Avocet Touring I, all of the above saddles cost between $20 and $35. If you buy a saddle for your new touring bike, you should get a discount for trading in the stock saddle.

Making Your Selection

By now you should have a pretty good grasp of the major basic components as they relate to the specific needs of the touring cyclist. OK, but which bicycle should you choose? You will probably be buying a bicycle all built up and will have to make compromises. If there were only a few choices and the models remained the same each year, the answer would be easy. But there are more than 25 major bicycle brands and who knows how many models. The obvious answer is that there is no one "best" touring bike. There are just different bikes representing various compromises according to the design ideas and sales data of various manufacturers. It is up to you to decide what is most important for your specific needs, then attempt to find a bicycle that comes closest to your ideal for the amount of money you have to spend.

A word about weight. Overall weight is not the most important factor when selecting a touring bike. The majority of moderately priced bicycles weigh under 30 pounds; a difference of 2, 3, or even 4 pounds among brands is not significant. Look instead at the quality of the components and their suitability for your needs. Once loaded with gear for a long tour, the difference between a 27-pound and a 29-pound bicycle becomes inconsequential. It is cheaper and healthier to remove 5 pounds from your own body (if you have them to spare) than to sacrifice quality or dependability for fewer pounds on your bicycle. Be wary of manufacturers' weight claims. The only sure way of determining weight is to weigh it yourself.

You will probably want to make modifications no matter what model you choose. This is where the dealer is important. Is he easy to get along with and willing to work with you or is he dictatorial and unwilling to listen to your wants and needs? Does he have a full line of accessories and parts or is he concerned only with selling you a bike "off the shelf," leaving additional modifications up to you? Will the dealer take trade-ins on stock parts toward other components not standard on that model? Who sets up the new bikes and how are they adjusted? Look at how the brakes are adjusted and aligned on floor models: Care there usually means care elsewhere. Check the crankset in the bottom bracket. Do the arms run smoothly and free or are they loose, sloppy or too tight? You will have to slip the chain off the inner chainwheel to feel this for yourself. Don't be shy; it is your money and might be your bike. If the dealer seems more concerned with moving bikes out the door than with providing honest, accurate information along with a correctly adjusted machine, you should move out too.

Stay away from chain store and discount house bicycles. They are generally of poor quality and usually don't have a service department to back up their product. Many have odd parts and modifications can be a problem or even impossible. Keep in mind that the bottom line for a quality touring bicycle is around $250. A survey by *Bicycling* magazine found that the average price paid for a bicycle by readers in 1978 was $277. That is not cheap but with loving care a bicycle can be a life-long investment. How many items in our society can lay claim to that? Prices are rapidly escalating. Due to the floundering value of the American dollar abroad, you can expect even more dramatic increases in bicycle prices. This is already happening for both components

and complete machines.

Because of the rapidly changing nature of the bicycle business and the time it takes for a book to move from the authors' desks to the bookstore shelf, we have opted not to make specific recommendations or list the better touring bicycles. Rather we are listing some of the major components we would like to see on a touring bicycle. Although many come close, there probably is no production-line bicycle that matches our suggested list of components exactly. Use our list as a guide, not an edict. Study this chapter if necessary, talk with knowledgeable touring cyclists, find and consult a responsible bike-shop dealer, then make a decision. This takes time and requires work on your part but if you are going to spend in excess of $250 for a bicycle, we want what you bring home not only to be worth the money but to be the best possible bicycle for your needs.

Shopping Guide

Frame
    Construction: double-butted, chrome-molybdenum or manganese-molybdenum (Reynolds 531)
    Seat tube angle: 72 or 73 degrees
    Chainstay length: 17¼ inches minimum
    Fork rake: 2 inches minimum
    Wheelbase: 40½ inches minimum (23-inch frame)

Crankset
  Cotterless alloy, double or triple chainwheels

  All chainwheels replaceable

  Additional chainwheels available preferably down to 34 or fewer teeth

Gears
  Rear derailleur: wide range (GS or GT) to handle up to a 34-tooth cog

  Front derailleur: wide range to handle up to an 18-tooth chainwheel difference

  Cluster: five cogs, low gear cog over 30 tooth

Brakes
  Cantilever, centerpull, sidepull (in order of preference)

  No safety levers

  Gum-rubber brake hoods

Handlebars
  Randonneur

Shifters
  Bar end

Wheels
  Hubs: low flange, quick-release

  Spokes: 14 gauge, four cross

  Rims: alloy box-type construction, $27 \times 1\frac{1}{4}$ inches

  Tires: clincher, $27 \times 1\frac{1}{4}$ inches

Saddle
  Solid leather

Chapter Three
Fitting the Bicycle to You

Properly fitting your bicycle to your individual body type is crucial to your enjoyment of the sport. Although rich in the positive versus negative aspects of various bicycle components, bicycle literature does not dwell much on the comfort of the rider. Instead there is a tendency to think that all problems can be solved with a better component.

There are two major stumbling blocks to the increased use of bicycles in our society: first, the general lack of physical fitness along with an unwillingness to undertake a gradual, systematic program of conditioning; and second, the discomfort and strain so often associated with bicycle riding. We think the latter dominates the former in that no matter the excellence of your physical condition, if your bicycle is not adjusted to your personal dimensions there is a reduction in efficiency and comfort and

an increased chance of injury.

The bicycle is the most efficient means of transportation yet designed but its efficiency is greatly affected by how well the rider fits the machine. Whether you are a Sunday afternoon recreational rider or a potential cross-country candidate, certain mechanical and human factors must be in adjustment to allow for the highest possible degree of energy production. Many times in our classes and on tours we have witnessed the transformation that occurs when an individual's bike is finally properly fitted. "I had no idea a few simple changes could make such a difference." That comment betrays the belief of most cyclists that they can eventually get used to any discomfort, as though a certain amount of physical stress is to be expected. Such may be the case if the enthusiast is an occasional rider but in general, discomfort should decrease on a properly fitted bicycle as the body's level of physical fitness increases.

Efficiency and comfort are good reasons for properly fitting your bike, but even more important is the prevention of actual injury. Many aches, pains and serious injuries can be traced to improper adjustment of various components. The machine and the body must be working together to insure a smooth, compatible system. If one component is out of adjustment then the system is interrupted with injury as a possible result. Let's look at some basic adjustments that can be made to a touring bicycle in order to insure efficiency, comfort and the prevention of injury.

Frame Fit

The most important fitting of your bicycle takes place when you make the initial purchase. Does your frame fit you? Proper frame size is like the foundation of a house; if it isn't right in the beginning, nothing else will be right through the entire building process.

There is a simple test to check for proper frame size. You should be able to stand over the top tube comfortably without your crotch touching yet with no more than a 1½-inch clearance. Try this with the tires fully inflated, while wearing your normal cycling shoes. The frame either fits or it doesn't fit. If the frame can't pass this simple test, no fa-

To determine correct frame size, straddle bike with no more than 1½ inches clearance.

vorite color, style, sales pitch or sale price should make any difference.

Many people are confused as to what constitutes frame size. We have heard 5'4" women say they need 27-inch bicycles. Twenty-seven-inch wheels, yes; frame, no. Frame size is determined by measuring from the center of the crank axle to the point where the seat tube joins the top of the top tube. Most adult bikes range from 19 to 25 inches with some models going up to 27 inches. The increment of increase is usually 1-1½ inches depending on the make and model. Some models skip certain sizes so it may not be possible to obtain a proper fit in certain styles. Keep this in mind before making any final decisions.

If you want a mixte frame (women's style), you should first fit yourself to a man's frame, then ask for the corresponding size in a mixte. Exceptions can be made, however. One advantage of the mixte frame is that it allows shorter men and women to comfortably straddle a bicycle with 27-inch wheels. Due to the difficulty of finding high-quality production-line bikes with wheels smaller than 27 inches, many short people can obtain a good fit only by using a 19-inch mixte frame.

At the risk of redundancy, let us say again that frame size is the single, most important fit on your bicycle. This is reflected not only in comfort when straddling the bike but in the lengths and angles of other tube members and in the sizes of certain other components. Be very sure that you begin with a proper frame size.

Bicycle with mixte-style frame for short people or people who prefer this style.

Saddle Positions

Given the right frame size, there are other adjustments you can make. First take a look at your saddle height. Having a saddle too low is the most common error made by beginning and even some experienced riders. This not only causes very inefficient riding but is murder on the knees and upper leg muscles. Your legs must be able to extend almost their entire length to obtain maximum push; this requires proper seat height.

To check for proper saddle height, wear your normal cycling shoes, place your bicycle next to a wall, and climb aboard. Sit in your regular riding position on the saddle. Using the wall to balance, put your heel on the pedal (the bottom of the pedal if you have toe clips), and revolve the crank backward until you reach the lowest point in the revolution. If your saddle is at the right height, your leg will be perfectly straight with your heel just touching the pedal. Now, take your heel off the pedal and place your foot on the pedal in the riding position. The ball of your foot should be directly over the center of the pedal axle. With the crankarm still at its lowest point, you should have a slight bend in your knee. Anything more than a slight bend means your saddle is too low; no bend at all means your saddle is too high.

The first step to determining proper saddle height is to sit with heel on pedal with leg fully extended.

The second step is to place foot in proper position on the pedal with leg slightly bent at the knee.

To adjust your saddle you must have either a small adjustable wrench, the right-size open- or box-end wrench (usually metric), or in some cases, one or two metric allen wrenches. If you do not have the proper tools, you would be well advised to purchase a high-quality, six-inch adjustable (crescent type) wrench, the allen-key wrenches for your seatpost (usually five or six millimeters) and handlebar stem fittings. A high-quality six-inch adjustable wrench will cost $5-$7 and allen-key wrenches from 50¢ to $1 each. Good tools are a wise investment; don't buy variety-store junk.

To determine how high you can raise the saddle, remove seatpost. Note warning line on post and seatpost binding bolt on frame.

Change your saddle height by first loosening the seatpost binding bolt where the post fits into the frame. Remove the saddle with its attached seatpost. Wipe off the seatpost and look for an engraved horizontal line or warning statement that indicates maximum height. This point should be 2-2½ inches up from the bottom of the seatpost. Engrave or deeply scratch a line at this point on your seatpost if there is not one there already. Next, remove the seatpost binding bolt. Clean and grease the threads before replacing the bolt in the seat tube. Grease the seatpost itself up to the warning line to insure its easy removal two days or two years from now. Replace the post in the seat tube, align the saddle with the top tube, then tighten the seatpost binder bolt. Don't overdo it; just so the fit is snug. Now, climb aboard and repeat the saddle height test. If it is not right, keep adjusting until you have reached the proper height.

If during this adjustment procedure you discover that you have to extend your seatpost beyond where the warning line is visible, stop. Many new bicycles have short seatposts and some people have frames that are too small to start with. In either case, you will have to buy a longer seatpost to reach the proper adjustment height. Take your old post along when you go to purchase a new one; they come in many different diameters and must fit exactly. Never adjust the seatpost to extend beyond the warning mark or you'll risk it breaking off or bending the seat tube. Either one could ruin your day.

When your saddle is first put at its correct height, you may feel as though you are sitting on a flagpole. Ride it awhile. We think you will notice a vast improvement in your cycling ability. If the increase in saddle height is really too much, lower it some and gradually increase the height by ¼ inch per week until you feel you've found the correct height.

The "scientific method" is another way to find your saddle height. Measure your total inseam length while standing barefooted; it is the distance from the floor inside the leg to the pelvic bone, which rests on the saddle. Be sure your legs are straight, close together, and that you push the tape measure right up

to the bone. Next, take this measurement (in inches) and multiply it by 1.09. The result is the recommended height of your saddle, measured from the top of the pedal axle to the top of the saddle when the pedal is in the down position and the crankarm is parallel with the seat tube. Care must be taken to insure that the measuring tape is kept exactly in line with the crankarm and seat tube. We find it easier to place a block of wood across the top of the saddle and measure to the bottom of the wood.

Once you have set your saddle height using the "straight-leg/heel" method, try the scientific method to see how close the one is to the other. You should be within ½ inch either way; if not, check each measurement again. Keep in mind, however, that these are recommended or approximate heights. Don't be afraid to experiment. Factors such as foot size, angle of saddle and pedal type will influence the results. Using both methods along with some critical analysis should give you a saddle height that is ideal for your specific situation. You will then be well on your way to more efficient and comfortable cycling.

Once your saddle is adjusted vertically, it is time to check its horizontal placement. Do this by placing your elbow against the foremost portion of your saddle keeping your wrist straight and fingers extended. In this position your fingertips should just barely touch the rear portion of the handlebars near the handlebar stem or extend no farther

Measuring saddle height using scientific method employing tape measure and block of wood. Try to keep tape aligned with crankarm and seat tube.

than the forward edge of the bar. If your fingertips don't reach the bars or extend beyond them, an adjustment must be made.

Depending on the type of seatpost you have, you must either loosen the one or two side nuts that hold the saddle clamp to the seatpost, loosen the two 10-millimeter bolts that hold the saddle on a Campagnolo-style seatpost, or loosen the single or double allen-key bolts on the underside of a "laprade"-style seatpost. Whichever style you have, once these bolts are loosened you will be able to slide or shove the saddle backward or forward.

Before tightening the seatpost

To check proper horizontal saddle and stem position with your arm, place elbow on front of saddle with fingertips just reaching to back of handlebars.

clamp, take a level or just sight across the saddle to place it in a level position. Now tighten the clamp. After all these adjustments are made, take your bike on a long ride. Experiment with changing the level of your saddle slightly. A degree or two is a big change so do it in small increments until you find the most comfortable position. Some prefer a backward tilt, others a forward one. Let experience be your guide.

To be sure that the fore-and-aft position of your saddle is correct, you must determine the position of the front of the saddle in relation to the center of the bottom bracket. Place one side of a yardstick or straightedge directly in line with the center of the bottom bracket axle. Use a level to make sure the straightedge is vertical (the bike must be standing on a level surface). Now measure the distance from the front of the saddle to the side of the straightedge resting on the center of the bottom bracket axle. It should be between 1½ to 3 inches. In other words, the saddle should be that distance back from the center of the bottom bracket. In most cases this measurement will agree with your fingertip/elbow method. If not, you must consider getting a handlebar stem with greater or lesser reach; then you will need to reposition your saddle to bring it to the proper relationship with the bottom bracket axle.

Remember as you are moving your saddle fore and aft that you are also changing the height because of the

Fore/aft measurement of saddle checked with straightedge and level from the center of the bottom bracket.

slope of the seat tube. Don't forget to check and make minor readjustments once the proper fore-and-aft position is determined.

Handlebar Adjustments

Handlebar stems are sold with 60-140 millimeter extensions — the distance between the center of the bolt or allen-wrench fitting to where the center of the bars pass through the stem. They also come in three common diameters so make sure you have the correct size when making replacements. Unless you are fairly skilled at bicycle repair, have the stem changed at a bike shop. One of the brakes must be removed so that the handlebars can be taken off the old stem and placed on the new one.

Another adjustment you should make at this time is the height of the handlebar stem in relation to the saddle. In theory, the saddle and the stem should be of equal height. In fact, this is seldom the case, especially on taller frames. Unfortunately, most stems are one specific height, usually about 150 millimeters from top to bottom. Due to this standard length many people have handlebar stems lower than their saddle. Usually they adapt to this unless they are troubled by severe upper back or neck pain. If you are so bothered, there is at least one stem available that may solve your problem. The SR Custom handlebar stem, 60-millimeter extension only, is about 180 millimeters long, giving you an extra inch to play with. This, coupled with the shorter extension, can make for a more comfortable ride although you may lose some efficiency.

As with seatposts, the amount of stem left inside the frame is critically important. We have seen a number of cases where the handlebar stem has been raised to the point where not enough is left in the head tube to prevent it from shearing off. Some were weakened by cracks that had developed. Most newer bicycles have a warning mark on the stem indicating the maximum rise allowance, but it is best to check the height for yourself by removing the stem.

To do this, first use your adjustable wrench or correct allen wrench to loosen the top bolt or allen fitting two complete turns. Next, place a piece of wood on top of the bolt and strike it with a hammer. This should drive the wedge down and allow you to remove your stem. Once it is out, clean it off and check for a warning statement or horizontal indicator mark. If you can't find one, measure up 2½ inches from the bottom of the stem or 1¼ inches from the top of the split or from the top of the wedge cut, depending on the type of stem you have. Make a permanent mark on the stem with an engraving tool or sharp object; do not raise your stem beyond this mark. While you have the stem out, grease the wedge bolt, threads and stem so that it can be easily removed in the future.

Once the stem is replaced and the bolt tightened snugly, there is one more adjustment to make. Take your wrench or allen key and loosen the pinch bolt that holds the handlebars in the stem. Loosen it just enough so that you can pivot the handlebars using some pressure. Take a long straightedge — a broom handle will do — and place it under and against the nut or tightening side of the quick-release mechanism on your rear wheel. Extend the straightedge forward until it touches the drop portion of your handlebar on the bottom side. Move the handlebar until the bottom of the bar lies flat on the straightedge while the other end rests on the bottom of the rear axle bolt or quick-release. When you have the right position, tighten the pinch bolt on the stem.

Consider this measurement as a starting place. Take your bike on a long

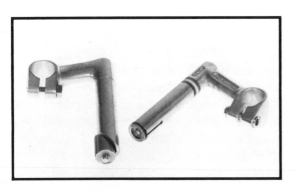

Two types of handlebar stems: the expander plug and the wedge.

Check handlebar drop alignment by using straightedge from the rear axle.

47

ride; you should feel an even pressure across the palm of your hand rather than in certain spots. Too much pressure in certain places can cause damage to the ulnar nerve that passes from the hand to the upper body through the narrow channel at the base of the palm. Tingling or numbness in the hands and fingers indicates trouble with this nerve. Change the angle of the bars by pivoting until you feel a good, even pressure on your hands while riding in the down position.

One more adjustment on the handlebars is the positioning of the brake levers. Most bikes are adjusted properly prior to sale, but you might as well be thorough in checking out how well your machine fits your body. The main criterion is whether you can easily reach them with the tips of at least two fingers while riding in the down position. You will probably have to shift your hands up from their normal placement but you should be able to do this with an easy, comfortable movement requiring no special gymnastics.

Check to make sure that you can ride comfortably with your hands on the brake-lever housings while in the up position as well. If your bike is not equipped with rubber brake hoods, you might try adding them if you like that hand position.

If you find you need to change the position of your brake levers you will have to disconnect the brake, unwrap a portion of the handlebar tape, loosen the clamping screw or nut, and move the brake to the desired position. If you don't feel competent performing any of these operations, let a bike shop do it for you. Remember that you must be there to insure a proper fit, however.

Toe Clips

The final adjustment we will discuss is the sizing and positioning of toe clips. Toe clips and straps have two important functions for the bicyclist. First, they increase efficiency in the pedaling action by allowing the rider to not only push down on the pedal, but also to pull up creating a much smoother, more efficient action. Second, toe clips keep the rider's foot in the proper position on the pedal making for a more efficient and comfortable pedaling action. They also lessen the danger of developing knee problems. Knee problems are a common ailment among cyclists, but properly adjusted toe clips can help in preventing or alleviating such problems.

Toe clips usually come in three sizes: small — men's 5-7; medium — men's 8-10; large — men's 11-13. You can sometimes get a satisfactory fit by just telling the salesman your shoe size, but it's best to take your bike along to the shop wearing the shoes you cycle in. The easiest way to fit a pair is to make a mark on the side of the sole of your shoes where the ball of your foot is. Now take a toe clip, hold it against the pedal, place your foot on the pedal and slide it forward all the way into the

Proper position of foot in toe clips and straps with ball of foot directly over pedal axle. Note how cleat bottom engages pedal.

clip. If the toe clip length is correct, the mark on your shoe sole should be directly over the center of the pedal axle. If not, try another size.

If you have especially big feet and small pedals, it might be necessary to use washers or spacers to extend the large-size toe clips even farther out. We have found through personal experience that even a two-millimeter extension can make a considerable difference in comfort, so be exact.

When installing toe clips, begin by aligning them directly on the centers of the pedals. If you notice any discomfort in your feet, ankles, or knees after riding awhile, adjust them sideways (laterally) until the discomfort disappears. It is very important that you find the position that allows your feet, ankles and knees to keep in the proper alignment so that lateral movement is kept to a minimum.

If you are new to toe clips, we advise you to ride without the straps until you have learned the necessary technique of getting into and out of the metal clip. There is a degree of skill in tipping the pedal to the upright position when pulling away from a stop. Once you feel confident, put your toe straps on but keep them loose. Then, after you feel at home with both clips and straps, begin to tighten the straps until your feet are held firmly in place. You don't have to pull your straps supertight. They should be firm, but not so tight that they put your foot to sleep or don't allow you to remove your foot without loosening the straps. Unless you are using shoe cleats (metal, leather or plastic plates attached to the sole of the shoe that have a groove into which a portion of the pedal fits), there is no reason to ever feel trapped in the pedals.

Once you have completed all of these basic adjustments don't think that you are finished. Most people find tremendous improvement in their comfort and riding efficiency, but that doesn't mean you can pedal away into the sunset never to be plagued by a body ache, or never to have to make another adjustment. You will have a basically well adjusted machine, but slight changes and experimentation are needed to obtain that ever elusive state of perfection. We are continually amazed at what minor adjustments do for our cycling comfort. Herein lies much of the appeal for many in the cycling fraternity; it is neither the machine nor is it the use of the human body that predominates, but a close, almost magical combination of human and machine that produces the most efficient means of propulsion yet devised.

Chapter Four
Efficient Cycling:
Gearing and Cadence

Although the bicycle is the most efficient means of transportation known to man, that efficiency depends on the rider's wise and correct use of the machine. The bicycle has the potential; man provides the energy and the intelligence to make it work.

When you are out there with your loaded touring bike facing 50 miles or more of rolling terrain, you need to be cycling as efficiently as possible. This is especially true on an extended tour where you are putting on high mileage over a varied countryside day after day. The ability to make full use of your energy resources without waste is what separates the apparently effortless cyclist from those who seem always on the edge of exhaustion.

Two factors directly affect the efficiency of the rider/bicycle combination: gearing and cadence. First, let's dispel a myth. Gears do not lessen the amount of work necessary to move a bicycle. They do make that work easier, or sometimes harder, depending on the degree of understanding the rider has about the gears.

Single-Speed Gearing

On a single-speed bicycle the gear consists of a front chainwheel and a rear cog connected by a chain. As the rider turns the pedals attached to the crankarms, the chainwheel revolves. That motion is transferred through the chain to the rear cog, which then turns the rear wheel. This propels the entire machine and rider. The amount of force the rider must apply depends on such things as his weight, the weight of the bicycle and its load, wind resistance (the major factor at speeds over ten miles per hour [mph]), the rolling resistance of the tires on the road, the frictional resistance of the various moving parts on the bicycle, the road surface and the type of terrain. The steeper the incline the more energy (work) is needed to move the bike and rider up the hill.

On the single-speed bicycle, the

With a touring load it is even more important that the rider learn the techniques which encourage efficient cycling.

front chainwheel is much larger than the rear cog, having many more individual teeth. Since the rear is smaller, it turns several times for every revolution of the chainwheel, an immediate savings in energy output by the rider. The rider can vary his pedaling according to the speed desired and the conditions under which he is traveling. On a flat section of road, turning the chainwheel at 75 revolutions per minute (rpm), the bicycle will move along at a constant speed of about 15 mph. As the rider approaches a hill things change rapidly. Either the pedaling (chainwheel) slows or the speed reduces, usually both. As the hill is climbed, chainwheel revolutions might slow to about 40 and the speed to about 7 mph. At the same time the rider is putting out a great deal more energy with each revolution of the chainwheel.

At the top of the hill things change once again. Suddenly the chainwheel revolutions are increasing dramatically, requiring less energy on the pedals as speed increases proportionately. Somewhere around 25 mph the rider's legs are flailing away at an attempted 120 rpm and there is no longer any force being applied to the pedals at all. The rider then finds it easier to coast until the next level terrain where the pedaling begins again.

As long as the hills are not too steep, the rider is in good physical condition and is happy to coast downhill, the 1-speed bicycle is satisfactory. However, given increasing steepness of terrain, there comes a point where the rider becomes physically incapable of propelling the bicycle up grades at a pace faster than he can walk. Considering the amount of energy poured into the effort, walking in fact becomes easier than riding.

Multi-Speed Gearing

This is where the multi-speed (gear) bicycle comes in, be it anywhere from 3 speeds to 18 speeds. The actual amount of energy required to propel the bicycle does not change (all other factors remaining constant), but through the proper use of the gears the production of that energy becomes easier for the rider of the multi-speed.

Instead of only one rear cog as on the single-speed, the multi-speed derailleur bicycle has several differing sizes of rear cogs. On 10 or more speeds there is more than one chainwheel, also with differing sizes. The rider has the ability to change the gear ratio of the bicycle by switching the chain among various-size cogs and chainwheels with the derailleurs. The rider can change the speed of the chainwheel in relation to the speed of the rear wheel without changing the number of revolutions his legs must perform. In effect, the rider has instantaneous choice of a number of gear situations to meet the variety of riding

53

conditions encountered.

Consider how a 10-speed would take the same section of road as a single-speed. On the flat stretch the rider still feels comfortable turning the chainwheel at 75 rpm at a speed of about 15 mph. Being on a 10-speed makes no difference at this point. However, as a hill is approached the speed begins to drop but the rider does not have to accept an increasingly hard-to-push, decreasing rpm of the chainwheel. He simply shifts to a lower gear to maintain a comfortable, less exhausting (more efficient), 75-rpm chainwheel speed.

There is no change in speed going up the hill between the 10-speed and the single-speed, rather the change is in the condition of the rider. As the hill becomes steeper, the rider continues to shift to lower gears (providing there are enough) while maintaining a comfortable chainwheel rpm of 75 or so.

When the rider crests the hill and begins to descend, he shifts to higher gears as downhill speed increases, maintaining pressure on the pedals with an efficient chainwheel speed. The higher the gear, the less likely it is that the rider will have to coast. The important thing to remember is that it takes the exact same amount of energy to propel either the single-speed or the multi-speed bicycle up a hill, all else being equal. What changes is the proportion of work done by the machine and the rider. The multi-speed can be shifted according to the conditions rather than having to change the speed of the motor (the rider). Using proper shifting technique, the multi-speed is simply easier to ride because the rider can maintain smooth, easy revolutions without wasting motion, expending huge outputs of energy on the uphill, and wasteful out-of-control flailing or coasting on the downhill. The hill is no less steep, it just feels that way to the rider. Such efficiency is especially important on long tours where your energy and enthusiasm must remain constant over a long period of time.

The Importance of Cadence

The primary function of gears on a bicycle is to allow the rider to maintain a good cadence (a smooth, comfortable chainwheel rpm). To better understand the importance of cadence, consider the motion of a fast-running animal. It is all grace and flow, no wasted motion at all, nothing to detract from the on-going energy of the action. Wasted, irregular motion is rare. When a cheetah is observed in slow motion, it seems hardly to be working at all. For comparison, go down to your neighborhood bicycle trail on a warm, sunny Sunday afternoon and observe. You will see a wide variety of style and rhythm, the sad majority of which is rough and irregular. You can almost see the energy falling by the wayside. Granted, if people are having fun and getting some exercise, so what?

But the point is to develop your touring efficiency through awareness and practice. So look once more at the normal recreational rider.

Two things contribute to a rough and irregular riding style. One, as we covered in chapter three, is a saddle that is too low. This causes a jabbing leg action where the rider is first pushing with one leg, then the next, rather than making a smooth, continuous circular motion. It almost seems like the pedal is pushing the leg back up for the next assault instead of the leg doing the work all the way around. Adjusting the saddle helps.

Cadence is another factor that influences riding style. Most of those rec-

In this instance, the saddle is too low, which will cause the rider to "jab" at the pedals rather than follow through the pedals with continuous rhythmic motions.

reational riders are pushing a very high gear, which requires them to turn the pedals at a slow and painful rpm. Instead of flowing along like fast-running animals, they are powering each stroke using legs like pistons instead of flywheels. There is frequently a pause after each downstroke to recover for the next. For the occasional, short-distance weekend rider; fine (although that may be partly why he or she is only a short-distance rider). But for you — the serious touring cyclist — a rough riding style can not only shorten your day on the road, but it can also lead to serious muscular and joint difficulties, especially in the knees.

Developing Cadence

How do you arrive at a proper, efficient, comfortable riding cadence? An easy method is to first make sure your bicycle is in proper adjustment (see chapter three). Then find a good route that includes a section of road about a mile long that is relatively flat and wind-free if possible. Now, put some miles on your bike over this route until you feel comfortable and relaxed as you ride it. Fasten a watch with a second hand to your handlebars or wrist. Once you feel you are riding in a normal, comfortable manner on the flat section, count the number of times your right pedal reaches the bottom of its stroke for one full minute. Do this several times to arrive at an average count. This figure represents your chainwheel rpm, which is also your own individual cadence.

You are exhibiting good, efficient cycling form if your cadence is in the range of 60-80 rpm. If you are under 60 rpm you have some work to do to develop your best touring potential. Above 80 you are doing something called "spinning"; it is a good training technique that helps to develop elongated muscles and loose joints, but is not too comfortable as a normal riding style. If you are spinning you are probably not just an occasional bike rider, either.

Try doing some spinning if your cadence is below 60 rpm to help you get the feel of pedaling faster. As your legs lose the feeling that they are flying out of control, you can begin to drop your cadence to within the 60-80 rpm range and exert more pressure on the cranks. Then it will feel more normal to you and your legs will have had some beneficial exercise. You will also find yourself pedaling more efficiently.

There is no one best cadence for which to strive; each rider must find his or her best individual pace. The majority of noncompetitive riders level out at between 60-80 rpm, but if you are a little below or above yet and feel that you have a smooth, comfortable riding style then don't worry about it. If, however, you are below about 55 or so, try some corrective action to pick up your pace.

As you develop and regulate your cadence on flat terrain, begin to consider the hills. On a single-speed bicycle you simply have to muscle your way up as the incline increases, trying to maintain your cadence with sheer will and muscle power. But on your 10-speed (or more) you have the option of maintaining your cadence through the use of gears rather than muscle. This is where gearing and cadence come together. The one simply facilitates the other; gears seem to flatten mountains and reduce headwinds because they allow you to maintain your own comfortable cadence no matter the changing conditions.

Know Your Gears

In order for gears to perform this almost magical function, the rider must be able to shift the gears properly and at the right time. To do that the rider must first understand what gearing is all about. It doesn't do any good to have a 10-speed if you are using only three or four of your gears. If, in addition, you are selecting those gears in a hit-or-miss fashion with no specific progression from gear to gear, you are losing much of the advantage of a multi-speed bike and you are most likely losing cadence as you make your shifts. It doesn't make any sense to invest $250-$1,000 in a fine touring machine only to ride it as though it were a single-speed

or 3-speed. Taking the time now to learn proper gearing can mean that your hours on the road will be longer, more pleasant and less tiring.

A common misconception among owners of multi-speed bicycles is that there are 10 usable gears on a 10-speed, or 15 on a 15-speed. The assumption is immediately made that you simply shift the rear derailleur five times in one direction, change the front chainwheel with the derailleur, and shift the rear five times in the opposite direction. Not so.

The best way to understand the shifting process is to chart the gears on your own bicycle. This will take a little time, but once done you will have a clearer picture of gearing. First, get a pencil and paper, a rag for cleaning your hands, and some sort of marking device such as a crayon. Start by looking closely at your chainwheel. On most models there is an engraved number on one side of each chainwheel that tells the number of teeth (the size). Check for that number. If you can't find it, or you just want to check it out for yourself, make a mark where you begin and count the total number of teeth on each chainwheel. Write those numbers on your sheet of paper, for example, 42 and 52. Next (this can get messy) count the number of teeth on each of your five rear cogs attached to the freewheel on the rear wheel. You will arrive at a series of numbers such as; 14-17-20-24-28. These are the sizes of your rear cogs. After cleaning your hands, sit down and get out your calculator unless you have a head for math; we are going to do some figuring to make up your gear chart.

When you shift your 10-speed bike, you move the chain into a variety of combinations of chainwheel and cog, thus changing the specific gear ratio. The mystical derailleur is simply a piece

A common mistake by a beginning cyclist is to push too high a gear, which results in rapidly tiring the leg muscles. Usually a rider demonstrates that the gear is too high by pushing through the pedal motions. Sometimes he will lean from side to side as he gives disproportionate emphasis to a particular pedal cycle.

of metal attached by cables to your shifting lever, in order to move the chain physically from one chainwheel to the next or from one cog to the next, depending on whether it is a front or rear derailleur. These various combinations are easier to deal with if we give them individual numbers rather than attempting to classify them with left-front chainwheel to second-from-the-inside or second-largest cog, and so on. So we will determine their numerical value (the size of the gear) by using a formula that breaks down the gear ratios into gear inches. The formula is as follows: The number of teeth on the chainwheel times the bike wheel size divided by the number of teeth on the rear cog equals the gear in inches. For example, given a front chainwheel of 42 teeth and a rear cog of 28 teeth on a bicycle that has 27-inch wheels (look on the tire if you are not sure of your wheel size), you will arrive at a gear of 40.5 inches.

$$\frac{42 \times 27}{28} = 40.5 \text{ inches}$$

This gear inch is relative, allowing us to make comparisons among the various combinations of gears possible on a multi-speed bicycle. It is not the distance your wheel travels in that particular gear. It originates from the old high-wheeler, penny farthing-type bicycle where the pedals were attached directly to the large drive wheel; a comparison of gearing between bicycles could be made by determining the diameter of the large wheel. If you want to know how far your bicycle will travel with one complete turn of the chainwheel in any one specific gear combination, just multiply the gear inch by pi (3.1416). In our sample gear of 40.5 inches the bicycle would travel 127 inches along the road for every complete turn of the pedals.

Figure the formula for a 52-tooth chainwheel and a 14-tooth cog, just for practice. Your figures should look like this:

$$\frac{52 \times 27}{14} = 100.2 \text{ inches}$$

$$100.2 \times 3.1416 = 314 \text{ inches of ground travel}$$

Looking at these two sample gears, it's apparent that the 40.5-inch gear is relatively low with only 127 inches of ground travel, while the 100.2-inch gear is higher with 314 inches of ground travel. That is what gears are all about; the actual distance you can travel per one revolution of the chainwheel or pedals.

On steep inclines you would gear down to your 40.5-inch gear to compensate for gaining less ground per revolution due to the resistance of going uphill. Your chainwheel would be turning faster in relation to your rear wheel than in a higher gear, making for an easier ascent. Going down, you switch to your 100.2-inch gear so you can turn the chainwheel a smaller number of times in relation to your rear wheel; this allows you to keep pedaling as your speed increases, rather than having to coast.

Now back to your individual gear chart. Determine your own gear inches by using the formula with the figures you wrote down for your chainwheels and cogs. It might look something like the following:

```
        Cogs—   28  24  20  17   14
                ┌
Chainwheel  42 │  40  47  57  67   81   ⟍ Gear
    Teeth   52 │  50  59  70  83  100   ⟋ Inches
```

Incorporating these into a straight-line gear progression you come up with: 40–47–50–57–59–67–70–81–83–100.

So now you have ten gears, right? Yes. But ten useful gears? No. When you use the smallest chainwheel in front and the smallest cog in the rear, the chain is at an extreme angle (from the inside to the outside). On our sample bike that would be 42/14, the 81-inch gear. This angle is so extreme that it will wear components (chainwheel, chain and cog) at a fast pace if used often. You can sometimes hear the friction as you ride in this combination. Try it briefly on your own bike to see for yourself. The same is true for the opposite extreme, the largest chainwheel and the largest cog; 52/28 on our sample bike, gear 50. These two acute chain angles are not recommended due to wear,

noise and shifting difficulties.

The straight-line progression now looks like this with eight gears remaining: 40–47–50–57–59–67–70–81–83–100.

There is an additional problem. The 57-inch and the 59-inch gears are very close together, a difference of only 6 inches in actual ground travel. Also, when shifting properly from lower to higher, the 59-inch gear requires that both front and rear derailleurs be shifted (double-shift). To gain only 6 inches on the ground you must shift both derailleurs, a difference you would hardly feel. The logical thing would be to skip that gear, going on to the 67-inch gear while remaining on the 42-tooth chainwheel. That now leaves a total of seven useful gear combinations: 40–47–50–57–59–67–70–81–83–100.

One more double-shift occurs between 67 and 70. If we are dropping the 59-inch gear because it is so close to the 57 and requires a double-shift, why not do the same with 70? There are only 10 inches of ground travel difference between 67 and 70, but skipping 70 means quite a jump to 83. It really depends on you and the conditions of your ride. You have the option of skipping it or working the double-shift. These midrange gears are used extensively in touring; sometimes when conditions are right the double-shift is no problem and well worth the gain. The option is yours, but notice that your 10-speed is now somewhere between a 6- and 7-speed. The chainwheel/cog combinations for usable gears in our sample bike look like this:

$$42/28 = 40$$
$$42/24 = 47$$
$$42/20 = 57$$
$$42/17 = 67$$
$$52/20 = 70$$
$$52/17 = 83$$
$$52/14 = 100$$

Do this with your own gear progression, noticing where there are double-shifts and which are the two extreme-angle gears you want to ignore. Don't be surprised if you end up with six or seven gears as we did above. The main thing is that you now have a clear idea of your gear capacity, progression, limitations and options.

You may want to make up a permanent gear chart to attach to your bike for reference while touring. We have done it for years; it is especially helpful if you have more than one bicycle. The easiest way to do this is to type or print the chart on a gummed label, then attach it to the handlebar stem or to the top tube near the headset. Use indelible ink or cover it with transparent tape to keep it from getting wet.

The trick is learning to distinguish, as you ride, exactly which cog and chainwheel you are using. Then you can quickly determine which gear combination you are in and what the next one is in progression. Glenda has always had difficulty using the gear chart as she is more receptive to size comparisons — largest, middle, smallest — than to what she considers an arbitrary number for each cog and chainwheel. The problem was even more complex on the 15-speed she frequently rode until she took a set of color Highliter pens to her chart. Using red for the largest, yellow for the middle, and blue for the smallest, she reports that her chart had instant visual meaning to her as she rode.

Run through your gears several times to become acquainted with your shifting progression before you actually get out on the road. To do this at home, put your bike in a stand or raise the rear wheel by tying a rope to a rafter or tree and attach it to your bicycle seat. With the rear wheel off the ground you can shift through the gears as the crank is turned by hand. (You might need a friend to help with this procedure.) After a little practice you will be ready for the road.

Once your gears are familiar to you, you can begin to combine the proper gear combination with your cadence to develop a smooth cycling style. Practice on a relatively flat roadway until you know automatically when your cadence is right. Then begin to tackle small inclines, gradually increasing the variety of terrain until your shifting becomes so automatic that you can maintain your cadence no matter what the hills and wind are doing. When you reach that point, you are riding at your maximum efficiency. Touring long distances daily will then feel as normal and comfortable to you as riding to the store for a bottle of milk. Well, almost.

Riding into a strong head wind can be more depressing and demoralizing than climbing an endless hill. A good, steady cadence along with gear shifting to match the force of the wind can reduce the devastating effect of a head wind.

Gearing Range

After all of this, if you are still having trouble developing a smooth riding and shifting style, the fault may be with your machine rather than with you. Now might be the time to examine the gearing range on your bicycle. Gear range is a highly individualistic matter; no one should be pressured into someone else's idea of the "ultimate." Here are some things to consider when looking at your own gear range.

Double-shifting is a pain (having to change both front and rear derailleurs to obtain a desired gear). It is not too bad in the middle and upper gears when you are pedaling along with a good deal of inertia going for you, but a double-shift in the lower gears can be your undoing while struggling up a steep hill. Check to see if you have a simple, straightforward shifting pattern with few double-shifts, especially in the lower gears. Halfway up the Rocky Mountains you will really appreciate it.

Another aspect to check out is the number of gear inches between shifts. You needn't translate them into ground travel inches; it is best to get used to thinking only in gear inches. The general practice is to keep about 10 or 12 inches between the various gears with wider gaps in the very low and very high ends. When using a fairly tight range like the one in our sample — 40 to 100 — you can have gears closer together through the midrange where most of the riding takes place. In the more widely spaced gear ranges, such as from the high 20s to over 100, difficulties arise that require decisions based on personal preference and experience. If you have not toured extensively with a heavy load, you will have to rely on others' advice and experience. Presumably that is one of the reasons you are reading this book.

We prefer low gears in the mid- to upper 20s with 5- to 10-inch jumps between gears, especially when touring with heavy loads in mountainous terrain. We like 10- or 12-inch jumps in the middle gears and 15 or more inches between the higher gears. In our experience, a steep grade is the toughest thing out there in the touring world. We need all the help we can get to maintain a smooth, nonexhausting pace to get up one.

Our preference for closely spaced lower gears and average jumps in the midrange necessitates either super jumps in the high gears or lower high gears to begin with. The latter has been our choice; we find it well suited to our needs. Our highest gear is in the mid-90s because we feel we have no business going faster than that downhill with a loaded bike. When we have toured with high gears in the 100s, we tended to use them; frequently arriving at the bottom with trembling arm muscles, weak knees and overheated rims.

The most controversial gearing subject is usually how low the lowest gear should be. Some cyclists spend hours debating this point, becoming very emotional in the process. What is frequently lost sight of is the element of personal need. The bike club president may well prefer a bottom gear no lower than 42 because the bulk of his riding is done in the suburbs with nothing heavier than a lunch in his or her panniers. He may also stand up off the saddle to "honk" up every hill on the Sunday ride. You have to decide if that is practical for you on your fully loaded touring bike when camp is 20 miles farther and 2,000 feet higher than you are right then. Honking on a loaded bike ruins your cadence, wastes energy through sideways motion and can do in your lungs. About the only thing going for it is the wonderful alleviation of that persistent pain in your bottom as you slide free of the saddle for awhile.

Gear your bike as low as you need to maintain your own comfortable pace carrying the load you expect to carry on tour. If necessary, pack up with five-pound bags of flour and go out to some hills for a trial run. You will find out quickly if your low gear is low enough. How will you know? By how soon you have to start walking. If you would rather use our experience for what it is worth, here are our recommendations: Stick to a low gear in the mid- to upper 20s for serious mountain travel with a heavy load (anything over 35 pounds); the lower to mid-30s for most standard touring with a moderate load. But it is best to find out for yourself before you set out cross-country or around the world.

It is not difficult to change your gear range if you decide it is not suited to your needs, but don't rush into it. Change only for the sake of change rarely brings improvement. Carefully analyze your gear chart and riding style for the gears you find most useful, those you seldom use and for convenience in shifting. Once you have these elements clearly in mind you can sit down to determine what changes are necessary and which is the easiest way to do it. Use the chart on page 65 for finding the various gear possibilities so that you won't have to work the formula each time.

In order to make changes in your existing gear pattern, you will either have to change one or more of the rear cogs, or one or both of the chainwheels. The changes are not difficult to make, providing you have the proper tools and know-how, but there are secondary problems associated with any gear change. These usually involve derailleur capacity.

Front and rear derailleurs have built-in limitations as to the size of cog or chainwheel combinations that can be handled. Before you decide on a specific desirable gear combination, check to make sure that your present derailleur can handle it. In other words, if you now have a 28-tooth large cog in the rear and you want to change to a 32-tooth cog, be sure your rear derailleur has the capacity for the increase. You must either talk with a competent bike mechanic about it or look at the August 1978 issue of *Bicycling* magazine. Beginning on page 28 you will find an excellent article by Richard Jow entitled "All About Derailleurs" in which is listed over 100 front and rear derailleurs and their various capacities. You might want to keep that article beside you for reference as you are planning out your gear changes.

Most people find it easier to replace some or all of their rear cogs than to replace their chainwheels. Even with the common 42/52 chainwheels, however, you can gear down to a 33-inch low gear with a 34-tooth large cog. That would require a large-capacity derailleur (G.S. or G.T. model); if your bike doesn't have one you will have to purchase it to make the change. Anything over 30 teeth will probably require the wide-range rear derailleur, meaning an investment of $12-$45

Our own choices among the many excellent rear derailleurs are, in order of preference, the Sun Tour VGT, Shimano Crane GS and Campagnolo Rally.

The VGT is the lowest priced, the Campagnolo Rally the highest. In wide-range front derailleurs we have had success with the Sun Tour Cyclone, Shimano Titlist and Campagnolo Record. Thse are not the only high-quality, wide-range derailleurs, but they are widely available and have proven themselves to us through the gamut of touring conditions and gear ranges.

When changing your rear cogs you must also consider the make of freewheel on your bicycle. Since some have limited capacities and are difficult to find replacement cogs for, you might have to obtain a whole new freewheel-and-cog assembly (cluster) to get what you want.

We have limited our freewheel selection to the Sun Tour (Maeda) Pro-Compe and the Perfect in order to suit our low-gear preferences and keep things as simple as possible. The only difference between them seems to be in the color. Each is readily available so cogs are easily replaced (an important consideration while touring), low in price, simple in design and highly reliable. For those especially strong riders who expect to be carrying very large loads, Sun Tour also makes a Tandem freewheel which uses the standard Pro-Compe or Perfect cogs. There are over a dozen types of freewheels, so make sure you know what you want and what you are getting. A competent, knowledgeable bike-shop crew can easily make all the necessary changes for you, but be sure to tell them what sort of

Gear Chart for 27-inch Wheel

Number of Teeth on Chainring

Number of Teeth on Sprocket	26	28	30	32	34	36	38	40	42	44	45	46	47	48	49	50	51	52	54
12	58.5	63.0	67.5	71.9	76.5	81.0	85.5	90.0	94.5	99.0	101.2	103.5	105.0	108.0	110.3	112.5	114.7	117.0	121.5
13	54.0	58.1	62.3	66.4	70.6	74.7	78.9	83.1	87.2	91.4	93.4	95.5	97.6	99.7	101.8	103.8	105.9	108.0	112.1
14	50.1	54.0	57.7	61.7	65.5	69.4	73.3	77.1	81.0	84.8	86.7	88.7	90.6	92.6	94.5	96.4	98.3	100.3	104.1
15	46.8	50.4	54.0	57.6	61.2	64.8	68.4	72.0	75.6	79.2	80.9	82.8	84.6	86.4	88.2	90.0	91.8	93.6	97.2
16	43.9	47.2	50.6	54.0	57.3	60.8	64.1	67.5	70.9	74.2	76.0	77.6	79.3	81.0	82.7	84.4	86.1	87.7	91.1
17	41.3	44.4	47.6	50.8	54.0	57.2	60.3	63.5	66.7	69.9	71.5	73.0	74.6	76.2	77.8	79.4	81.0	82.6	85.7
18	39.0	42.0	45.0	48.0	51.0	54.0	57.0	60.0	63.0	66.0	67.5	69.0	70.5	72.0	73.5	75.0	76.5	78.0	81.0
19	36.9	39.7	42.6	45.4	48.3	51.2	54.0	56.8	59.7	62.5	64.0	65.4	66.8	68.2	69.6	71.0	72.5	73.9	76.7
20	35.1	37.8	40.5	43.2	45.9	48.6	51.3	54.0	56.7	59.4	60.8	62.1	63.4	64.8	66.1	67.5	68.8	70.2	72.9
21	33.4	36.0	38.5	41.1	43.7	46.3	48.9	51.4	54.0	56.6	57.9	59.1	60.4	61.7	63.0	64.3	65.5	66.8	69.4
22	31.9	34.3	36.8	39.2	41.7	44.2	46.6	49.1	51.5	54.0	55.2	56.4	57.7	58.9	60.1	61.4	62.6	63.8	66.2
23	30.5	32.8	35.2	37.5	39.9	42.3	44.6	47.0	49.3	51.6	52.8	54.0	55.2	56.3	57.5	58.7	59.9	61.0	63.4
24	29.3	31.5	33.7	36.0	38.2	40.5	42.7	45.0	47.2	49.5	50.7	51.7	52.9	54.0	55.1	56.2	57.3	58.5	60.7
25	28.0	30.2	32.4	34.5	36.7	38.9	41.1	43.2	45.4	47.5	48.6	49.7	50.8	51.8	52.9	54.0	55.1	56.2	58.3
26	27.0	29.0	31.1	33.2	35.3	37.4	39.5	41.5	43.6	45.7	46.7	47.8	48.8	49.8	50.9	51.9	53.7	54.0	56.1
27	26.0	28.0	30.0	32.0	34.0	36.0	38.0	40.0	42.0	44.0	45.0	46.0	47.0	48.0	49.0	50.0	51.0	52.0	54.0
28	25.1	27.0	28.9	30.8	32.7	34.7	36.6	38.6	40.5	42.4	43.4	44.4	45.3	46.3	47.2	48.2	49.2	50.1	52.0
29	24.2	26.0	27.9	29.7	31.6	33.5	35.3	37.2	39.1	40.9	41.8	42.8	43.7	44.6	45.6	46.5	47.4	48.4	50.2
30	23.4	25.2	27.0	28.8	30.6	32.4	34.2	36.0	37.8	39.6	40.5	41.4	42.3	43.2	44.1	45.0	45.9	46.8	48.6
31	22.6	24.4	26.1	27.8	29.6	31.4	33.1	34.8	36.6	38.3	39.2	40.1	40.9	41.8	42.7	43.5	44.4	45.3	47.0
32	21.9	23.6	25.3	27.0	28.7	30.4	32.1	33.8	35.4	37.1	38.0	38.8	39.7	40.5	41.3	42.2	43.0	43.9	45.6
33	21.3	22.9	24.5	28.2	27.8	29.45	31.1	32.7	34.4	36.0	36.8	37.6	38.5	39.3	40.1	40.9	41.7	42.5	44.2
34	20.6	22.0	23.8	25.4	27.0	28.6	30.2	31.8	33.4	34.9	35.7	36.5	37.3	38.1	38.9	39.7	40.5	41.3	42.9

Gear ratios not shown above may be calculated as follows:

$$\text{Gear} = \frac{\text{number of teeth on chainring}}{\text{number of teeth on sprocket}} \times \text{diameter of rear wheel in inches}$$

gearing you want to begin with so there are no surprises.

Efficient Riding

We will assume now that you have a gearing system suited to your personal requirements and that you have developed your cadence and shifting to a smooth degree. Let's look into a few of the finer points of efficient cycling that will be of help to your touring.

Riding as smoothly as possible is the major factor associated with efficiency in cycling. By learning and concentrating on the proper shifting sequence along with developing a steady, 60-80 rpm cadence, you have already done most of the work. This isn't to say there will never be any variation in your cadence; rather as you become more skilled and experienced you will find you rarely vary from your norm by more than a plus or minus 5 revolutions no matter the cycling conditions.

Cyclists frequently interrupt their cadence when they shift. It pays to learn to anticipate your shifts before they become necessary or even impossible without breaking into your rhythm. You have probably seen two riders closely paced going up a hill, only to see one suddenly drop behind dramatically, never to catch up. It isn't that one was stronger; more likely one was anticipating the shifts while the other waited too long only to lose all upward momentum while trying to get into a lower gear. The opposite extreme is when a rider shifts down too soon on approaching a hill, sometimes going into the lowest gear because he knows it will be needed before getting to the top. Then you see a wild spinning of pedals with dramatic drop in momentum until finally the hill matches the low gear; you will slow down much sooner than would have been the case had the shifting been done properly.

As you approach a hill, wait to shift just until you begin to feel increasing resistance to your stroke, then drop down only one gear at a time while maintaining your normal cadence. It takes practice. As you shift the gear, momentarily ease up on the pedal. You can't expect the derailleurs to move the chain while you are applying full pressure to it. The trick that comes with practice and experience is to learn just how much to let up pressure to quickly make the shift without breaking your cadence or losing momentum.

There is sometimes a tendency to overshift, that is to move the derailleur (the chain), a little too far on the cogs. With experience you will learn to automatically adjust the derailleur to center it on the cog when you overshoot. A sudden noise in the area of a derailleur made by the chain rubbing against the adjoining cog indicates an improper alignment that can be quickly cured by moving your shift lever slightly in one direction or the other. It doesn't take much, just a slight adjustment will do.

As you are progressing up a hill,

dropping into lower gears one at a time, you will eventually reach the point — if the hill is long and steep enough — where you arrive at your last, lowest "granny" gear. From there on you will be exerting steadily increasing pressure on the pedals and your cadence will necessarily begin to slow down. Things are getting tough. By this time you should have your hands in the full drop position on your handlebars and be leaning forward. This lets you bring your strong back and arm muscles into play and to literally pull your way up the hill. One thing to watch for here is to guard against shifting your weight from side to side as you pull. Such swaying back and forth is a great waste of energy and tends to make your course erratic. Try to maintain a stable body position and a straight line of travel.

A good way to check on your upper body stability is to suspend a small object from a string around your neck (a simple pendant necklace would work fine). Glance at it as you cycle up hills; it should remain hanging straight down, not swinging from side to side.

When the going gets tough, some of the toughs start "honking," standing up off the saddle to pressure their way up. Try to resist the temptation. Honking is a real strain on your legs, arms and body in general. With good gearing you can conquer almost any hill sitting down. When all is lost and you are almost at a standstill, swallow hard, ignore your pride, step off your bike and walk. You will be amazed at how good it

To check on your upper body stability, suspend a small object (a pendant necklace would work). Glance at it as you cycle up hills. If your body position is correct, it should remain hanging straight down, not swinging from side to side.

feels to use different muscles for awhile, not to mention how nice it is to really look at the view. If you are worried about what your better-conditioned (or more stubborn) cycling companions will say, whip out your camera and take a picture. They'll never know the difference.

One final technique in efficient cycling is called ankling. It is a difficult maneuver to learn only by reading about it; it is even harder to teach by writing about it. Basically, ankling is the maintenance of constant pressure on both pedals throughout the entire 360-degree rotation using a maximum number of muscles in your legs, ankles and feet.

In order to do it successfully, your bicycle must be adjusted to you exactly (see chapter three) and you must be using toe clips and straps.

Beginning at the top of the pedal cycle, the 12 o'clock position, the foot is flat or horizontal. As the pedal passes the 3 o'clock and approaches the 6 o'clock position, there is a digging into the toe clips. As the pedal passes the 6 o'clock position the foot is definitely tilted downward and there is a feeling of pulling, or clawing, of the foot backward on the pedal. As the 9 o'clock position is reached the foot is beginning to flatten out again until at the 12 o'clock position it is again horizontal and ready to start downward once more. This continual digging and clawing, done in a smooth, steady manner for the entire rotation, should employ all the muscles possible in the lower leg, ankle and even the foot. Don't be surprised if you develop sore ankle joints, calves and insteps as you are learning and practicing the process. Persevere, your body will soon adjust to this new development.

Proper ankling will add greatly to your overall efficiency because you are applying power throughout the entire rotation of the chainwheel, spreading the effort over a greater number of muscles, and sharing the load, thereby increasing the energy output as well.

After writing this section, Tim went out for his usual daily ride to put ankling into practice as though for the first time. He reaffirmed that it is definitely much easier to do than to write about. Simply concentrate on maintaining pressure throughout the entire chainwheel revolution by digging down and clawing back up. Chances are, if your bike was properly adjusted in the first place, you have been ankling all along and were not even aware of it.

Chapter Five
Choosing
Auxiliary Equipment

Assuming you are progressing through this book chapter by chapter, you have now chosen a touring bicycle, fitted it exactly to your body specifications, and are acquainted with or have modified your gearing range to suit your particular style of riding. We will now consider basic safety and auxiliary equipment as well as how to hold onto your investment.

Helmets

Aside from the bicycle itself, your most important piece of equipment is what is on your head in addition to what is in your head. You may think a helmet is not very important, or perhaps even detrimental, to your touring pleasure. We find life on a bicycle preferable to life in a hospital bed, or no life at all. Tim

would have lost a number of friends — which he claims he can hardly afford — and in fact would be a widower with two small children were it not for bicycle helmets.

Accidents don't always happen to someone else. If one happens to you, most of your parts can be pinned, stitched or taped back together. However, you've got real trouble if you spill any of that gray matter inside your skull. If the $35 or more cost deters you, consider that you couldn't even see a neurosurgeon's receptionist for that price. From the neck up is no place to economize.

Some cyclists object to the extra weight of a helmet. The better ones weigh just over a pound. Our daughter wore one almost every day for more than two months when she was nine years old and never once complained about the weight. Your neck will manage to hold your head and your helmet up without much additional effort.

Another argument against helmets is that they are hot. We have crossed the Mojave Desert in July when temperatures exceeded 110°F. and toured in both Hawaii and the eastern states when temperatures and humidity were in the upper 80s. Our experience is that wearing one of the better helmets is cooler than wearing no helmet at all. The bright shell reflects the sun's rays and holes allow air to pass through cre-

ating an evaporative cooling effect on the perspiration occurring inside.

As you have figured out by now, we are real helmet fans. There is admittedly one major drawback that involves the ego. What are people going to think when you are out there riding around with half an eggshell on your head? If you ride with a club or group, chances are that many of them ride with helmets. You feel like one of the "in" group when you have numbers on your side. It can get rather touchy if you ride alone or as a family, especially if people in the

Racers in action wearing strip helmets.

area are not used to such sights. The only advice we can give you is that, like seat belts in automobiles, helmets have been proven to save lives again and again. By wearing one you are showing intelligence, good common sense, and that you value your life. Drivers will see that you are serious about your cycling and will be more apt to share the road. You are also helping to educate people by familiarizing them to the sight. If these arguments do not totally convince you, keep in mind that by the time you are fully outfitted and packed up for a long tour you will look something like a traveling circus anyway; what difference in your appearance does a little thing like a helmet make?

There are a number of helmets available but only a few function. Don't attempt to save dollars or cut corners when it comes to your head. First, let's talk about the leather- or plastic-strip headgear, the one that looks like you have an octopus wrapped around your head. These were the first on the block and are still popular with the racing crowd due to their light weight. Fortunately, however, racers are beginning to want more protection than that offered by the strip helmets, which is practically nil. If you ride only on a smooth, wooden racing track with no rocks, curbs, trees or posts, they might be of some help. In the real world there are too many objects that can do serious damage to your skull between or even through the open, thin padding of the strip helmet. It might hold your head

Child wearing hockey-type helmet (CCM).

together, however, until you get to the hospital.

Next on the scene was the hockey helmet. This has a hard plastic shell with thin foam padding inside. Up until the early 1970s it was the best thing around, mostly because there wasn't much else available. But this helmet is generally very hot, uncomfortable and offers little protection against impact at high speeds given the distance from the ground of the falling object (your head). The hockey helmet has had a place among children as some can be adjusted to a small size, but specially made children's helmets are now entering the market. With a knit hat or two as padding, the hockey helmet can be worn by infants. For an adult, there isn't enough protection to warrant its use.

In the past few years a number of specially designed bicycle helmets in a wide variety of styles have come on the market. Some have undergone extensive testing and are excellent; others seem only to fill a void with no testing or evaluation. As usual, the buyer must beware; insist on proven quality.

There are only two helmets we feel confident in using; one is the MSR, the other the Bell. Both products have been thoroughly tested with the companies standing firmly behind their products. Both are light, cool, comfortable and offer the best protection available to cyclists. Do yourself or a loved one a favor — invest in a good helmet.

MSR and Bell helmets.

Aids to Visibility

Once your head is protected, look out for the rest of your body. Bright clothing is the best guarantee that you will be seen out there in the jungle. We go into greater detail about clothing types and materials in chapter six, but we mention it here as a prime component of safety while riding or touring.

Other products that aid your effort toward visibility are bike flags, bright vests and safety patches. Bike flags are the subject of much controversy in the bicycling world. Many cyclists feel that flags are amateurish and in fact slow you down. As to their lack of professionalism, it is true that you don't see many Tour de France racers with bike flags flapping in the breeze. However, they are not worried about lumber trucks and semis either. As to being a drag, Chester Kyle permanently put that argument to rest in the March 1976 issue of *Bicycling.* In a series of tests, Kyle determined that a bike safety flag offers no more air resistance than a frame-mounted water bottle. The touring cyclist should be at least as concerned with safety as with dehydration. If flags have any serious drawback it is the gymnastics required of the rider when mounting or dismounting. If you choose to use one, you soon become accustomed to it.

We believe in bike flags for several reasons. They greatly increase your visibility because they are continually moving, thereby better attracting the attention of motorists than relatively stationary bright clothing or bike packs.

Also, they extend into the air above the height of the rider. This is especially helpful in crowded, urban situations.

There is no longer the choice among bike flags that there used to be both due to the crash of the bike boom and their disfavor among so-called serious cyclists. Those that are on the market are generally sad items, at best. We use and prefer those made by Schwinn. Since they cost more you might have to special-order from the factory through your local Schwinn shop. Schwinn flags are superior because they are tapered like a fishing pole. This gives a lot more action at the tip where it counts and the amount of action is not dependent on your speed. They have a small ball on the upper end to protect your eyes when the pole is bent. Pull that off and reattach it with good glue as it is prone to disappearing.

Flags usually come in international orange or bright yellow. Yellow is more visible in green, wooded areas such as the eastern United States, but orange is best in the dry West and the central states. One flag will survive a cross-country trip, but you will probably have to replace the pennant for cycling beyond that. We have had good success with red and orange ripstop nylon replacements Glenda sews on the sewing machine.

If flags don't appeal to you, or you want to double your protection, try the safety vests you see highway-repair people wearing. They are a good idea if you don't mind looking a bit like an orange-breasted fly catcher. Choose one made of material that can breathe or make your own.

A popular item, especially with American Youth Hostel, Inc., (AYH) touring groups, is a bright orange or red triangle of material worn on the lower back or on the bike packs. This is the standard symbol for slow vehicles and is readily recognized as such by most motorists. We are for anything that improves your chances of being seen. Take your pick or use them all.

Rearview Mirrors

As important as being seen is to see for yourself. For that the rearview mirror is a critically important piece of equipment. We don't mean one that attaches to your handlebars, rather the small dental-type mirror that fits onto the temple of your glasses or to the rim of your helmet. Most cyclists are paranoid about being attacked from the rear by a Detroit gas guzzler. It rarely does any good to point to statistics, which prove that few cyclists are hit from behind; they understandably do not want to be one of them.

Without a mirror you must turn your head to look behind. Not only do you lose sight of what is ahead, but there is a natural tendency to drift to the left as you twist around. It is small comfort to learn that you have drifted directly into the path of a Peterbilt truck instead of the Greyhound bus that you thought

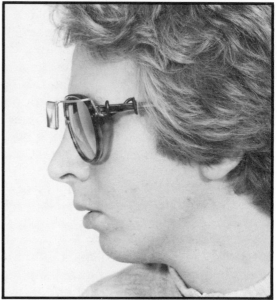

Cyclist wearing simple wire-style rearview mirror attached to regular glasses or sunglasses.

you were turning around to see. A rearview mirror attached to your glasses or helmet keeps you aware of yet out of the traffic with a simple movement of the eyes. You should, of course, be wearing glasses while you cycle whether you normally wear them or not. Glasses, regular or tinted, protect your eyes from flying insects, stones and other roadside miscellany.

Rearview mirrors, like the proverbial mousetrap, are always being improved. We like the original style made of stiff wire that slips on the temple of your glasses. Glenda tried a plastic model while crossing the Mojave Desert; four days of extreme heat and rough shoulder riding rendered it useless. The fewer joints, clips and plastic parts, the better. You want that mirror to fasten in the exact same position every time you use it and you want it to stay there no matter what road conditions are. If you can't depend on it, you are better off without one.

They come in two or three styles to fit different-size glasses and cost $3-$5. The mirror itself may be square, rectangular or circular; pick the one that shapes the world as you like it.

Once you have your mirror, do the basic adjustments while standing with both feet firmly on the ground. Bend it so you can just see the edge of the center portion of your left ear (naturally you wear the mirror on the left side where the traffic is). That should be fairly close to where you want it. Now, get on your bike to try it out. If you find it is not quite right, STOP to make your final adjustments. This may take awhile, but once it is right you should not have to adjust it again — unless you sit on it.

Hand Protectors

Another item that we consider part of auxiliary safety equipment is some sort of padding between you and the handlebars. As mentioned in chapter three, many cyclists experience numb or tingling fingers when cycling for long periods of time. There are three approaches to dealing with this problem; use of randonneur handlebars that provide a variety of hand positions (as discussed in chapter two), use of riding gloves that pad the palm, and use of some sort of padding on the handlebars themselves. If a person is particularly sensitive, it can take all three.

Riding gloves look like golf gloves with cutoff fingers, an open-weave knit top and a leather, padded palm and fingers on the underside. The padding not only protects the ulnar nerve from being pinched but offers some protection against road shock by making it generally more comfortable to grip the bars. Road shock can really take its toll. On our cross-country trip Kirsten wore through the leather-padded palms of her gloves in about 2,500 miles. Gloves also offer some protection if you ever make that infamous trip over the handlebars with a scream on your lips and your hands extended in front of you. Such a maneuver is hard on your palms and on emergency-room personnel who hate all the work it takes to remove the gravel. Riding gloves help.

There are only a few varieties of gloves available and most are good quality. They cost $10-$15. One way to preserve your investment is to wash them occasionally in cool water with hand soap. Allow them to line dry a little, then put them on to finish drying. This insures a good fit by preventing the cotton-knit backing from shrinking.

Aside from protection, other serious cyclists will recognize you as one of them by the little round patches of tanned skin on the backs of your hands. That alone should be worth the money.

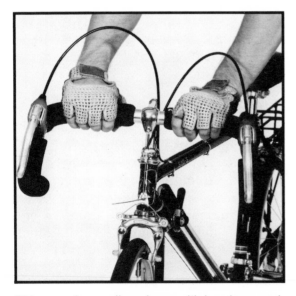

Rider wearing cycling gloves with hands on padded randonneur handlebars.

75

If you need still more padding, you will have to add it to your handlebars. Most production bikes come with cotton cloth tape wrapped on the bars. Although far superior to plastic tape, cloth tape offers little protection to the hands from road shock or pressure on the palms. If you have never been troubled with ulnar nerve problems and your tours are generally short, you can probably do without handlebar padding, especially if you wear riding gloves. However, for long tours some sort of padding would be a wise investment, even if you have not had problems to date.

We have tried many of the handlebar padding tapes available. Until recently we always used Bailey III tape ($4). It is a rubberlike product with tapered edges that can be wrapped on the bars like regular cloth tape. It is rather sticky and attracts dirt, so we put a layer of cloth tape ($1 per roll, two required) over the Bailey III. The cloth not only feels better and stays cleaner, but protects the padded tape from wear and tear. When this outer cloth tape begins to wear, we simply wrap another layer over it.

If you prefer very heavy padding on your handlebars, you might try a product called Grab-On ($8). Tim has been using it recently with good results. It is a black foam-rubber tubing about ¼ inch thick that looks like it might have been designed as refrigeration pipe insulation. Depending on the model, it either slips on the bare handlebars in one piece, or is split down one side to be placed over the bars and glued together. Buy the solid variety as the other has difficulty staying glued together. Both come so that one section is placed above the brake lever, one below. Tim doesn't use the lower section because of the way it feels as the brakes are applied. Many people use it there and don't see it as a problem. We don't think the Grab-On will last as long as Bailey III with cloth over it, but it certainly provides a smooth, comfortable ride over even the roughest road.

The best piece of bicycle-touring safety equipment cannot be purchased at any price. It is common sense. Even if you are fortunate enough to have it, it is a good investment on your part to add the few items we have just discussed. Everything we advocate to this point, including the helmet, costs about $60-$70. That is pretty inexpensive insurance against injury.

Tire Pumps

Some other touring equipment items are not necessarily safety related but can be important for your comfort and convenience. At the head of the list is the frame-mounted tire pump. If you live in a metropolitan area it is sometimes hard to imagine that there are miles of country out there without gas stations at every corner. Even if you won't be touring in open country, gas-station air hoses are notoriously hard on bicycle tires. Th scenario usually goes like this: "Hey, lady, let me help you with those tires." BLAM! "Wow, you must have had a bad tire there. Here, let me do the other one." BLAM! "Imagine that, lady, two bad tires. You better get those fixed."

If you insist on inflating your tires at gas stations, do it yourself, slowly. Those air hoses have in excess of 100 pounds of pressure and it comes out fast because they are designed for very large-volume automobile tires, not small-volume bike tires. Keep your fingers pressed on the tire to monitor the inflation rate and use short, quick blasts of air. Don't trust the gauge on the hose as it surely has been dropped and probably has been run over a few times. Take your own along to use. Better yet, avoid the entire process by carrying your own pump with you, neatly attached to the frame out of the way on your bicycle.

Only a few of the many pumps on the market are dependable. If you ride with tubular tires or have Presta-valve clincher tires, the Silca pump is a tried and true companion. A new model is now available to fit Schrader valves. It comes in colors to match your bike and in varying lengths (frame mounted) to fit between the bottom bracket and the top tube.

We consider the Zefal pump best for touring with clincher tires and Schrader valve stems. It has a quick, thumb-lock device, which attaches to the valve stem so that it goes on and off without significant loss of air. Avoid any pump with a screw-on valve fitting; you are apt to lose more air getting it off than you put into the tire.

The Zefal comes in three models; the Zefal hp made of lightweight silver metal that fastens to your frame with an umbrella clip; another hp made of plastic that fits on the frame like the Silca; and the hp like the plastic hp but with a built-in gauge to allow you to set the desired pressure, so the air automatically bypasses the valve when that pressure is reached. All models come with a conversion unit for Presta valves.

Any one of these pumps will give you years of service and is capable of inflating your tire to over 100 pounds,

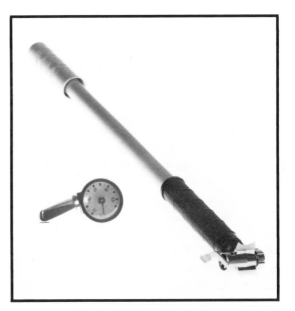

Zefal high-pressure (hp) pump alongside of Pressograph pressure gauge.

depending on the strength of your arm. Prices range from $10-$20; the built-in-gauge model is the most expensive.

You should have a good, reliable gauge in your equipment if you don't have one on your pump. Be sure the gauge you buy is for bicycles, not automobiles. Car gauges usually do not register high enough for bike tires and are not designed to attach tightly to the valve stem. A good bicycle gauge will have a spring-loaded gasket inside the stem that makes complete contact with the top of the tire valve stem before allowing air to pass from the tube into the gauge.

We use and recommend the Pressograph dial-type gauge. It is accurate, reliable (if not dropped), and registers up to 115 pounds of pressure. It sells for over $6 and is available for either Presta or Schrader valves. The pencil-type gauge made by Dunlop is less expensive but also very good.

Water Bottles

As devastating on tour as not being able to put air into your tires is not being able to put water into your body. Dehydration is a serious problem that we will discuss later, but even for short rides you should have a water supply literally at your fingertips. The quickest and easiest solution is the frame-mounted water bottle or bottles. You could carry your water supply in your handlebar bag or rear saddlebags (panniers), but that requires stopping to drink. With the bottle(s) attached to your frame in plain view, it is easy to remember to fill them and with a little practice you can use them adeptly while riding. Water-bottle holders (cages) can be attached to the down tube, the seat tube or even to your handlebars. Most riders prefer the tube locations.

Your bicycle pump will already occupy one of the tubes, probably the front of the seat tube, so you might mount your water bottle on the down tube as close to the bottom bracket as possible. It will be within easy reach while pedaling after you become accustomed to its location.

Cage types include those that attach directly to the frame with small bolts (if your bike has braze-on attachments), those with a permanently affixed clamp that attaches to any tube, and those with a removable clamp that fits either way. They are made of chrome-plated steel or aluminum alloy in either silver or black. Prices range from $2.50-$10. The TA alloy cage is more expensive; the cheaper steel weighs more and will eventually rust. Higher price usually means that the method of construction is more lasting and secure as well.

As for the water bottle itself, look for TA, Maraplast, REG or A.L.E. They all give good service and cost from $2-$3 each. If a plastic taste prevails when the bottle is new, put in ¼ cup of vinegar and fill with warm water. Let that sit overnight; don't forget to drain and refill with fresh water before you use it.

Lights

Most touring bicyclists prefer and plan not to ride after dark. However, it may sometimes be necessary; that is no time to realize you do not have a light. On our cross-country trip, we rode through the western deserts in July. It was far too hot to be on the road after the noon hour, so if we had a long stretch to cover before the next camp (water), we had to get up to be on the road as much as an hour before daylight. We never rode at night, yet we sometimes rode in the dark. On tour you never know when an emergency or an entertainment may delay your arrival at an expected place until after dark; it is best to be prepared for the possibility.

There are two main types of bike lights — generator powered and battery powered. If you do a good deal of riding after dark, either on tour or around the neighborhood, the generator light may be best for you. It has a relatively high output of light and you do not have to buy batteries or a battery charger. The disadvantages are high cost, the drag it places on the bike tire and its somewhat delicate nature. We personally dislike the fact that it goes off when the bicycle is stopped. Intersections are the most dangerous places for bike riders, yet the generator light leaves you without illumination when you need it most.

If you decide that the generator light best suits your needs, we recommend the Soubitez and Union models at $10-$15. Find a bike shop that stocks the rubber cap that fits over the generator wheel; it helps preserve the sidewall of your tire where the generator wheel rubs.

The battery light also has disadvantages. Some do not provide much illumination and batteries are expensive. But it is light in weight, dependable (as long as your batteries hold out), remains on no matter what the bicycle is doing, and — perhaps its greatest advantage while touring — it can be removed and used around camp. If you plan to camp out you will need a light anyway. Why not have one that serves two purposes?

For bicycle touring a battery light must be bright, legal, lightweight, reliable and it must fit your bike when the bike is outfitted with racks, packs and panniers. These requirements negate a lot of lights, including the arm/leg light; it is not legal in many states when used by itself because it is not bright enough. As for the popular Wonder Head Lite, you will frequently be wondering where you can buy another battery.

For a long time Tim used a chrome lantern ($4) that used two D cell batteries and had a swivel head. It served its purpose but offered little illumination. He has since discovered the Berec ($6), made in England. It is plastic, uses two D batteries, which can be found even in Hanksville, Utah, and comes with a mounting bracket for the handlebars. It is of superior construction and has a fine, specially formed tough plastic lens. He has yet to find a light of comparable weight that is as good. Berec makes an excellent red rear light ($4) that uses two D batteries and we have heard good reports on the CEV 181 ($5) powered by two C cells.

Whatever kind of light you choose, there are some tricks to using one. The light not only lets other vehicles see you, but it shows the condition of the road immediately ahead of you. Always assume there is a huge chuckhole or dead muffler just beyond it waiting for you; keep your speed down and your attention sharp.

Be sure that your light will stay together and on your bike when you hit rough roads or bumps. Tape over the battery compartment if necessary (it is with the Berec rear light), and reinforce the mounting system. Try to mount the light low so you can better see the road. Tim used a front reflector mount that fit onto and extended in front of his front brake, but now uses a hard-to-find English light bracket that is held in place by the quick-release mechanism on the front wheel.

Always carry an extra bulb; unusual ones can be hard enough to find but when one goes out in the dark, any stores around are likely to be closed. On some models the extra bulb can be taped inside the light. Use heavy-duty alkaline batteries for obvious reasons. Finally, when it is not in use, either reverse the batteries or tape the switch in the off position. It won't do any good to have well-lit pannier interiors all day and no light at night.

Whether you plan to do any night riding at all, or if you simply want to be legal, you must have a full complement of reflectors. That means a red one to the rear, a white one to the front, amber ones on both sides of the pedals, an amber or white one on the front wheel, and a red or white one on the rear wheel. If you have a choice use white on the wheels as it reflects better than either red or amber. If you swear you will never ride at night and you don't care what the law says, at least have a red reflector to the rear. It may give a driver a few seconds of reaction time before he plows into you on that one time when you just couldn't help being out there after dark.

Kickstands

A kickstand is a piece of auxiliary equipment that we feel is very helpful to the cyclist. Most "serious" cyclists wouldn't be caught dead with one but we are more concerned with practicality than style and highly recommend one. Without a kickstand you must lean your bike against some sort of support. Many times the support doesn't do the job so your bike is on the ground with a few more scratches in the paint and maybe worse damage elsewhere. If there is no support handy, the bike gets put down on its side, packs and all. This is just too hard on everything and not practical besides.

There are two real objections to kickstands. First, they are heavy. They add some extra weight to your bike but it is relative to other important considerations mentioned above. Second, they can damage the chainstays if clamped on too tight. So, don't tighten them down too much. Use a small wrench and just get the bolt firm, don't see how far you can turn it. We use kickstands on all our bikes, including some with very thin tubes, and have never had any problems.

If you do use a kickstand, make sure the end is on firm footing. Hot asphalt, soft mud or grass won't do the job. Always turn your handlebars in whatever direction will give the bike the best support when the kickstand is in use. Make sure the kickstand fits the bike properly so that it leans over about eight to ten degrees when the stand is in use. Cut it to the proper length and angle with a hacksaw if necessary. Finally, buy a quality kickstand; the Esge ($4) is the only one we use.

Fenders

Fenders (mudguards) are another controversial item. Some tourists wouldn't use a set even in pouring rain, while others wouldn't ride across the desert without them. Fenders not only keep you drier by stopping the wheels from spraying water on you in the rain or on wet pavement, but they also keep your bike about 75 percent cleaner in dry weather by keeping dirt and dust from being thrown by the wheels onto your bike.

On the minus side, fenders add wind resistance and definitely slow you down a bit. They make it harder to service your bike, and they are useless under some really muddy conditions. Thick mud jams up between the fender and the wheel, making it impossible to move. All in all, they are just one more thing to hassle with. We have ambivalent feelings about them but use them on both our town and touring bikes. We think the protection is worth the negative aspects. Better fender sets are made by Bluemel and Esge ($8-$12).

Time/Distance Instruments

Many touring cyclists enjoy using a speedometer and odometer; the first clocks your speed, the second your distance. It is fun to know how fast or far you have gone at the end of a long touring day. We have used both and now don't use either.

We bought a very expensive English odometer to use on our daughter, Kirsten's, bike as we began our cross-country tour; it lasted 14 miles. Tim tried another variety later but the clicking on the spokes of the little metal stud that strikes the star wheel attached to the odometer, just about drove him nuts. He has a low threshold for such things. He also worried about protrusions that could catch on something and cause trouble.

A recent newcomer to the market is the Huret Multito Cyclometer ($10). This device fits on the front axle and is driven by a belt instead of the usual pin-and-star-wheel arrangement. It is silent, compact and looks like the best odometer to come along. The Multito just may make us believers again.

Speedometer/odometer combinations are now usually made with a wheel that runs along the side of the tire, turning a cable that is attached to the main body of the device; it registers both the speed and the distance traveled. These little gadgets are great fun to use, but are relatively fragile. Costs range from $10-$15. We used one on our Hawaii tour but found it inoperable after an overly exuberant baggage clerk bent it while loading the bike for an interisland flight. From that point on we decided to let the road map tell us how far we had traveled. As for how fast (or slow) we are going, sometimes it is better not to know.

Child Seats

If you have a family and want your cycling pleasures now, you will need to acquire some rather specialized equipment. Let's first cover the child seat that mounts over the rear wheel of the adult bicycle. We are ambivalent about it. On the one hand, we want to encourage as much family participation in bicycling as possible, especially family long-distance touring. On the other hand, we are well aware of the danger of transporting a small child on the back of a bike; if the bike goes down, so does the child. We used one when our son, Erik, was between 14 and 18 months. Prior to 14 months he rode, well padded with blankets and knit cap in a Gerry carrier, on Glenda's back. We don't recommend it; we simply did it without mishap.

Shop for a child seat of the tough plastic, wraparound high-backed type with a built-in foot area. Make sure it has, and that you use, a safety belt and a spoke protector. It should mount well forward so the weight is centered over the rear axle. There are several on the market now that are improvements on what was available when we needed one. Check them carefully for durability, construction and lack of protrusions.

More important than the seat itself, perhaps, is putting some sort of hard-shell helmet on the child. We eagerly watch the developing market in children's bicycling helmets for one comparable to those now available for adults; but until that happens, use something even if you have to pad it with knit hats to make it fit snugly. Up to two years of age, we used an adjustable hockey helmet for Erik, which only required one thick knit hat and that more

Mother and child on bike with child strapped in well-designed bike seat positioned over rear wheel. Of course, helmets are desirable.

for shock absorption than sizing. For the cross-country trip we used the smallest adult Bell helmet, fitted with their thickest sizing pads glued to a Styrofoam spacer inside. Bell, Inc., does not recommend or guarantee it, but we decided it was certainly better than nothing.

Bike Trailers

It has been our experience that once the child is over 20-25 pounds, de-

pending on the pedaling parent, he simply becomes too mobile and tipsy to use a child seat. It is time, then, to consider a bike trailer.

There are several bike trailers on the market, but the only one with which we are familiar is the Bugger made by Cannondale Corporation. The Bugger is a two-wheeled trailer framed with steel tubing, which incorporates a nylon sling between the wheels to support the load. An option is a child seat made of durable black plastic, which fits directly onto the Bugger frame. It has a safety belt, will hold two children, and has a capacity of about 85 pounds. It attaches to the bicycle with a semiflexible hitch at the seatpost, which allows the bike to tilt to either side, independent of the trailer. The Bugger tracks beautifully and its approximately 25-30 pounds of drag do not affect the handling qualities of the bike. In fact, Glenda reports that it has a stabilizing effect when the bike is being knocked about by truck turbulence.

The Bugger transforms a bicycle into a really practical utility vehicle. That is enough to make a lot of cycling purists cringe, but most parents are reconciled to station wagons over sports cars anyway. Things that you would never be able to carry on a bike can be easily handled with a trailer. When Erik was small, Glenda found the Bugger actually promoted her use of the bicycle because she could haul library books, dry cleaning and groceries, in addition to Erik. She appreciated being able to pedal right up to front doors with no parking hassle. With the child carrier in place, she could carry Erik plus four or five regular-size grocery bags. Of course it is nice to live downhill from town for the loaded return trip.

Even though the Bugger, including child seat, now costs in excess of $180, it is worth the price considering its versatility and potential for long-term use. We first got our Bugger when it became too risky to carry Erik on the rear of the bike — brought home by an incident on a lonely stretch of road where Glenda had her hands full of bike and baby. He then weighed about 20 pounds. Almost five years later, at about 50 pounds, he is getting a little heavy for either of us to haul around for fun. Luckily, he can now pedal his own small bike up to ten miles. The Bugger, however, still serves as the family errand runner.

We are convinced that a trailer is a good deal safer than the bike-mounted carrier primarily because the Bugger remains upright in the event of a fall, something we have unintentionally proven. Also, the child is much more comfortable because there is room to move around or even to lie down for a nap within the confines of the safety belt.

If you plan to use a Bugger, there are some modifications you might make. First, install thin, $3/16$-inch-plywood fenders on the side of the child carrier to keep small hands out of the spokes. Second, put on both an upright and a horizontal bike flag. The horizontal one should extend 12-15 inches on the left (highway) side to act as a warning for passing motorists to keep their distance. The flags can be attached by drilling small holes and wiring them to the frame. We also attached a water bottle to the arm portion of the child carrier so we wouldn't have to stop every time Erik got thirsty. It has been a good investment.

For long-distance touring with small children, you can do as we did and use two Buggers — one for the child and miscellaneous gear, the other without a child carrier for camping gear.

Adult pulling child in a trailer with a child seat.

It is still cheaper than hiring a babysitter for several months, even if you could find one. Be prepared to pay the price in energy for the weight you will be pulling. It is a good pace equalizer, however, if you have other children on small bikes along with you.

Protecting Your Bike

Now that you have finalized your investment in your touring bicycle with the necessary and nice in safety and auxiliary equipment, how do you hang onto it all in the face of constant bike thefts? Over 75 percent of bicycles stolen are left unlocked. No matter what lock you choose, if you always use it the odds are in your favor.

As to the type of security you need, your decision will rest to a great extent on where you live and where you are going to be parking your bike. In Wolf Hole, Arizona, you wouldn't even need a rubber band through the spokes, but in New York City a Brinks armored truck might not do the job.

The most popular form of bike locking device is a self-coiling, plastic-coated wire cable. These range in thickness from about $3/16$ - $7/16$ inch (this does not include the coating). Most are 6 feet long. This is perhaps the handiest bike security system when combined with a good padlock whose hasp is at least as thick as the cable. In low-crime areas, the $3/16$-inch cable is a good deterrent to spontaneous rip-off. It is cheap, easy to use and light in weight. If the bike is to be left unattended for a long period of time, the heavier 3/8-inch cable with comparable lock might be a better idea. Be forewarned, however, that all of these cables can be easily cut with rather small wire snips and bolt cutters. The thickness of the cable does not make all that much difference. On tour we use $3/16$-inch cable simply for its light weight and compactness. But when Tim used to leave his commuter bike unattended all day at the bus stop, he used a 3/8-inch cable. However, that was in a low-crime area.

Chains are also available for bike security, but their disadvantages include bulk, shortness, cost and ease of cutting with bolt cutters. Since 85 percent of stolen locked bikes have had bolt cutters used in the process, a chain does not represent much of an advantage over a cable; each will readily separate with a 24-inch pair of bolt cutters. With the more-resistant, case-hardened, four-foot-long, 3/8-inch-diameter chains and a heavy-duty padlock to match, you are talking of an investment of over $25 and a weight of

over 6½ pounds. That is a lot to haul around and it can still be cut with 48-inch bolt cutters.

The ultimate in bicycle security are the Kryptonite and Citadel bike locks. These locks are so secure that they are guaranteed against theft when properly used, even on the streets of New York. They look like oversize horseshoes, cost in the vicinity of $25, and weigh about two pounds.

No matter the system you choose, it is worthless if you don't use it correctly every single time you leave your bike. A cable or chain should be extended through the front wheel, around the frame, through the rear wheel, then around or through a solid, permanently fixed object. It does little good to lock

To secure your bike, lock it to a solid object with cable running through front and rear wheels, through frame and around solid object.

your front wheel to a bike rack unless the front wheel is the only thing you value.

Park your bike in open, public view. Don't hide it around the back of a store where no one will see it except the thief who will be well protected from view as he works on your cable or lock. When touring, it is especially important to keep your bike in sight at all times, even if locked, because on it are all your worldly possessions with only a zipper or Velcro tab to slow down a thief. We generally leave one person with the bikes while the others are off shopping or, if we are eating out, we park them near the restaurant window and then ask the waitress for a seat where we can see the bikes. At tourist attractions or when everyone has to go at once, we lock everything securely together in one big tangle of wheels, then try to find a friendly ticket taker or shopkeeper to leave the baggage with or just to watch it for us. That is in theory; in practice we have been known in some quiet, rural

areas to totally forget to lock anything as we sip sodas at some back-of-the-drugstore counter.

While camping at night on tour we remove all gear from the bikes and lock them together to a solid object such as a picnic table. The gear goes into the tent with us. In over 30 years of camping and touring in many countries of the world, we have only suffered the loss of one pair of cycling shoes; right out of our tent as we slept at a campground in Hawaii. If we're staying at a motel, we take everything, including bikes and Buggers, into the room with us. That has been rather interesting in some of the smaller places we have stayed.

Your security consciousness should not stop when you are at home. In our garage we hang all our bikes by one wheel on J hooks along the rafters, putting the most expensive bikes at the ends. A Kryptonite lock goes through the bike at one end, a Citadel through the other (we try not to show favoritism) and a heavy cable runs through the middle bikes to connect everything to the superlocks. A really good lock goes on the outside of the garage door. We haven't lost a bike yet, although a friend's was taken out of our front yard once when she dropped in for a visit.

It is a good idea to engrave your state driver's license number into the bottom bracket of your bike. Don't use your Social Security number as it is almost impossible for law-enforcement agencies to trace. With your driver's license number all they do when they catch a thief or find an abandoned bike is run a computer check; in a matter of seconds they know who the bike belongs to. In California, the ID engraving would look like this: CA D.L. #G937064.

Keep a record of that number (in case you move to another state) and also of the serial number along with a good, clear photograph of your bike. That way you will have something to show the police and your insurance company if it is stolen. You will also have something to remember it by.

Chapter Six
Clothes for Bicycle Touring

What are you going to wear while touring? To some this is of grave importance, perhaps of more importance than what to hang on the bicycle in the way of equipment. Others will be tempted to skip this chapter entirely, figuring they will wear what they always wear or whatever strikes their fancy at the time. Whichever you are, at least strive to maintain harmony between yourself and your environment, both in physical and psychological terms. If your body is as comfortable as possible given the weather conditions, yet you feel at ease with yourself alone in camp, in the midst of a group of tourists or walking around a small town square on Sunday afternoon, then your tour will be that much more enjoyable for you and for those exposed to you.

There is an increasingly varied selection of clothing and shoes available for bicycling. A trip through any large bike shop, the sport clothing section of a department store or a mail-order catalog will bombard you with a confusing array of colors, styles and materials. Unfortunately, most bicycling clothes and shoes are designed for the racing set. Bicycle touring shares some of the same needs, but has its own particular requirements. Rather than attempt to discuss the selections of brand names, which are constantly changing, expanding and expiring, we are going to give you criteria of choice that you can always use when selecting or replacing your touring wardrobe.

Comfort

The most important single factor in touring-clothing suitability is comfort.

89

No matter what other features an item has, if it is not comfortable you have lost the game. By comfort we mean off the bike as well, mental as well as physical. Something may feel great as you put in your mileage for the day, but as soon as you stop in town to shop for dinner you feel like hiding behind the produce counter anytime someone approaches. We do not consider that being comfortable.

On most bicycle-touring adventures you are outside urban areas. What is accepted dress in the city or suburbs may be outlandish in the country. Do you care? Should you care? That depends on your feelings about what other people think of your appearance, which is the only thing they have to go on until you open your mouth. If your appearance is weird to them, you may never have a chance to say a word. Perhaps that isn't how people should judge each other, but the fact remains that it is the first consideration of the majority.

We are not advocating that you cycle in coveralls and boots in the country. Just be cognizant of your own attitude toward acceptance. If you truly don't care what others think, then physical comfort is your only concern. Others are more sensitive to opinions and will consider psychological comfort as well as physical. Cycle touring in most areas of the world and in many parts of the United States is an unusual occurrence. You will be an object of curiosity no matter how you dress. This can work to your advantage in getting to know

people if you don't scare them away with unnecessary eccentricity. It is possible to have comfortable cycling clothing that fits in just about anywhere even when you are off your bike; just remember to remove your helmet and rearview mirror.

Physical comfort means the item is not binding or constrictive; there are no ridges, grommets, zippers or other protrusions between you and the bike; and the item is conducive to a comfortable body temperature in any weather conditions. Whether it is binding has to be determined by trying it on. Protrusions and ridges can be seen on examination, and temperature comfort is largely a matter of material type.

Breathability

When you are riding a bicycle with an eye to getting somewhere, you are going to get hot and sweaty no matter what gears you have. Your clothes must allow passage of perspiration from your body to the outside where air can evaporate it. Otherwise you might as well be pedaling in a sauna. Besides being uncomfortable, saturated clothing can be dangerous. In hot weather you overheat because evaporation cannot take place fast enough to cool your body. In cold weather, or simply going down a long grade, saturated clothing increases the windchill factor to an uncomfortable degree. In either case, a breathable fabric is essential for touring comfort.

Weight

Overall weight is a critical factor in any self-propelled vehicle; you don't want clothing to be heavier than necessary either on your body or in your panniers. We have seen people that were concerned that their water-bottle cage be the lightest available jump on their bike to tour in a pair of heavy jeans, carrying an army-surplus parka for evenings. If you order clothing from a catalog, total weight is usually given. In person, you can judge for yourself. If all else is equal in considering several articles of clothing, opt for the lightest.

Durability

You are carrying the bare essentials while touring so every piece of clothing counts. If something critical falls apart, you could be losing one-fourth or more of your wardrobe. Don't count on being able to replace an item at the next town as many towns do not have the selection or quality you need. Even the major department stores vary widely in what they carry for different sections of the country. Test items before going on an extended tour; if seams are going to rip out, they usually do it early. Wash everything several times before a long tour. The middle of the Mojave is no place to find out your shirt is suddenly too short.

Washability

This is an area where touring clothing requirements differ from those for racing. You might have the finest wool, chamois-lined riding shorts, but what will you wear during the two days they take to dry? Worse yet, what happens when you put them in the dryer out of desperation or forgetfulness only to find that they fit your kid brother back home but no longer fit you?

Touring clothing must be machine washable and dryable. Even if you wash by hand, as you must in many countries, easy-care fabrics dry quicker. In the United States there are self-serve laundries in most small towns with a business district. With easy-care clothing all you have to do is stop every couple of days for an hour or so. For a nominal fee you can start out fresh. Most have soap dispensers and some even have showers.

Bright Colors

You needn't look like a court jester in an orange-and-red-striped jersey, but make yourself able to be readily seen for safety's sake. This can be as simple as choosing lighter, brighter colors over darker ones. Being seen is critical, especially in the United States where drivers tend to mentally block out anything on the road that doesn't have four wheels. Bright colors are a morale booster too.

You may want dark colors, however, in the shorts department. Any type of riding pant, short or long, should be dark if you have a solid-leather saddle. You may already have discovered that the black dye used on many of the better saddles rubs off on your pants. This can add greatly to that psychological discomfort we talked about. Now you know why most chamois-lined professional cycling shorts are black.

Cost

Economical does not necessarily mean least expensive. If something you bought cheap proves totally unsuitable or does not wear well, it can be very expensive indeed. Much of the cycling clothing now available, and some of it is truly great for touring, is highly priced. We don't think the manufacturers are trying to rip off the consumer, rather the market for specifically designed items is not large. However, something costing a great deal initially can prove to be a very economical item in performance and durability.

Don't overlook the possibility of adapting some common piece of clothing or footwear to your cycling needs. We all wore ordinary, wash and wear shirts, shorts and blouses on our cross-country tour; they were physically and mentally comfortable, and fit all of the criteria listed here. Better yet, choose the material to your liking and get acquainted with a sewing machine (or someone who has one). You determine the quality of workmanship and the price is right.

○ ○ ○ ○ ○ ○ ○

Comfortable, breathable, light-weight, durable, washable, bright and economical — use these criteria when selecting any item of touring clothing or footwear. A lot depends on the type of material an item is made of. The choice is usually wool, cotton, man-made fiber, or a combination of these. Wool and cotton are more popular for sport-clothing construction.

Wool is common in the manufacture of cycling clothing for a number of good reasons. It is breathable and readily wicks moisture away from the rider's skin. It can hold almost one-third of its own weight in water without being saturated, which makes it comfortable to wear even when the rider is perspiring heavily. When it is cold, even if you are wet, wool will keep you warm and comfortable. Wool items are now available that are lightweight as well as brightly colored, making them hard to beat for cycling wear.

On the negative side, wool is not as durable as some man-made materials and it can be very expensive. More than that, wool clothing has traditionally been difficult to care for; it must be hand washed and line dried, sometimes requiring dry cleaning and blocking.

That is no problem for occasional use or weekend trips, but it is a huge stumbling block for the long-distance touring cyclist. Frequently, you simply don't have the time, inclination or weather to hand wash and line dry clothes. Dry cleaning means a planned layover of several days, not impossible but not always convenient either.

Some wool clothing is treated with a process called SUPERWASH so the item can be machine washed and dried. We haven't used a SUPERWASH product, mainly due to the high cost, but it might be the answer if you definitely prefer wool.

Cotton is used in many sports clothing items because it is comfortable, breathable, lightweight, easy to care for, durable and economical. All of these are criteria for good cycling clothing. It has, however, one predominantly negative feature. It is cold and clammy when wet. When saturated with sweat or rain it holds moisture and does not readily release it to the atmosphere. Even in hot weather this is uncomfortable because your clothing clings and sticks to you.

Man-made fibers have the advantages of cotton — economy, light weight, durability and ease of care — but they do not breathe as well and do not wick moisture away from the body. They are not comfortable under many climatic conditions.

The solution seems to be in the many blends of natural and man-made fibers. Some fiber blends incorporate wool, but it is not yet a common procedure and they are difficult to find. Cotton/man-made fiber blends are abundant.

Our own choice in touring-clothing material is a blend of cotton and polyester. This meets all the above criteria except that it is cold when wet; only wool can overcome that. The secret about using blends for cycling clothing is to keep the man-made fiber content at 50 percent or below. Otherwise the blend does not breathe well and the material holds perspiration odors in spite of frequent laundering. We try to purchase items that are 50 percent cotton, 50 percent polyester; they are sometimes hard to find. We never settle for more than 65 percent polyester.

Using the criteria above you should be able to judge most items offered for touring, especially when it comes to determining properties of the material. Beginning at the bottom and working up, here is what you need to tour anywhere.

Shoes

It is generally true that any lightweight, comfortable sport shoe is suitable for touring. However, there are specialized models that have certain advantageous features. The most efficient shoe available is a leather cycling shoe designed strictly for riding. It is tight fitting and low cut and has soft leather uppers with holes punched throughout to help cool the feet. The hard leather or plastic sole incorporates a nylon, leather or aluminum-alloy cleat. The cleat attaches to the sole so that the groove in the cleat lines up with and fits down over the rear cage of the pedal. When you tighten the toe strap, your foot is locked into the pedal. This insures that your foot is always in proper alignment to exert maximum force on the pedals. Your feet actually become extensions of the pedals.

For sheer efficiency this cleated cycling shoe is ideal; every racer wears a pair. For the touring cyclist there are some problems. With the stiff sole, no heel and cleats they are hell to walk in. Besides ruining the rider, the rider can also ruin the shoes by walking in them. It breaks down the sole, loosens the cleat and generally destroys the rigidity of the shoe. Yet a touring cyclist can count on doing a considerable amount of walking, whether up some impossible hills or around town and camp. Cleated shoes are also dangerous because the

Leather riding shoes. On the left, note the holes in the shoe that permit ventilation. On the right, note the cleat attached to the shoe.

slick leather sole slides in wet conditions. Wearing them on cement is a bit like a horse trying to tiptoe.

Some touring cyclists opt for the advantages of a cycling shoe and carry a regular pair for walking. This is a viable alternative, but remember that you are then not saving any weight and we have yet to see a rider change shoes halfway up a difficult climb. However, the choice is yours. Another idea is to wear the cycling shoes without cleats. You lose some efficiency, but are left with a lightweight shoe that can be worn for walking if you don't mind not having a heel.

Cycling shoes cost a minimum of $20. If you decide to purchase a pair, be very careful in sizing. Most, especially those manufactured in Italy, are cut narrow; many Americans have difficulty getting a good fit. If you have wide feet, try Dutch or English shoes. Also the cleats come in a variety of styles; find an experienced person to help you as they must fit exactly.

A few manufacturers now offer a touring shoe due to growing interest in touring and recreational riding. It looks basically like a cycling shoe but is wider and more flexible and has a small heel for more comfortable walking. The rubber soles do not take cleats, but there is a steel shank under the ball of the foot to take the brunt of the pedaling shock. They are not as comfortable for walking as running shoes are, but they are far better than regular cycling shoes when you are off the bike.

Two of the most popular touring shoes are made by Bata Shoe Company and Avocet, Inc. The Bata is made of canvas and rubber; the Avocet, of leather at twice the price. If this type of shoe appeals to you, try on both and make your choice. You should not then have to carry an extra pair while touring.

Many tourers use a regular running or lightweight tennis shoe. This has been our choice and we are well satisfied with the results. The running shoe is stable both on and off the bike, has a thick-enough sole for pedaling, looks "normal" everywhere and doesn't necessitate that you carry an extra pair. There are so many running shoes on the market that your choice will be highly personal. Look for comfort, a sole that is fairly thick through the ball of the foot (about ⅜ inch at minimum), quality construction, and nylon or nylon/leather uppers. Nylon keeps the foot cooler and dries faster when wet. If the running shoe you choose has a wide heel, check that it will clear the chainstays as the pedal revolves.

Socks

We like the thin socks sold in backpacking shops and called inner or liner socks. They are available in all wool (Wigwam Mojave), 70 percent wool (Wigwam Summit), or olefin (Wigwam Dry Foot Sock). All are machine washable and dryable. The Summit is the most practical as it maintains warmth when wet yet wears better than an all wool sock.

A lot of women, Glenda included, do not like the ankle sock. Glenda wears half socks, or golf socks; they don't extend over the top of the shoes and have a pom-pom at the back to keep them from slipping down. They are not available in wool or cotton, but are quite cool and comfortable and would be suitable for men who have no "macho" thing about the pom-poms.

Pants

What you wear between you and the saddle is a great determinant of how happy your tour will be and how many miles you will be able to put behind you each day. Soldiers walk on their stomachs, but cyclists ride on their butts.

There are riding shorts specially designed for bicycling. They are tight fitting, long in the legs and made of

Bata and Avocet touring shoes.

Black cycling shorts. The pair on the right is turned inside out to reveal the chamois liner.

stretch material — usually black — with a piece of chamois leather sewn inside the crotch. There are no seams to rub or chafe so they are worn without underwear. The chamois is soft and smooth and absorbs perspiration.

All racers, many dedicated recreational riders and a few touring cyclists wear cycling shorts. As with other bicycle items, what is good for the racer is not necessarily good for the tourer. The primary disadvantage of the chamois-lined cycling short is the laundering care required. Many are made of wool, which cannot be machine dried. Even those made of dryable man-made fabrics have a chamois lining that cannot be dried by machine. The chamois becomes stiff and hard and will eventually break down if dried with heat.

Cycling shorts must be washed by hand in mild soap and left to dry out of direct sunlight. The chamois should then be rubbed with chamois fat or some type of skin cream to keep it soft. Even with two pairs of shorts (about $25 each), we doubt that you could keep up with the washing and drying while touring. Such shorts, worn without underwear, should be washed after each day's ride to keep the bacteria count within limits, but even if you let it go for two days it would be difficult to dry the other pair out of the sun while on the road. Besides this care problem and cost, the chamois quickly gets saturated with sweat. Even on day rides a change of shorts at noon can be a necessary luxury.

There is a hiking-type trail short on the market — you've seen the khaki ones with all the pockets — that manufacturers have lined with chamois and called a touring short. It has none of the advantages and all of the disadvantages of the cycling short as far as touring is concerned. Because the legs are too short, they ride up and are uncomfortable, besides being hard to care for.

A few manufacturers are coming out with snug-fitting touring shorts of synthetic-blend stretch material, long in the legs, with a liner of absorbent, fast-drying, towel-like material in place of chamois. These are the best answer yet for the tourer. The shorts fit well, give without sagging, can be worn without underwear, and can be machine washed and dried. The man-made fiber in the lining dries quickly, even on a lunch break, without removing the shorts. The better brands are difficult to find. They can be confused with a walk-

Touring shorts. The pair on the right is turned inside out to show towel-like liner.

ing short now available with a cloth crotch liner, also called a touring short. Make sure that the legs are long enough to cover your seat entirely when you're bent over the saddle and that the fit is right before you lay down your money.

If you can't find a suitable touring short in your area, or you are on a tight budget, there are some options. But be cautious as any old short will not do for cycle touring. Stay away from cutoff jeans or any short with heavy double seams as they are very uncomfortable for sitting over a period of time. Women are cautioned against wearing short-shorts, no matter how great they look on the models in the bike ads. You end up sitting half on the hem and half on the bare saddle, uncomfortable at best, impossible at length. Look for shorts with fairly long legs (what used to be called Jamaica shorts — not Bermudas) and smooth seams, which are loose in the thigh or — better — slightly stretchy, and easy to wash and dry.

For years Tim has been satisfied with Sears' or Penney's cotton/polyester work pants cut off and hemmed with a six-inch leg. They wear like iron, cost under $10 and fit great. Glenda wore a pair of double-knit, polyester stretch shorts cross-country and in Hawaii, but they caused rash problems due to heat retention. She now wears a pair of cloth-lined touring shorts of stretch khaki material that she is well satisfied with. If you are clever with a sewing machine you might try sewing your own chamoislike liner into a favorite pair of shorts. Look at a pair of chamois-lined shorts or a replacement chamois at your local bike store to see how it is cut and sewn in. Don't, as we did, use too thick a piece of material. Something with the thickness of a worn, thin towel is best, preferably 50 percent cotton at the least. Good terry cloth does not have to be hemmed, which minimizes seams you are sitting on. For less than $20 (using work pants with do-it-yourself liner), you can have two pair of riding shorts. Whatever materials you choose to use, experiment and take your time.

Any pair of shorts is improved by applying baby powder, cornstarch or a medicated cream several times a day and overnight as well if you really have a problem. Above all, keep yourself clean; take advantage of every shower that comes along. If you are touring in an area where showers are out of the question, at least make good use of soap and water before you go to bed each night. A little prevention works wonders in this area.

Shirts

Here you have more latitude to let your personality show through. A top is important but not for the critical reasons that shoes and shorts are. There are cycling shirts (jerseys), again designed with the racer in mind. They are knit with long or short sleeves and a zippered neck opening, are long at the bottom — especially in back — and have a food storage pocket(s) in the rear. Available in a wide variety of bright colors with intriguing combinations of stripes and patterns, they fit the needs of the racer or day rider nicely. They can be used on tour if they are machine washable and dryable. They are relatively expensive (above $20) but that does not mean they are uneconomical if easy to care for and durable.

Other than jerseys, your choices are limitless. Keep protection from the sun in mind in addition to the criteria already presented. Some thin materials do not keep out dangerous rays, although they provide some protection from sunburn. Glenda found that she must wear long-sleeved shirts on extensive tours due to an allergy to the sun's rays that causes a rash on her arms and legs. Very sensitive to heat as well, she found she could tolerate a light-colored 50/50 cotton/polyester shirt, which was loose enough to provide good ventila-

tion yet covered her arms and torso completely. Wear whatever is comfortable for you both mentally and physically. Bright colors heighten visibility; remember this when choosing your shirts.

Jackets and Leggings

You have even more choice in warming-up gear because it is specialized for certain conditions and need not be worn all the time. A warm-up suit, wool sweater, down or Dacron vest, or even a heavy shirt will meet the need. Keep in mind that you will probably be wearing it more off your bike than on. Choose the lightest, most compact item that gives the protection you need.

You should carry some protection for the lower half of your body in case of cold conditions. The bottom half of a warm-up suit or a pair of long casual pants is better than nothing, and may be all you need under most touring conditions except in high mountains or during winter.

If you are concerned about weight, you can purchase specially designed leg and arm warmers at your local bike boutique. They are stretchy double knit and slip on to meet your jersey or riding shorts. Usually available in basic black, they are made of a variety of materials and work very well. Their appearance is something else again; wearing them off

Cyclist wearing riding jersey, black riding shorts, arm and leg warmers. This tourist has chosen traditional racing garb.

the bike or around town depends on how thick-skinned you are.

Rainwear

Carrying rainwear is like carrying a bike light; you may not plan to use it but when needed, nothing else fills the bill. How you prepare for rain will depend to a certain extent on your basic philosophy toward it. Tim hates it. At the first drop he either makes a beeline for the nearest sheltering roof or throws up the tent fly in a panic to wait it out. Fortunately, the longest we have had to wait is two days. If we ever tour the Northwest, it will most likely be by bus. If caught in a cloudburst or drizzle, Tim rides in an attitude of general reluctance and great disgust, ever on the lookout for escape. Because of this we seldom carry a full complement of rain gear.

When riding in rain you have two choices; either to be wet and warm or wet and cold. Most rainwear does an adequate job of keeping rain out. It also keeps your perspiration and body heat in. Either way you end up wet. If you ride without rain gear, you will be wet too, but also cold — even in tropical conditions — due to the windchill factor. Especially going downhill.

The rain cape has been a traditional solution. This is a round, poncho-type garment with a hole in the center for your head. The cape covers you to the knees and is held down in front by thumb loops on the underside. The rear is held down — in theory — by a waist tie on the inside. The whole thing is so loose that it allows good air circulation around your body to help perspiration evaporate; you remain essentially dry. Most capes have sewn-in hoods that are too small to go over your helmet and

Cyclist riding in a rain cape, which provides protection and ventilation.

too hot to wear under the helmet over your head. You end up stuffing it down the back of your neck, along with a good deal of rain that drips from your helmet, your nose, your ears, your hair or whatever. See why Tim hates rain?

If you are really determined to ride in the rain, a pair of chaps can be worn along with your cape. They tie to your waist to protect your legs. Fairly cool and comfortable, they have no crotch to trap moisture.

The biggest drawback in rainwear has been lack of breathability. Gore-Tex seems to have the answer. Gore-Tex is waterproof yet breathable, allowing wa-

ter vapor (sweat) to pass out of the material from the inside yet blocking water penetration from the outside. Test reports and recent experience indicate that the fabric does indeed do what it claims. However, under heavy touring conditions — hill climbing with a loaded bike — you can expect some condensation on the inside; but nothing like with old-style rain gear. Gore-Tex loses its breathable properties if body oil gets on the underside of the fabric. This means always wearing it over a long-sleeved shirt or, better yet, getting Gore-Tex rainwear lined with nylon.

The big disadvantage with Gore-Tex is the price. Expect to spend in excess of $70 for the parka alone. Acquaintance with a sewing machine can save money, but the material is expensive (about $9 per yard) and it should be lined — not a job for novices.

We carry a minimum of protection; only enough to keep us dry during our mad dash for shelter. Several years ago we purchased lightweight, snug-fitting waterproof nylon jackets that fold into themselves to form neat little storage packets. Glenda opened the underarm seams from the elbow along the side and inserted wedges of good-quality nylon mosquito netting. This allows air to circulate while we are pedaling yet keeps perspiration evaporation continuing while we stay reasonably warm and dry. We don't worry about the lower body as we do not stay out in the rain that long. We always have long pants with us, however, if the need arises.

Windbreakers are excellent shells over a sweater or wool shirt on cool nights or mornings in camp.

One other alternative for the dedicated rainy-weather cyclist is to have a good set of wool underwear, tops and bottoms. When the rain starts just slip on your long johns, put your shirt and shorts over top (this really looks classy), and carry on through the storm. You will be wet but the pure wool keeps you warm enough for survival if not comfort. Wool underwear is a good guard against any cold conditions, wet or otherwise. If the appearance bothers you, dye them black to look like a racing pro.

Feet can develop problems in the rain. One solution is to carry special rubber or plastic shoe covers. More simply, put your feet into plastic bags, then slip your shoes over them. Your feet will stay reasonably warm if not dry.

Another problem is rain being sucked up into the ventilation holes of your helmet. Your choices are to stuff them with cork, rags, waxed paper, chewing gum, or any combination of these, or to purchase a ready-made helmet rain cover.

Clothing for Desert Conditions

Sometime during your touring life you will encounter hot weather, whether in the summer heat of the United States or the shimmering sands of the Sahara Desert or Australian outback. Actually, deserts offer some of the most enchanting bicycle touring around. The trick is to understand what you are getting into, prepare yourself adequately and accept, rather than fight, conditions.

The temptation in the desert is to think that the fewer and lighter your clothes the better. This is definitely not the case. You must strike a balance between clothes that are cool and light, yet protect you from the intense sun and dehydration possibilities of heat coupled with very low humidity. You don't have to look like a Bedouin on a bike but neither should you cycle in your shoes only.

Even if you are well tanned, you should use a sun-protection cream (sunscreen) rather than a sun-tanning oil. Check labels to be sure the product screens out the sun's rays; look for PABA in the ingredients. If a cream isn't enough — and it isn't for sun-sensitive skin — you should wear a loose, long-sleeved shirt. The shirt not only protects you from the sun, but allows your body to cool more efficiently by slowing down the evaporation of sweat from your skin. That is why desert people traditionally have worn long, loose robes as opposed to G-strings. In the extremely low humidity of the desert your perspiration will dry as it is formed. A garment slows this process enough to give an illusion of cooling, especially as you move through your bicycle-created breeze.

You will need to protect your legs, especially the upper thighs, if you are sensitive to the sun. Long pants might be your only answer if a sunscreening lotion doesn't do the job. Tim uses loose-fitting, cotton/polyester work pants. Glenda sewed a piece of matching Velcro to the outside of each front crease, its other half to the outside seam. Both cuffs can be closed to keep them out of the chain or to keep bugs out in camp, but are loose enough for air to circulate. Off the bike, Tim releases the Velcro and they look like ordinary pants. Glenda prefers a gaucho skirt (culottes) if she must cover her upper legs when the sun is particularly intense. They are loose and comfortable with lots of room for ventilation, yet are too short to get caught in the chain. Whereas Tim's long pants can double for protection in cold weather, the culottes do not serve this dual purpose. If you prefer double duty you should choose long pants when encountering both heat and cold on a tour.

A useful article of clothing for desert conditions is the bandanna. The large arteries that service the head run very close to the surface as they pass through the neck. Thus they are especially susceptible to heat and intense sunshine. Tie a bandanna loosely around your neck; if you have sufficient water, keep it wet for added protection and comfort. When not used for that, a bandanna is an emergency hat, pot holder, washrag, towel, first-aid device, strainer, all-purpose rag, diaper or handkerchief. A couple of bandannas are useful on any tour.

Desert conditions demand a head covering, whether you have taken our advice to wear a helmet or not. Only a fool would walk or cycle in the desert without some sort of light-colored, breathable, brimmed hat. We carried white, net-ventilated tennis hats for use in the desert portion of our cross-country tour. After extensive experimentation with these hats, dry and wet, without any head covering, and then with the Bell helmets, we decided that helmets were coolest of all.

Unfortunately, neither Bell nor MSR offer a smoke-colored, plastic snap-on visor for their helmets. This would be a welcome addition for extensive desert touring. Such visors are available at motorcycle-equipment stores and, as with motorcycle helmets, attach with snaps. Visors are especially helpful during the early-morning and late-afternoon hours when the sun is low on the horizon shining directly into your face. They can be stored away until high sun hours, otherwise wind resistance might be a disadvantage.

Clothing for Cold-Weather Touring

Cold conditions are not confined to winter months; they occur in high altitudes and during unseasonal weather. There is no reason to avoid high altitudes during your tour only because you might encounter cold. A little preparation will see you through.

Use the layer approach instead of cramming your polar-weight parka into your panniers. Carry light- or medium-weight warm clothing that you can wear simultaneously. Conditions change rapidly while cycling; you may be sweating and shedding shirts on the up-side of a mountain, but literally freezing at the top or down the other side when you are no longer working hard. You need to be able to change your clothing without a thin shirt and a heavy parka being your only choices.

For cold weather, we each carry a fishnet T-shirt, a lightweight long-sleeved shirt, a wool sweater, or a down or Dacron vest (it need not be machine washable as it is not always worn), and a waterproof nylon jacket or light parka. If expecting severe conditions, we add a long-sleeved wool or wool-blend long

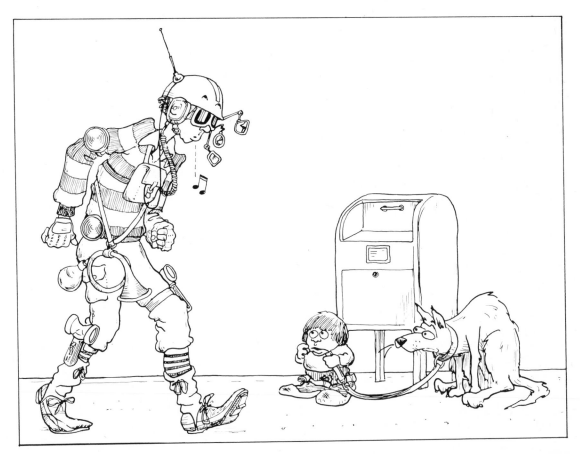

john top to be worn over the fishnet shirt. Long john bottoms to be worn under long pants or warm-up suit pants complete the outfit for really cold weather. In an emergency a newspaper placed between layers of clothing in the chest area can get you through an especially cold morning (or night).

The hands, feet and head require special consideration in cold-weather cycling because of their extreme location and the windchill factor. Cold-weather cycling gloves with full fingers are available for this type of weather. In an emergency you can wear a pair of socks (wool ones are best) over the hands. By placing your thumb in the heel area you should be able to grip the handlebars and apply the brakes, but practice this maneuver before mounting up. If you happen onto unexpected cold weather and it isn't raining, you can get an ordinary pair of cotton gardening gloves at almost any grocery or hardware store in the United States.

The feet can be a real problem. Wear double socks if your shoes are large enough. If not, put a pair of cheap, heavy socks over your shoes. It looks strange but works OK. In an emergency, plastic bags between your socks and your shoes will help, but not for long. For extensive cold-weather cycling, one company makes small shields that fit on the pedals and over the toe clips for good protection from the cold. Check the ads in *Bicycling* magazine for a mail-order source for these Polar Pals.

Ventilation holes in good bike helmets work a bit too well in cold weather. Either plug the holes or use a helmet cover. For extensive cold-weather riding wear a knit hat or balaclava under your helmet; you might have to adjust the sizing to do this. If while wearing a balaclava with only your eyes and mouth showing, foot covers, gloves and long johns you are still cold, forget the whole thing. Find a warm spot to hole up in until spring. You won't be alone.

Chapter Seven
Carrying Gears:
Racks, Packs and Panniers

Bicycle touring differs from recreational riding in the distances involved and in the amount of gear carried along. How to carry gear is one of the most complicated elements of successful touring because you must make decisions regarding relatively expensive equipment beforehand, based on experience that you most likely do not have.

You can always "just get by" like the fellow we met in Washington, D.C., at the end of our cross-country trip. He was heading for Texas for the winter and had stuffed all of his gear into a huge backpack strapped to his back. He had neither toured before nor read anything about it, but he figured that bikepacking couldn't be all that much different from backpacking — "except maybe a little easier." He assured us he had everything under control and would be just fine as soon as his neck muscles got used to the load. He had been on the road eight days and was still expecting a muscular miracle. All we could do was wish him well and hope that the Good Bicycle Fairy who watches over such as he would give him special attention.

Carrying gear in a backpack is definitely not the way to go on long trips. Or any trip. The load is dangerously high, making it difficult to balance. A rapid shift of weight can send the bicycle out of control. It places added strain on the neck and shoulders, and the extra weight puts unnecessary stress on the buttocks, exactly where you want the least-possible pressure. Finally, a large pack should be used with a waist belt — a highly uncomfortable prospect as it cinches just where your body bends the most on a bicycle. If no waist belt is worn, you risk dislodging the pack up or sideways in a quick stop or evasive action, causing entanglement that can have severe consequences. (If you use a light book bag for short trips of a day or less, use a belt or tie to hold the pack securely to the lower part of your back.) Besides these dangers, consider wind resistance and the heat generated on your back by a large backpack. There are far more efficient ways to carry a load on a bicycle.

An experienced long-distance tourer carries gear distributed over the bicycle in such a way that he or she is totally unencumbered; the bicycle handles almost as well as when unloaded. At first glance it is difficult to tell where the bicycle leaves off and the baggage begins. It is a picture of function in motion with a place for everything and everything in its place.

A lot of bicycle-touring gear is sold on form alone with little regard for function. It is your job to know the function you desire and to let that determine your choice of form. We assume you are reading this book to supplement your own experience or even to substitute for it until you get some. We are not going to present you outright with extensive lists of suggested equipment and recommendations, although it would be easier. We hope that you will develop your own reasoning behind choices. Everybody is different with different goals, expectations and desires. We will point out things to be aware of when selecting gear so you don't learn the hard and expensive trial-and-error

way. Listen to what we and others have to say; consider your own values, needs and ideas; then make your decisions.

How you plan to use the racks and packs should determine your choice more than any other factor. What do you, not the salesperson or the writer of the slick brochure, need them for? Wait a minute, you say, all anyone needs is to carry stuff, right? Basically, yes. But sales pitches are made far and wide of this assumed function. Consider the pair of panniers now on the market whose major advertising gimmick is that the packs can be securely snapped together to form a single piece of luggage. They also have flat bottoms to keep the panniers sitting up whenever off the bike. That's just wonderful if you plan to do most of your cycling with your panniers snapped together and sitting on the ground somewhere. Better yet, use suitcases. On the other hand, if you plan to tour the four main islands of Hawaii where you are flying between islands, loading and unloading your panniers for carrying onto the airplane or checking separately, then connecting panniers with flat bottoms would be a distinct advantage.

You will likely be touring a number of places; do not restrict yourself with packs that have built-in limitations. If the feature is in addition to convenience and efficiency in carrying your gear, fine. Make sure though that it is not instead of convenience and efficiency. Never lose track of the function for which a product is designed. Look beyond form, style, popularity and Madison Avenue packaging.

Racks

If you plan to carry gear for long-distance touring, you will need secure racks to support the load. The load must be evenly distributed and not interfere with the working of the bicycle or the rider. There are dozens of racks from which to choose. What are the basic requirements? Most important are rigidity and strength. Without these a rack will not be functional for long. The rear rack will be carrying up to 80 percent of your total baggage load. Both strength and stability are determined by the number of struts (legs) the rack has and by how it attaches to the bike.

Single-Strut Racks

The single-strut rack will suffice for loads not exceeding around 15 pounds, depending on the thickness of the strut and how it is attached to the main body of the rack. When overloaded, this type has a tendency to sway from side to side (fishtail) when the bike is under heavy pressure as in hill climbing. At high speeds or on rough roads, the load itself sometimes initiates a fishtailing action, making the bicycle much harder to control.

Frequently, the single-strut rack simply is not strong enough to support a heavy load. It usually breaks where the strut is attached to the main part of the rack. You have real trouble if this happens out in the desert somewhere or, worse yet, going downhill at high speed.

On some single-strut racks it is hard to keep the panniers out of the spokes. A strong gust of wind or a sudden maneuver on the bike can turn them into the wheel and really ruin your ride. Make sure the pannier attachment is firm and sufficiently sturdy enough to prevent this.

Better single-strut racks include the Pletscher, Eclipse Nomad, Esge and Caleisure; just remember their limitations — light loads on a casual basis. Prices range from $6 to $15. If you plan to stay in motels and carry a minimum of gear, these racks will function well;

Pletscher rack with support plate.

don't load them down with 35 pounds of camping gear.

Many of the single-strut racks mount onto the upper part of the bike by a plate that goes across both seatstays. This has been a problem as a loaded rack sometimes slides down the stays until it comes to rest on the rear brake, taking the paint with it. There are now two or three varieties of aluminum or vinyl-covered steel support plates that connect to the brake-mounting bolt, then to the rack-mounting bolt. These keep the rack in place and save the stays. It is worth the $1 investment if you use a single-strut rack.

Multiple-Strut Racks

Some racks, including the Karrimor and Claude Butler, use a double-strut support system; others, like the Eclipse and Blackburn, use triple struts. Any of these provide adequate support for heavy loads. Your choice will depend on other variables such as the material used in construction. Aluminum alloy and steel are the two basic types. Your intended use and what features are more important to you will determine which is best.

Alloy racks are lighter than steel. Two of the newest and best available, the Eclipse and the Blackburn (both made in the United States), are alloy with triple-strut construction; Eclipse has enlarged one of the stays for added strength. Both are excellent in design and workmanship. Disadvantages are cost (Blackburn — $20, Eclipse — $25), and if you crash or otherwise bend your

rack, they are difficult to fix. Alloy is very light and strong but it cannot be bent in one direction, then bent back without the risk of snapping. Chances are you will never bend your rack so severely that the straightening process might break it, but it is a possibility and something to consider if you are planning to tour in isolated or Third World nations where replacements are not available. Baggage handlers may be rough on an alloy rack.

Steel racks are heavier than alloy and will rust when the chrome or vinyl wears off. They can, however, be bent back to their original shape if necessary with little difficulty or danger of breaking. The Karrimor and the Claude Butler (both made in England) are steel, costing about $12 each.

Method of Attachment: All racks, except some custom models, attach to the eyelet on the rear dropout (at the junction of the rearstays). All bicycles designed for touring should have this eyelet, or even two, on each front and rear dropout. Many are threaded (metric) to take the proper bolt through the bottom of the rack struts. Leave enough of the bolt extending through the eyelets so a lockwasher and locknut can be attached to insure that the bolt doesn't work loose, or use a small amount of Loc-Tite on the bolt so a nut is not needed.

The rack also attaches to the bicycle at the top in front of the platform, but methods vary according to the model of the rack. One of two basic types is a

Blackburn rear rack with double arms attached to the seatstay.

Claude Butler rear rack. Note mounting tang on rear brake bolt.

two-arm bracket that extends from the rack platform and is secured to the seatstays with a vinyl-covered clamp. On custom touring bikes there is sometimes a braze-on eyelet to which a rack can be attached without using a clamp. This two-arm attachment is the strongest of the types normally used, but it may be necessary to bend the arms of the rack somewhat to get a proper fit. The Eclipse rack has adjustable arms although modification is still sometimes necessary. Karrimor uses the double-arm attachment as does one model made by Blackburn.

The other type is a bendable or adjustable tang (metal protrusion) that extends from the front of the rack platform to the brake-mounting bolt. This is not as rigid as the two-arm method but is

easier to fit on the bicycle initially. The Claude Butler and one Blackburn model use this method.

Mount the rack on your bicycle using the best hardware and greatest care. Adjust the rack to be as level as possible. Make sure that no part of the rack interferes with the brake mechanism; this may be difficult as centerpull brakes may require a longer or shorter transverse (yoke) cable to insure proper brake operation. Don't settle for less than a perfect job as the rack is an integral part of your touring system.

Special Features: Some racks have a protective shield on the front of the platform just behind the brake. This keeps baggage from creeping forward into the brake cable, especially with centerpull brakes. The Eclipse, Blackburn and Butler racks have this safety feature, Karrimor doesn't.

Another feature you might want is a means of hooking a rear reflector to the rack. The Butler and Karrimor have an integral mount for this, the Eclipse and Blackburn don't. Blackburn markets a clamp to be used for this purpose, however. This same clamp — with a ⅜-inch wooden dowel as a spacer — can be used on the Eclipse rack.

Some racks are made to carry a specific make and model of panniers. You don't have to purchase the matching set; simply be aware that such things exist and know why you do or don't want the combination.

Front-Load Carrier

When loading a touring bike, approximately 20 to 30 percent of the baggage weight should be over the front wheel. About 60 percent of your body weight is already concentrated over the rear wheel; if your entire equipment load is on the rear wheel as well, the handling properties of the bike are going to suffer. A bicycle overloaded in the rear is hard to steady just standing still, let alone on the road. The more weight that is placed on the rear wheel, the more stress there is placed on the spokes and the more potential there is for spoke breakage.

The solution is to apportion part of your touring weight to the front. The general practice is to do this with a handlebar bag. This is fine if your total

weight is less than approximately 35 pounds (your handlebar bag would then be carrying about 10 pounds). More than that puts too much stress on the arm, shoulder and neck muscles and adversely affects the handling characteristics of the bike.

Front panniers let you put the weight right down over the axle where it belongs. This improves the handling and is easier on the rider's upper body muscles. You can also carry bulkier gear up front in panniers than in a handlebar bag. Front panniers were rare in this country until a few years ago, but now they are more common and several manufacturers make them.

Front pannier racks should exhibit most of the properties of the rear racks that we have covered. There are two readily available in this country; Karrimor makes one of steel and Blackburn has an alloy model. Both are excellent. However, a front rack takes some of the spring out of the fork since it attaches to an eyelet on the dropout and to the front brake bolt above. This makes for a stiffer ride. The Blackburn is definitely stiffer than the Karrimor. We personally dislike this aspect of using front panniers and you should consider it when deciding whether to use them yourself.

Some of Karrimor's front racks have a flange at the front for mounting a light. Most British lamps, including the Berec, fit perfectly into this excellent position right over the wheel.

Mounting a front rack can be more difficult than mounting a rear rack. This is caused by differing fork rakes on various brands of bicycles. A little bending and the drilling of a new hole for the eyelet bolt (on the Karrimor) solves the problem.

Which Is Best?

Each rack has advantages and disadvantages, the choice depends on what is important to you. Eclipse is more rigid; Blackburn is lightest; Claude Butler with its chrome finish and smooth line is the most attractive; both Karrimor and Butler are least expensive and easiest to repair. All are good choices. We have used each of them with satisfaction of our particular needs at the time.

Panniers

Many experienced tourers will tell you that choosing panniers carefully is almost as important as choosing a bicycle carefully.

Size

This is the most difficult factor for inexperienced tourers to understand; the assumption is usually "the bigger the better." To the contrary, the size of the pannier should reflect the type of touring you plan to do. Whereas staying in motels on a weekend excursion requires a minimum of gear, a two-month camping tour could require the maximum (see Appendix A for a list of equipment for trips of various lengths). Our experience leading tours and teaching cycle touring at the college level indicates that people fill up whatever space they have, whether they are going 15 miles or 500.

Analyze your touring style. Do you hate camping of any sort? Are a shower and soft bed pure luxuries to you or absolute necessities? Will you end up eating out no matter what cooking gear you have with you? Do back roads and near-wilderness attract you or will most of your touring be to and among urban attractions? If your policy is cash instead of carry, then you will need a small-capacity pannier set, or perhaps only a stuff bag or handlebar pack. Look for the right capacity to hold your kit rather than at the last minute packing into your bags anything that will fit.

The following is a general guide to matching your pack outfit to the type of touring you will be doing:

Weekend Touring (motels):
    Small rear panniers of approximately 900 cubic inches or
    A 10 × 20-inch stuff bag that can be strapped on the rear rack or
    A large seat bag or
    Handlebar bag (optional)

Weekend Tour Camping:
    Medium rear panniers of approximately 1,500-2,000 cubic inches
    Handlebar bag

Extended Tour Camping:
    Large rear panniers of more than 2,000 cubic inches

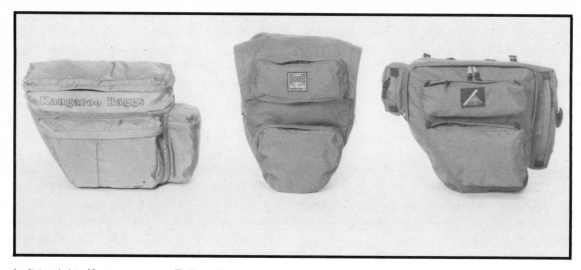

Left to right, Kangaroo rear, Eclipse Transcontinental rear, and large Cannondale rear panniers.

Handlebar bag or
Front panniers

Expedition Touring (long periods in isolated areas):
Large rear panniers of more than 2,000 cubic inches
Front panniers
Handlebar bag

Material

Since almost all American-made panniers are of nylon, most people assume that nylon is the only material worth having. Many excellent European panniers are made of high-grade cotton canvas. Europeans know from experience that canvas wears well, holds its shape better than nylon, won't leak as much because the material expands when wet and is less expensive. They are seldom found in the United States but if you should happen onto a good set of canvas panniers, give them careful consideration.

Nylon panniers come in differing types and weights. The strongest material that is most resistant to abrasion is eight-ounce Cordura nylon. This cloth has a coarser texture on the outside and is generally used on most top-of-the-line products. The majority of panniers are either six-, seven- or eight-ounce pack nylon that is smoother than Cordura; hence slightly less resistant to abrasion. All else being equal, the lighter the material, the less rugged the final product.

All of these nylons have a waterproof or water-repellent coating. Many salespeople will tell you the pannier is waterproof. Not so. The material is waterproof or water repellent, but not along seams where a sewing machine has punched thousands of holes. Neither are zippers waterproof. Hold one under a faucet if you don't believe it. So how do you protect your gear in a not-so-waterproof pack? You can (1) hope it won't rain that much, (2) coat all the seams with sealant, (3) buy or make waterproof covers like those Eclipse sells, or (4) put everything you value into plastic bags inside the panniers. We do (4), have (3), have done (2) and always hope for (1).

Construction

Are the seams straight and professionally sewn? Is there enough seam allowance so they will not pull out? Is the stitching tight and evenly spaced? How many stitches per inch are there? (We consider any less than six per inch to be too few.) Are there double stitching and reinforcements in areas of stress? Are the seams accessible so they can be restitched if they pull out on the road? All of these factors determine the quality of construction; check them out.

Closures

The trend in pannier closures is definitely toward zippers. They are tidy, fast, relatively tight (not waterproof), and convenient. They also restrict the quantity of stuff that can be squeezed into a given space. Sometimes, however, it is nice or even necessary to be able to extend your pannier capacity to take on an unaccustomed but consum-

able load such as a loaf of bread, a jug of wine or who knows what else. An extension of material with a drawstring can save the day. If there is a top flap held down by a buckled strap that is also expandable, so much the better.

Zippers can also be a pain on very small pockets, especially on the back of some handlebar bags when you try to close them with one hand while cycling. Velcro on an overlapping flap comes into its own in such situations. Zippers can and do fail, and sometimes simple repairs are not so simple in touring situations, especially if you have lost the metal slider. Straps and buckles are more dependable, though their flaps may gap and let in water thrown up from the road.

Just because you select the "best" and most expensive gear, don't think it will be immune to failure or accident. Things have a tendency to go wrong at the wrong moment, especially if the item is so specialized or complicated that you cannot fix it yourself. Opt for simplicity instead of complication. Think function instead of style.

Mounting on the Rack

Whatever the method, it must be foolproof. Many touring accidents are attributed to bikepacking gear getting tangled up with moving parts of the bike. If a pannier comes loose or shifts into the spokes, you could be in for an asphalt encounter of the worst kind. Make sure the method of attaching the pannier is simple and secure.

Eclipse rack with the panniers attached. Note new-style tang attachment.

Some panniers are designed to fit specific racks. Be sure you are aware of this as it can influence the final unit price considerably. The best example of this type of union is the Eclipse line. Designed as a system, the racks and panniers are matched specifically to one another, providing a very secure, convenient attachment. The total package is clean, functional and innovative, well worth the investment if the Eclipse panniers appeal to you. Eclipse does market an adapter plate ($5) so their panniers can be used on other racks; this is a necessity for the front panniers since there is no Eclipse front rack.

Karrimor panniers are also designed to fit their own rack best as the clips are spaced exactly so there is no forward or backward sliding. They do fit most other racks without a special adapter.

A factor in how well panniers attach to the rack is how easily they are removed. Imagine standing in the rain trying to undo semipermanent attachments so you can move your gear into the tent. We had that type on our cross-country trip and usually ended up scooping all of our gear out in one untidy heap rather than try to get the panniers off. Fortunately, the manufacturer has changed the design.

Design and Shape

The primary idea with any load-carrying system on a bicycle should be to get the weight as low and as centered over the axles as possible. The higher the weight, or the more it extends behind the bicycle, the more top-heavy the bicycle becomes. That is why panniers were designed in the first place. Otherwise you could simply stack suitcases on your rack and pedal off. Many people, especially in Third World countries, do just that or something similar, but it is not recommended for long distances and efficient cycling. To the opposite extreme are the systems used by experienced cyclists in Europe and Japan where specially designed racks extend from below the top of the wheel down to within six to ten inches of the ground. With panniers attached they have a very stable riding experience with no sway or top-heaviness. This is the system to have if money were no object. The rest of us must make do with mass-produced systems.

As you examine your potential panniers, determine how low they are carried on the rack. Most square or rectangular panniers look neat and roomy, but do not offer the air-flow advantages of the tapered panniers and carry most of the weight too high. They are easier to pack but we do not believe that ease of packing should be valued ahead of handling characteristics on the bicycle.

Many such panniers extend above the top of the rack. This really doesn't make much sense when you look at the way it limits the load-carrying capacity of the rack. A sleeping bag can be strapped lengthwise on the rack between two panniers, but this space must usually also hold a sleeping pad and a tent. There are definite problems with stability and getting it all tied down if you try to stack it all on top of the lengthwise bag. The answer is to put everything on sideways, but then you discover why you don't want panniers that extend above the level of the rack. If you manage to get everything on and tightened down, it is almost impossible to get anything out of your panniers without undoing the entire package. This is especially hard to do if you have zippered openings on your panniers, unless the zippers extend well down the sides. Insist on panniers that are flush

with the top of the rack; the weight is lower, as it should be, and the openings should be accessible even when everything else is mounted on the rack.

Another advantage of tapered over rectangular panniers is heel clearance as you pedal; this is greatly appreciated if you happen to wear a size-11½ shoe as Tim does. You can always move rectangular panniers back if this is a problem, but then you are putting the weight back into that zone of instability behind the center of the wheel. Tapered panniers put the weight right where it should be, over the axle.

Another design feature is the pocket. Many cyclists say that you can't have too many; to a certain extent we agree. But each pocket adds to the cost of the product. They are useful and convenient, but how many do you really need for your type of touring? We like at least one good-size outside pocket for those frequently needed items, which eliminates having to dig through the entire main compartment. The best arrangement we have seen is the Eclipse Transcontinental with three well-thought-out exterior pockets, all with convenient two-way zippers. There is another zipper in the middle of the main compartment, which allows access to the bottom portion without digging from the top. A final touch of class is the zip-out divider separating the main compartment, giving the option of two smaller units or one large one. However, the cyclist pays dearly for such conveniences, so consider your needs carefully.

Backing Material

Most panniers have some sort of permanent or removable, rigid or semi-rigid material to keep the backside of the pannier flat and out of the spokes. This is an essential safety feature. Common materials are hardboard, aluminum, corrugated plastic, stiff foam or nylon. All of these do an adequate job if the system of attachment to the rack is adequate. The only time we had a problem along these lines was with a set of panniers with a soft foam liner. When not fully loaded they would turn into the spokes in a side wind, not only because of too soft a backing but also due to an inadequate tie-down system on the struts. Take your bike with you when pannier shopping (if you already have a rack) and try them on before making your purchase.

Off-Bike Handling of Panniers

If you foresee much traveling by public transportation where you are separated from your bike for fairly long periods you will want to carry your panniers with you or check them separately as baggage. Most can be tied together at the tops and bottoms with short pieces of nylon cord, or even strapped together. But some sort of carrying handle is mandatory. Carrying bulky panniers under your arms as you rush for a plane or train is not the way to go. Some panniers have an optional single or

Kirtland rear panniers filled, snapped together and being carried by their handle.

double shoulder strap (backpack type) arrangement. The latter usually is designed to carry only one pannier with any degree of comfort; since you are apt to have your handlebar bag suspended from a shoulder as well, you might find this as awkward as we do. The first time you strip your bike for a trip by public transport you may decide that nothing is so important as a decent off-bike carrying system. Remember, however, that the majority of the time your baggage will be on your bike, not on you.

Color

Logically, the only consideration here is safety. Panniers should be as bright and easy to see as possible. But

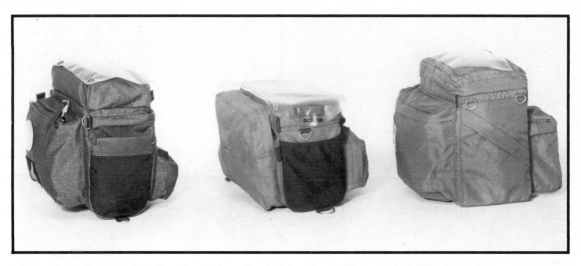

Left to right, Cannondale Trestle, Eclipse Professional and Kirtland S/T Elite bag.

most of us are not logical creatures so we choose what is pleasing to our senses or matches our bike. Try for safety and color coordination. Most brands of panniers come in red, blue, orange, yellow or sometimes green. (Karrimor has a black, cotton canvas model although it is next to impossible to get in the United States.)

Handlebar Bags

Most of what we have said about panniers applies to handlebar bags with a few specific differences.

Attachment

Make sure the handlebar bag will not interfere with your brakes or limit the places you can put your hands on the bars. The better bags use a twin metal fork that hooks around the handlebar stem and extends toward the front of the bike to support the bag literally free of the bars. This system is far superior to any that attaches the bag directly to the bars. The only problem is that there is more muscle strain in steering with the weight of the bag so extended, with a slight reduction in stability. The only way to get away from this is the arrangement used by many European tourists where a small rack to support the bag extends out from the front brake just slightly above the wheel. This is better but is difficult to fit on a wide variety of bicycles.

If you choose a bag without a rack, you can sometimes use one of the other racks available (like the Eclipse or Kirtland) or purchase a Park Tool Company front-bag support. Insist on the steel model instead of the alloy if you expect

117

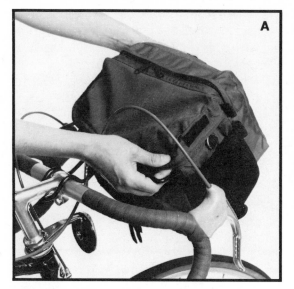
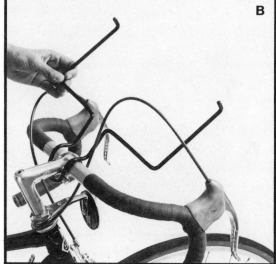

Eclipse front-mounting rack for handlebar bag (A). Note how rack is mounted on stem and how bag fits on support rack (B).

to carry more than a few pounds. All other handlebar racks are of steel. Since you will be taking the bag off a number of times a day, look for an attachment method that is simple but sturdy.

If the bag is suspended by the rack alone, most models have a tendency to jump around on rough roads or when going over bumps. Some manufacturers use elastic stretch cords that extend from the bottom of the bag to the front forks where they hook to the eyelet, rack or fenderstay. These work well, but we don't like the potential for breaking or becoming unhooked and getting wrapped up in the front wheel. Others use a short elastic cord that wraps around the head tube.

Pockets

Like panniers, handlebar bags are greatly enhanced by pockets. They add to the cost, of course, but they also aid your sanity as you try to find some item while cycling. Your handlebar bag is somewhat like a desk where all sorts of handy and necessary gadgets can be stored at your fingertips. Pockets and dividers keep things organized, but they must be large enough to be useful yet small enough to separate. On many bags the rear pockets are so small as to be almost impossible to get into; with zippers they are impossible to get into safely while pedaling.

Two-way zippers are handiest, but we also prefer the main compartment to have a flap and Velcro closure as we leave the zippers unzipped most of the time for easy access. You need plenty of flap over the zippers to keep rain out. It is most convenient if the main compartment opens toward the rider, both for ease of access and for protection against rain.

Lining

Many riders carry their camera gear in the handlebar bag. You need some sort of stiff foam or plastic liner for this and to give the bag shape. Some of the better bags make such excellent camera bags that we use ours continually even when not on tour. If you are serious about photography, then give special attention to your choice of handlebar bags. Many bags come with detachable shoulder straps, but you can always make or buy one if not.

Map Case

This is by now a standard feature on most bags. It is usually a built-in clear plastic cover under which you slide your map so you can, in theory, read the map as you ride along. In reality that is a good way to end up in a ditch, down a grating, or wrapped around some car's fender. Besides you can't read it anyway because the road is either too bumpy or you've stuck it in upside down.

Map reading is for the side of the road, preferably while sprawled under some shady tree sipping orange juice. If you don't want to remove your entire handlebar bag for this, look for a map case that is detachable. Years ago we

made our own out of soft plastic pencil holder envelopes using Velcro patches glued to the bag and the map case. They worked great. A detachable case can be replaced after the sun and weather have rendered it opaque.

Size

Handlebar bags range from 400 to 700 cubic inches; the size you buy should reflect how much you plan to carry. Consider weight as well as the volume of your gear. How much will you put in it? How heavy is your gear? Will you be using front panniers too? Do you plan to use it as a tote bag when not touring? Will it safely hold your camera gear plus other essentials you want at your fingertips?

We began touring with very large handlebar bags and are now using smaller ones. Tim is getting away from using a handlebar bag at all when not touring; he uses small or front panniers mounted on his rear rack for day rides and errand running. Glenda prefers riding with the handlebar bag since she uses it as a purse while shopping. Handlebar bags definitely affect the steering and handling of a bicycle; buy only what you think you need, not what you think you can fill.

Miscellaneous Packs and Gear

Although panniers and handlebar

bags are the accepted standard for most bicycle tourers, there are a number of specialized items that can sometimes be used to fill a particular need. Eclipse has several innovative minipacks on the market. One is their Omni Pack ($10), which is about two inches high and fits on their handlebar bags where the map case attaches. This minipurse or large wallet keeps all your valuables in one small place and can be quickly removed for shopping or carrying with you. It can also attach directly to your handlebars or belt with two Velcro straps.

Eclipse also makes a Rac-Pac ($13.50) that attaches with Velcro to the rear rack. It is a rounded rectangle and will hold 380 cubic inches of stuff, about equivalent to a quart of milk, a dozen eggs and a loaf of bread.

You can carry your handlebar bag

on the rear with Eclipse's clever alloy post. It attaches to the seatpost and accepts a standard handlebar bag rack. You have all the advantages of the handlebar bag without the detrimental effect on your steering. This interesting device is called the Seat Post Thing and sells for $10. It can be used on frames that are 21 inches or larger.

You sometimes see riders with a narrow pack hanging from the top tube to fill the space between the main tube triangle of the frame. It looks neat but has definite drawbacks. You are, of course, limited to carrying very thin things in the pack to prevent rubbing against your knees as you pedal. It takes the brunt of any crosswind, and it uses up the space you need for mounting a water bottle. It might work nicely for artists or architects who need to transport sketch pads, but its uses are limited for cycle touring. A Midframe Bag model is available from R.E.I. (Recreational Equipment, Inc.) for $12.

R.E.I.'s Pannier Extension ($9) does have great possibilities for touring. It is a rectangular nylon bag, 4 × 12 × 15 inches, which snaps onto the top of one of their pannier sets. It is designed to carry a sleeping bag, tent, sleeping pad or whatever else you want in there. It's a good idea if these particular items happen to fit into that amount of space. If you are handy with a sewing machine, however, you could make your own to custom-fit your gear and simply strap it onto the rack. For light load carrying, such a solitary stuff bag might be all you want or need.

Eclipse Rac-Pac in Eclipse rear rack.

A common minipack is the seatbag ranging in price from $3.50 to $35, depending on size and complexity. Most are used as utility bags to carry tools, locks, lunches or such on day rides. They can be used on tour although the sleeping bag is usually taking up that space. For motel touring with limited gear a seatbag could be a worthwhile investment, especially if you leave most of your stuff in the motel while sightseeing. The seatbag will hold your essentials for the day so you can ride unencumbered. If you want a very small seatbag only for tools and lock, the Keithley Nylon Tool Bag is available from Third Hand for $3.50.

In Europe, especially in England, seatbags come in large sizes and are used by tourists to carry all their gear for staying in hostels or hotels. The behind-the-saddle location is excellent but we have had problems keeping these large bags in place and out of the way of the brakes. Karrimor makes three very nice, large seatbags but we have yet to be able to get one mounted right. We ended up adding Velcro to each corner so the bag could be mounted lengthwise on the rear rack like Eclipse's Rac-Pac. Mounted in this manner, Karrimor's large seatbag has ample room for all the gear necessary for weekend motel touring.

When selecting a seatbag in the normal 100- to 300-cubic-inch capacity, check for a shape-retaining liner and a two-way zipper that wraps around three sides for easy access. Better bags are priced in the vicinity of $10.

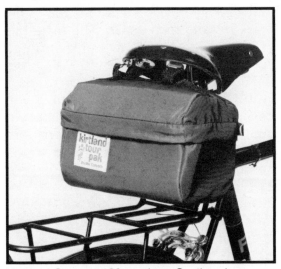

Kirtland Century 100 seatbag. Seatbag loops are available if saddle is without them.

Modifications: Doing It Yourself

Many bikepacking items, especially the less-expensive models, can be and sometimes must be modified to suit your needs. People and bicycles vary widely; don't feel restricted by what you buy. Modify factory gear to satisfy any peculiarities you have. By the time we finished changing and adding to our first handlebar bags, they bore little resemblance to the original articles. Most of the better gear today is of excellent and thoughtful design, but go ahead with any changes you need to do to make a good piece of gear better.

If you really enjoy doing your own

thing, or finances dictate that you must, make all your own packs. The materials you need are readily available through such mail-order houses as R.E.I. and EMS (Eastern Mountain Sports, Inc.). With a little ingenuity and patience you can end up with really superior products. Our next set of expedition panniers is going to be homemade so we can put some of our ideas and experience into practice with no compromises. When making it yourself you are only restricted by your capability and imagination; you need not worry about whether it will sell.

If tackling the entire thing from the ground up is too scary, there are a number of kits available with complete instructions for sewing your own bags and panniers. The quality is generally good but the designs are somewhat limited. You are, however, free to make modifications as you go along.

Recommendations

"OK, but what do you recommend?" Inevitably at the end of the lecture, or after a long pitch in the bike shop, this is the question. The choice is yours, but what if you can't decide even after looking at the selection in view of all the above considerations?

We hesitate to make outright recommendations, partly due to the huge variety of bikepacking equipment available. Sometimes it seems that everyone in Boulder, Colorado, with access to a sewing machine is turning out panniers. It is impossible for us to have seen, let alone have used, everything on the market. Tim has spent considerable time, aside from his research and teaching, with Two Wheel Transit Authority, possibly the most fully equipped bicycle-touring shop in the West, so he is familiar with most major brands of touring equipment. Yet we firmly believe that final selection is highly personal, and should be based on individual needs, desires, values and finances. We rarely use the same gear on each tour, varying our choice according to the type of tour and its particular set of circumstances. But we are fortunate in having a large selection from which to choose.

If you insist on recommendations, the following is as close as we can come. Use it only as a guide, not as an edict. As you know by now, bikepacking gear is not cheap. Shop carefully for equipment that meets your needs, is of good quality and is durable. With care it should last your whole cycling career. You can be pessimistic and dwell on the fact that everything costs much more now than several years ago; or you can be optimistic and realize that everything is much less now than what it will likely be in the future. As always, the choice is yours.

Shopping Guide

Top-Quality Manufacturers
  A.Y.H.
  Cannondale

Carrying Gear

Eclipse
Kangaroo
Karrimor
Kirtland
R.E.I.
Touring Cyclist

Preferred All-Around Pannier Set
Eclipse Transcontinental ($85)

Preferred All-Around Handlebar Bag
Eclipse Professional ($46)

Preferred All-Around Front Pannier
Eclipse Superlite ($40)

Best Overall Value (Panniers)
R.E.I. Pannier II ($42)
A.Y.H. ($32)
Karrimor ($45)

Best Overall Value (Handlebar Bag)
Cannondale Casey ($15)

Best Overall Value (Front Pannier)
Karrimor ($20)

Chapter Eight
Planning Your Tour

The best place to begin bicycle touring is at your own front door. You can start today. Pack a little food, fill your water bottle, check your bike and head out. Where? Does it matter? OK, that is a little unfair. To some it matters, but to others. . . .

To us, the archetypal cycle tourist is one who cycles purely for pleasure, for the experience itself. There are no goals, no restrictions, no reservations, no time schedules. If a philosophy exists at all, it is that it is better to travel than to arrive. The means and the end become one. Impossible in this world of clocks and fences, tickets and timetables? Perhaps. But a bicycle is a very good vehicle for easing through the barriers that we build around ourselves. You can only go at a limited speed; you are subject to every whim, whiff and wayside attraction; you have every ex-cuse in the world to totally flow in the "now" of experience.

If you can, give yourself a chunk of time and try a nondestination bicycle tour. Pick a direction and set out. In most areas of the country there are campgrounds, towns and motels in which you can pass a night without advance notice after you have put enough miles in for the day. In spite of our seemingly innate need for routine and structure, you can cater to the craving for adventure in your nature simply by cycling out of your confines on a bicycle — if only for a weekend.

As ideal as this may seem, it is not everyone's idea of a good time. It assumes a certain expertise on wheels, a familiarity with touring and tripping that you may not feel you have at this point. So how else does one begin touring by bicycle?

It is best to start slow and gradually build toward your personal touring goal, whether that is to go overnight to a nearby park with the family or to try for a coast-to-coast summer on wheels. Naturally, we advocate building up physically, dealt with more extensively in chapter twelve, but you must also build up psychologically for touring. This is especially true if you are easing a reluctant spouse or friend into cycling and cycle touring. You need to build on positive experiences; frequently the most positive experiences of our lives are the small ones, the little things that may not have seemed at the time like an "experience" at all.

Initially, if you have not yet cycled distances, you need to learn that a bicycle will truly get you from here to there and back again. Ten miles in one day may seem mind boggling at first; it did to Glenda when she began. And it is. But the next time is easier, with each ride bringing greater distances within the scope of possibility.

Begin with day tours. Pack a lunch or pick a distant, favorite restaurant and spend the day on your bike. If there is a cycling club in your area, join the club members on shorter rides — don't pick a 50-miler if you are just beginning. Trying to keep up with the Joneses is the best way to end up hating your bicycle. Most clubs have beginner rides; if not, have your own. Is there a favorite area near your home? A museum, theater, park, zoo or simply a scenic view? Pick a relative or friend you enjoy visiting.

The important thing is to get there and back again by bicycle.

Increase the amount of time you spend on your bike for each day trip. As your cadence and riding style improve, your range will extend, opening new possibilities of pleasure.

At some point you will resent turning homeward midway through your day. The hills or fields or sights of the city will beckon and you will wish you could cycle the whole weekend instead of a single day. It is time to plan your first overnighter.

By now you know how far you can comfortably travel in one day. Plan your first overnight tour for around that distance. Don't give into the temptation to exceed your maximum distance to date. Remember, you must be able to get out of bed and do the same thing the next day, hopefully with a smile on your face. If you have done 35 miles in a day, try an overnight round trip of 60 miles. You will no doubt feel like going farther the first day; adrenalin works muscular wonders but it has a way of deserting you overnight. Resist the temptation, lie down on the grass until it goes away if need be. The best time to determine how far you should go the first day is at the end of the second day.

On your first overnighter, treat yourself to a motel, a hostel, or some soft place to land. Your equipment needs are then minimal yet you have maximum comfort at the end of the day. Many reluctant riders have been hooked on cycling because a considerate companion smoothed the rough edges off a first tour. A credit card is the lightest piece of touring equipment yet developed. If you possess one and are not averse to using it, why not let it ease your entry into the wide world of bicycle touring?

You can keep your baggage needs lower by eating out. If you can't afford it or can't hack the state of American culinary art, either take along or buy your food at a market at the end of the day. Meals are easy with cold foods or supermarket deli specials on paper plates. As soon as you feel comfortable and competent putting any number of miles under your seat on a two-day tour, begin carrying whatever gear you desire for fun, food and fulfillment. If camping is your idea of heaven, go at it with tents, panniers and Primus stove (see chapter nine). If city life is your bag, pack an evening gown or tux and cycle to a downtown hotel for an evening at the theater. Have to attend a family reunion 50 miles away? Get there by bike. You will find things to talk about with relatives you never knew you had anything in common with, or you might simply confirm their already "iffy" opinion of you. Either way, it will liven up your visit. Your weekend touring possibilities are only as limited as your imagination.

Frequently, the best weekend tours begin at your doorstep. The less you involve other modes of transportation, the more time you have for the pleasures of cycling. If you can plan circular trips with a minimum of backtracking, so

much the better. The only guide you need for this type of tour is the basic automobile road map. If you live in a major metropolitan area, there is probably a bicycle-touring guidebook that outlines day and weekend trips. Many regions and states have such guides; ask at your local bicycle shop, bookstore or library. Check with your local bike club for good trips, or join them on rides in your area. Some state automobile clubs have bicycle-touring guides; if not, the local office should have knowledgeable people who are familiar with the surrounding area and could suggest possible routes. At the least, auto clubs have high-quality road maps. County maps are frequently the best for detail, yet cover enough area to keep you cycling in circles for weeks or months of minitrips. If you aren't already a member of an auto club, consider joining one. Sometimes the maps, tour books and camping guides alone are worth the membership cost, even if you don't own a car. As a cyclist you share the same roads, enjoying both the rights and responsibilities of a motor vehicle.

Sooner or later we hope you find yourself with a chunk of time and the inclination to cycle somewhere far, far away. This might be a 400-mile trip through your state that begins right at your door, or it might mean a transport somewhere for two weeks of cycling in a totally different area. Try Utah in the spring, southern Arizona or Hawaii in the winter, New England in the fall, or how does an Alaskan cycling summer sound? How far can you cycle in how long? You probably know your "comfort range" by now, but a safe average to plan on is 50 miles a day when fully loaded; 60-80 miles with a minimum of gear or with more touring experience.

Knowing how far you can go in a day, plus the known amount of time you have available, you can sit down with a map and gain a realistic idea as to what the world offers you and your bicycle. Now the fun begins. As we said, the best touring begins at your doorstep. Better yet, it can begin in your living-room easy chair right now. Pick up a map, lean back and follow us.

Route Selection

You must first decide where you want to go. The safest, fastest, easiest route in the world is no good whatsoever if it is not where you want to be. Once your ultimate destination is decided, then you can begin to plot out the best route to or through it. By best we mean limited traffic, paved shoulders, small gradients, predominant tail winds; all those things that seem to smooth the road so you can enjoy the aesthetics of the area.

Trying to find all of those elements in one route is at best extremely difficult. But you should have them in mind as you select one road over another. Most rural secondary roads offer the least traffic unless they pass through recognized vacation areas. The most

unlikely roads can be unbelievably congested on weekends until you discover that a good fishing lake is nearby. Hunting season can do terrible things to an otherwise deserted road. Look for major roads or interstate highways that drain the majority of traffic from secondary roads nearby. In an earlier day, these smaller roads were direct routes into and through an area; they are ideal for cycling.

When selecting routes we frequently opt for off-the-beaten-path areas that most tourists bypass. Many motor tourists drive directly from one resort area or scenic attraction to the next. We usually note where those areas are and try hard to skirt around them. Our policy is to stay away from popular attractions and concentrate on quieter, more secluded countryside where the cycle tourist has a chance to experience the totality of the environment in a leisurely, personal manner. The Grand Canyon is awe inspiring no matter how you get there. But it takes a bicycle to really experience the tiny Mormon settlements of southern Utah, the vast expanses of a ranch in Wyoming or the small seaports of Maine.

Where to Stay

Whether you are just taking mini-tours or you are planning a big one, you want each night's stay to have as little fuss as possible. If you don't camp, your choices are pretty well limited to private homes, motels or hostels. Private homes are up to you to find and treasure, unless you can take advantage of the system of private homes that serve as "tourist inns" offering economical lodging and sometimes meals. This is worth asking about in towns you pass through, especially in the central and eastern United States.

Motels offer a sometimes expensive, yet very available nationwide accommodation alternative. There are numerous state and nationwide chains that you can contact for advanced reservations, sometimes toll free from your home phone. Of course, you must then stick to your planned cycling schedule, something hard to do given the delights and distresses of bicycling. If you are not sure of your distance capabilities or would like to wander without restriction, there are usually older independent motels and hotels where reservations are seldom necessary. We have found these to be generally inexpensive if we are willing to forgo swimming pools, saunas and free ice.

When stopping at a motel, give yourself time to cool off before entering. Take off your helmet and rearview mirror (best done out of view of the office), and run a comb through your hair. We have been refused lodging only once due to our cycling appearance, but others — especially lone males — report problems more frequently. Sure, as long as you can pay the tariff, appearance shouldn't count, but to many people it still makes the difference between the good guys and the bad guys. Always present yourself in the best possible light and explain as soon as feasible that you are bicycle touring (not cycle touring). They may think you're crazy, but at least not malicious or dangerous. We never ask ahead about taking our bikes and gear into the motel room; we do it as a matter of course. We have yet to run into any trouble, even at major hotels, but we do opt for unobtrusive entries and out-of-sight elevators whenever possible.

For lodging somewhere between the minimal expense of camping and the maximum expense of moteling, hostels are the answer. Most hostels provide dormitory-style sleeping accommodations usually with blankets, cooking facilities and sometimes showers provided. Costs run $1-$4 per night, with chores occasionally required in addition to the fee. Hostels were originally intended for traveling students, but adults are welcomed in most countries of the world. A membership card is required and may be obtained for a small fee from American Youth Hostels, Inc., National Campus, Delaplane, VA 22025; it is accepted all over the world.

In Europe, youth hostels are found everywhere; daily cycling between them is easy. In the United States there are only about 200 hostels, mostly situated in the Northeast. It is possible to tour using hostels for all of your accommodations, but this gets tricky for extended touring. Every year legislation is introduced into Congress to subsidize the building of more hostels, but it has not yet been passed.

Meeting nice people is one of the nicest things about staying in hostels. It is perhaps the quickest way to learn the ins and outs of inexpensive travel. Hostels are a great medium for fostering international understanding and friendships; we highly recommend them for your use.

Maps

Planning your long-distance tour can be almost as much fun as doing it. You can begin as soon as you decide where you want to go. If you are not familiar with an area, or even if you want only to update your information, there is a huge amount of material available to you. The best place to begin is with maps.

Maps are to the bicycle tourist what recipes are to the cook. Good ones are full of general and specialized information just waiting to be discovered. Most people read a map; maps really come into their own when they are interpreted. A good text for developing your map-reading skills is *Mapping* by David Greenhood, but you will find that maps bend to your will if you simply ask the right questions and take the time to find the answers.

Maps are basically representations of the earth's surface on a flat piece of paper. There are specialized maps of just about any phenomenon, but the

better automobile road maps are adequate for most cycling purposes. Topographic maps, those showing relief (the ups and downs of the land) using contour lines, can be useful but are by no means necessary. Although they show many cultural features such as roads and towns, they are not as up to date as most road maps. Good coverage with topographic maps on a long tour would mean a big expenditure and a storage problem due to the size and number of maps that would be involved.

If you want to use them for shorter tours, they are available at many backpacking stores or directly from the government. Request an index for your state, pick out the specific maps you need, then order them at a cost of $1.25-$2.00 each depending on the scale. If you live east of the Mississippi write: Branch of Distribution, U.S. Geological Survey, 1200 South Eads Street, Arlington, VA 22202. If you live west of the Mississippi write: Branch of Distribution, U.S. Geological Survey, Box 25286, Federal Center, Denver, CO 80225.

Good local and county maps are available from auto clubs or bookstores. Rand McNally has excellent state maps, as does Texaco and a few other gas companies. Many gas stations now charge for maps but they are still a bargain. State-supplied road maps are usually of poor quality. For Europe, the Michelin 1:200,000 series is excellent as are Bartholomew's maps of the United Kingdom. In the United States, Michelin's maps are available at PO Box 5022,

New Hyde Park, NY 11040; Bartholo-mew's maps from the American Map Company, 1926 Broadway, New York, NY 10023.

Any of the better maps will show you the current road situation, but they also contain many cultural and physical features. Some are shaded to indicate major physical relief. Elevation is the distance of a point above sea level; relief is the local difference in topography (how much one point is above or below another). An area may be 7,000 feet in elevation yet relatively flat with little relief, such as a high plain or plateau. Conversely, a road might parallel the coast at only 100 feet average elevation, yet that road may be very hilly with steep gradients due to rugged relief.

General relief can be interpreted from unshaded road maps if you look closely at available data. Town elevations and passes are usually marked, or town elevations can be found on the back of the map in the index section. If town A is 1,050 feet and town B is 1,330 feet with a 4,000-foot pass in between, then you can figure on some pretty hard pedaling to the pass and a nice, long downhill to town B. This is general and not to be read as absolute reality, but it does give an indication of what is in store for you on a particular road. If you want to know if a stretch of road is uphill or downhill, check for a stream or river flowing beside it. Follow the stream until you can determine its point of origin or exit, then you can determine the nature of the road. By looking closely you can tell a little about the lay of the land by stream patterns. Short, relatively straight streams can mean steep, rugged topography; long, winding streams usually indicate gentle valleys.

Using these clues along with your general knowledge of an area, you can make good decisions about what you can expect in any given region and what routes to choose. Maps provide an excess of information; it is up to you to ask the right questions and interpret the data on the map for the answers.

Maps tell you much more than physical and road information. The cultural data is sometimes of greater importance to the touring cyclist. The population of a town according to the latest census not only satisfies your curiosity but gives you a valuable clue as to the services you might expect to find there. A village of 400 may not have a grocery store, but a town of 3,000 surely does. With some road experience you will even be able to make an educated guess as to whether a store would be open on Sunday. (Very likely in a town of 3,000, if there are no really large towns nearby.) With practice you will be able to predict fairly accurately if services and facilities are available; be aware however, that customs vary in different states or even in differing ethnic areas within the same state. In some sections of the country, markets never seem to close; in others, 6:00 P.M. is the absolute end of the business day. In one area, stores may close on Mondays and remain open on the weekend; in others, Sunday is the observed non-business day. Be flexible and always carry emergency rations.

Most good road maps show public campgrounds; some even show private ones, but we have found it best to supplement this information with campground guides published by map companies, travel trailer groups and auto clubs. In the West it is particularly important to know whether campgrounds provide water; the guides tell you this, road maps do not. Many public campgrounds are located in national forests, which are usually shown as green shaded areas on road maps. These areas usually mean trees, and in the West trees mean higher elevation with improved scenery; clues important to the cycle tourist in planning a route.

Roadside rests are another feature shown on good road maps. In some states these are no more than a trash can or table; in others they might mean running water, flush toilets, phones and even overnight camping. When planning critical aspects of your tour such as water-supply points and overnight stops, don't rely on a single map source, no matter how good it is. On their road maps, Arizona and California use the same symbol for roadside rests. California interstates provide full service at these with water, making bicycle touring possible in large areas of desert where it would otherwise be difficult if not risky. However, when the tourist enters Arizona conditions change radically. There, roadside rests can be very

primitive with no water available. The cyclist cannot make assumptions when it comes to important things like water. He should use more than one source of information.

Road maps frequently designate scenic routes. When venturing into new areas you can see the best of the region by planning your trip along such routes. Be aware, however, that some of these might be heavily trafficked, especially on weekends and during peak summer months. Off-season and during the week these routes can be delightfully lonely.

In addition to being critical to planning and carrying out your tour, maps offer unlimited hours of enjoyment, relaxation and education to the armchair portion of your tour. Every good tour consists of three definable segments: the preparation, the actual tour and the memories of it all. Maps are important to all three. If you are using your map only for the actual tour, you are missing out on two-thirds of the pleasure. If you are like us, you will never be able to realize all of your touring ambitions, but that doesn't stop us from enjoying many tours vicariously by selecting a route and traveling it from the softness of our living room using pretend wheels over paper roads. Whether you are actually planning a trip or just taking a magical mystery tour you will be sharpening your map skills and broadening one very real aspect of the bicycle touring experience. No one is born with map-reading skills.

As hard as it is for us to imagine, not everyone loves maps or feels comfortable trying to unlock their secrets. It is certainly easier and may even be necessary for you to follow someone else's route. They are available, planned in detail down to each rest stop, along well-thought-out, safe (hopefully) routes, through towns willingly playing host to many cyclists. Traveling that way relieves you of much of the responsibility and a lot of the advance planning of a bike tour. Beware. It can also rob you of the joy of complete independence, of charting your own way in the world, of getting where only you want to go, and perhaps of your being the only one who happens along that way.

Gathering Information

You will need and want more information about an extended tour destination than is available on road maps alone. If you are totally unfamiliar with an area, anything can help give you insight. A lot of advance information may seem superfluous when it comes to actual planning, but it can add appreciably to your enjoyment on tour, sharpening your view so that you can look deeper into an area because you are already familiar with surface things.

Allow yourself time to write for information that might not be readily available to you. Whenever you write, be specific about what you want to know and where you are going to be touring. Make it as easy as possible for the informant to answer you, even to listing questions that can be checked yes or no, or at least answered very briefly on your same sheet of paper. We were deluged with requests for information following the publication in *Bicycling* magazine of articles on our cross-country trip. Most were broad requests for information, some wanting us to "tell anything you know" about bike touring or a specific route. Tim's article "Four Across America: Afterwards" in the May 1978 issue was in partial reply to these requests; this book will have to take care of the rest. Obviously, we weren't able to write the amount of information requested in one reply. When you ask for information, be specific.

Most countries in the world and each state in the United States has a department of tourism. You may contact it through the U.S. consul or state capital to request information on a specific region. You will usually be deluged in return with loads of information on cultural and scenic attractions. Describe exactly or as closely as possible where you will be touring and ask for any other information they might have on that particular area. Be sure to mention in your request that you are bicycle touring.

Other sources to approach in writing are the chambers of commerce in towns along your route. Write directly to the chamber of commerce addressed to the town (using zip codes) and it will get to the right people. If you ask specifically about accommodations and services, you will sometimes get detailed lists including lodging prices. Many towns have climate charts that can help you to decide when you would prefer to tour and the sort of clothing and equipment you will need. If you want, ask the chamber of commerce to include an issue of the local paper.

More information is available in general and regional tour books from your local library. Let the librarian in on your plans and you will have access to a vast amount of information you probably never dreamed existed. Many large libraries have newspapers from various regions around the United States, some have international periodicals as well. These are good for the type of information we discussed, which gives you a feeling of familiarity in advance so you can use your touring time to really get into the more unknown aspects of an area.

Also at the library, again the larger ones, is perhaps the greatest single source of really important information for the bicycle tourist in the United States. This is the *National Atlas of the United States.* The amount of information that can be gleaned from its pages is astounding. Plan several hours to pour over it; be sure to have a notebook for jotting down important data. It is fairly large and it is difficult to photocopy selected pages, but not impossible. This book is available from the U.S.

Government Printing Office (see address below) for the sum of $100; better hope your local library has it.

The *National Atlas of the United States* has maps of just about every mappable phenomenon in this country from air pollution to public lands to wind direction. Anyone anticipating an extensive tour in this country should be aware of this source of information. The map of prevailing wind direction is of particular interest, since wind is one of the major weather elements that affects your tour. There is nothing worse than gearing down to struggle along on a level or even downhill section because of a strong head wind. Day after day of fighting head winds can be the most demoralizing part of any tour. You can't do anything about them, but you can attempt to plan your tours around known prevailing winds. That is why most cross-country tours are planned from west to east, also why most West Coast tours start in the north and proceed south. Using the wind direction maps in the *National Atlas* will give you an idea as to "normal" wind patterns. Don't be too shocked, however, if you happen to encounter abnormal winds while touring; it happens all too often.

Weather Information

In addition to the *National Atlas,* there are more specific sources of weather information for the entire United States that are of value to the cycle tourist. The U.S. National Oceanic and Atmospheric Administration puts out a series of pamphlets entitled *Climates of the States.* In theory there is one for every state but some are out of print. Write the U.S. Government Printing Office, Cap Street, Washington, DC 20402 for the state or states you want (about $1 each). If you live near a major college or university, its library should have a government publications section where you can look at and reproduce what you want. The *Climates of the States* pamphlets give you specific data on high and low temperatures, precipitation and frost-free periods for climate stations around each state as well as detailed information for selected stations in the state. There is a synopsis for the entire state with a breakdown of climatic regions within it. If you use these pamphlets you will have no excuse for not knowing what to expect climate-wise where you are touring. They are only describing climate, the long-term trends in atmospheric condition, not the weather, which is the daily mixture of elements through which you will be riding. Weather and climate can vary drastically, but you will at least have a guide as to what is probable.

If your touring is limited to one specific area, write for "Local Climatological Data," available through the National Climate Center, Federal Building, Asheville, NC 28801. For a small fee (20¢-40¢), the center will send you a climatic data sheet for almost any town or city in the United States. Each sheet gives you specific information on temperature, precipitation, wind direction, percentage of sunshine, record highs and lows, amounts of snow, rain, hail and humidity. Simply request the sheet(s) for the town or city you are interested in. Great for the planning stage of a tour, these sheets give hours of enjoyment to the armchair tourer as well.

Road Conditions

As you gather data on scenic wonders and possibilities of sunshine, you might also obtain what advance information is available about road conditions — shoulders, traffic hazards, gradients, and perhaps large-scale construction projects — that might detour or detain you. If you have settled on a specific tour and route, with leeway for the inviting and the unforeseen, there really isn't a whole lot you can do about road conditions. But like the weather, it is good to know the possibilities. The best, single source of road information is the state's highway department. Some states have a centralized data-gathering department, others handle it on a regional or county basis. Phone or write your local office and ask how you can acquire traffic flow, gradient and road shoulder information. If they can't help, then ask for the address of the state office. Most states have specific information on road conditions that is valuable to the cycle tourist, but many charge for the data. Some states, like Washington and California, have an office just for providing information to bicycle travelers on routes and road conditions. Ask the states you are interested in for any information specifically on bicycling in their state. Whatever you do, don't ask for road information on the whole state. Decide beforehand what roads you most likely will be traveling, then ask about those routes and any alternative routes they might suggest. Also, ask about any planned construction or repair projects on your route during the period you will be touring. Bicycling over wet tar behind motor homes and trailers is no fun.

Wide paved shoulders are a cyclist's dream. They can also be frustratingly rare or intermittent for unexplained reasons. You may be better off trusting to luck and taking what you get. In some states, almost all primary and secondary roads have some sort of paved margin to the side. Even if only a foot or two, it is important to the cyclist — not as a steady path, but as an escape hatch when traffic pressures dictate. Many roads are only two lanes on which the cyclist has as much right as a vehicle. Unfortunately the typical American motorist does not always agree, even though it is the law.

Somehow, sharing the road with a cyclist is a blow to the ego of many drivers, especially if they have to pull out of their lanes to pass. Even if there are no cars approaching in the opposite direction, many drivers will not pull out to give the bicycle a few extra feet. In other areas of the world, it is an accepted practice to pass cyclists as one would any other slow-moving vehicle on the road. While riding in Mexico we were pleasantly surprised that the Mexican driver almost always moves over to the opposite side of the road when passing a cyclist. However, when American tourists came along they seldom did the same, and instead inched by dangerously close and frequently forced us off onto the dirt path at the side of the road.

Time after time on our cross-country trip we were passed dangerously close by motorists who refused to slow down as they approached us in the lane, even though they could see us and our Buggers far ahead and could also see that we had no shoulder on which to pull off. Many times we were passed on blind curves or on "no passing" sections of hills, simply because drivers would not slow down and observe the legal method of passing another vehicle, evidently because we were on bicycles. Tractors and horse-pulled wagons get more road courtesy than the cyclist.

Lack of shoulders on lightly traveled roads is not a tour-stopping problem. We have traveled thousands of miles on two-lane roads, and many of those miles have been the most pleasant we have known. There are dangers however. The ignorant, in-a-hurry motorist is one. Another is the recreational

135

vehicle looming up behind you on that narrow road with its mirrors extending two feet into your backside, or even worse, you see it approaching blithely from the rear with its metal steps dangling dangerously out from beneath the door. That is the time to abandon the road. Take their license number if it makes you feel better — although it won't do much good unless the protrusions put them beyond the legal eight-foot width requirement — but don't decide that this is the time to lay claim to your piece of road. You may get six feet of ground out of it, but not pavement. On heavily traveled tourist routes with limited or no shoulders (such as California's coastal Highway 1) the bicyclist is at the mercy of RV drivers who are sometimes inexperienced and unaware of the danger they represent for cyclists. Use your rearview mirror constantly and keep an escape route in mind.

Recent passage of federal legislation allows highway funds to be used for bikeway construction, which now includes the widening or paving of road shoulders. If all states would pave just two feet of shoulder on all their roads, think what a boon to bicycle touring that would be. Maybe someday . . . Until then, you can write to the state department of highways to ascertain where paved shoulders exist if you want to limit your touring to those roads. Otherwise, take what you get, keep your ears and eyes open, and help make states aware of the need for paved shoulders.

You may want to take road gradients into consideration when planning your tour. An all-flat tour might be easy, but it might be boring too. Road maps give you some indication of the terrain, using the clues of elevation and stream-flow we mentioned. If you want more detailed information about a specific route, the state highway department might be able to help you. When we tour we try only to avoid the steepest passes if possible. Don't fall into the trap of thinking that all passes must be circumnavigated. Some of the finest country is found at high elevations; you will miss a lot if you don't attempt a big one now and then. Mountains can be deceiving. We found crossing the Rockies through an 11,000-feet pass more enjoyable than passing through the Appalachians over a seemingly endless series of 3,000-feet passes. It is all relative to your outlook and whether you are where you want to be or just on the way there.

Getting to Your Jumping-Off Place

Although the ideal is to tour from your front door and back again, we realize that it is not always possible or desirable. Perhaps second best is to drive your car to a safe place (such as a 24-hour service station, police station or ranger station), then pedal off to return by a circular route or public transportation from the termination point of your tour. All you really need is a secure means of carrying your bicycle on your vehicle and the will to put some time in behind the wheel before you can put some time in on your wheels.

If you don't have a car or time and distance negate its use, public transportation will have to get you where you want to tour. The transportation of bicycles via public conveyances in the United States is in a continual state of flux and uncertainty. Due to rapid changes in policy and price, we can only give you hints and guidelines, leaving final arrangements and details to

Many cyclists find the train a very convenient way to get to the starting point for a tour.

you. Always check the regulations and procedures of public carriers with at least two employees of the company you are dealing with, preferably at least a day apart. Take names and numbers when someone tells you something so that you have at least that much to back you up if things are not as they should be when you reach your destination.

The train seems to be the best public transport available for bicycles now in the United States, and in Europe too. Train travel is sometimes comparable to the cost of similar bus transport and, more important, your bicycle is usually handled with less hassle and greater care. Unlike Europe, the United States has limited passenger-train service now, with probably even more restricted travel in the future. When planning rail transport to your jumping-off place, make sure at the beginning that there is passenger service available there; many routes are freight only. Get a copy of Amtrak's (National Railroad Passenger Corporation) national timetable, which includes a map of its service-including stops. Write to PO Box 2709, Washington, DC 20001. If you know specifically where you are going, call Amtrak's toll-free number (in your phone book or ask information) to check on service and timetables. Be sure to verify that your bike can be loaded or unloaded at that point. Amtrak has many stops where freight cannot be handled due to lack of baggage-handling facilities and personnel. Unless you find out absolutely, you

may find yourself standing at Podunk Station, U.S.A., while your bike passes on another 200 miles to Bigville. Sometimes freight can be loaded or unloaded only on certain runs. Know where your bike is so you don't have any surprise eight-hour waits for another train.

Amtrak now requires the boxing of all bikes. Because of changes in Amtrak requirements, we advise you to check with them before traveling. Amtrak sells boxes for $4 at its major urban stations. There is also a $5 handling charge for all bikes.

If you plan to box your bike, call ahead to the station to insure that boxes are available or get your own from a bike store. Plan to arrive at the station at least an hour early so you can remove your pedals, lower the seatpost and turn the handlebars for boxing. Be sure you have both the tools and the know-how to do this. (Loosen your pedals before you leave home. Few tourists carry a 12-inch pedal wrench in case you can't break them loose at the station.) If you aren't boxing your bike, still plan to arrive at least 30 minutes ahead of departure. Baggage clerks are notoriously inflexible about receiving bicycles late; be nice to them and they will be more likely to be nice to your bike.

If you are returning to the same jumping-off point, don't count on Amtrak — or any other public carrier for that matter — to store your box for you. It is your box and they figure it is your problem. This all sounds pretty bad;

certainly it is worse than in Europe where people have been hauling bikes around for decades. Protect yourself by planning ahead, checking and double-checking all steps where you are relying on someone or something else. Have enough cash for any unexpected delays, be flexible and smile a lot.

Buses are another way of getting there with your bike. In the United States and Latin America buses run just about everywhere at one time or another. The cost is usually low, but your bike must be boxed or covered in an acceptable manner so as not to damage other baggage. Bus baggage compartments are more restrictive than trains, so make sure you box it well. Put a block of wood between the fork blades to insure that they don't get compressed. The box has to be smaller than those for trains and planes; use the bike-shop kind, which requires removal of the front wheel. All this takes time and a knowledge of what you are doing and how you can undo it when you want to put it all back together again. Check with the bus company for exact size restrictions so you are sure that the box you use is right, but many times bikes are excused from size regulations.

We have heard that bike boxes will fit standing upright in Continental Trailways bus baggage compartments. On Greyhound the box has to lie flat on its side, usually under all the other luggage. Be there when your bike (box) is loaded so you can attempt some control over the process (suggest nicely that it go in upright if possible and please don't put the box of rattling liquor bottles on top of it). Also make sure your bike changes buses whenever you do.

Airplanes are the fastest and most expensive means of getting you and your bike on tour. Within the United States, most airlines allow you to take your bike along for about $10; most also insist on it being boxed. Some carriers have large boxes that don't require removal of the front wheel; there is usually a charge for these. Always check with at least two airline employees, including one at the airport itself, to insure that a box is available when and where you need it. There is nothing worse than getting to the airport only to find that they just gave out the last box. Make sure you have the tools accessible to box your bike and leave yourself plenty of time to do it right.

On international flights, regulations regarding bicycles are varied and changing all the time. Most certainly, however, your bike will have to be boxed in the smaller bike-shop-type carton, or in some sort of specialized bag. On some international carriers your bike goes as part of your weight allowance, on others you pay an excess weight fee even if your baggage total is not in excess. Sometimes the same carrier will charge you one time, but not the next. Confusion reigns. Keep your bike and baggage below the maximum weight allowed if possible and if you

139

care. This can sometimes be assured by wearing your heaviest clothing and carrying tools and cooking gear in your carry-on luggage. Pack your bike in the smallest possible box, smile a lot, and hope for an understanding person at the check-in counter. You have of course checked regulations and know who told you what if a problem arises.

When you first make your plans to use public transportation, call around, check carefully and travel the line that is most sympathetic to your needs as a bicycle tourist. It won't hurt to let them know that that is why you are traveling with them instead of with a competitor. Smooth the way for the next cyclist.

No matter how you get to your jumping-off point, there is real joy in unloading your bike, attaching your gear, and pedaling off self-contained and self-propelled while others hassle with suitcases, taxis, schedules and reservations. Point your wheels in the direction

140

Boxed bicycle, ready for transport.

you want to go and head out. Such independence and self-sufficiency in a complex and frustrating world are two of the primary advantages of bicycle touring. If you have your sleeping bag and cooking gear on behind as well, you are even that much further ahead on your way to cycling pleasure.

Chapter Nine
Camping by Bicycle

Bicycle camping is the most challenging and rewarding type of bicycle travel. With your complete home on your bike you are free to wander anywhere; such is the essence of bicycle touring. Self-containment and self-sufficiency are approachable ideals on a touring bicycle loaded with camping gear.

A touring bicycle camper has a complete shelter and a cooking and sleeping system and is able to carry two or more days of food and water. Independent to a great degree, the cycle tourist travels anywhere the road leads without consuming nonrenewable fuel and without depending on a massive industrial complex to keep his or her machine running. Fuel for the body, and perhaps a little for the cookstove, is all that is required.

In addition to the aesthetics of such freedom, the economics are hard to beat. It is possible to tour in most parts of the world for $5-$10 a day depending on your eating habits and the camping facilities you require or prefer. With another $20-$40 per month for incidentals such as laundry, sightseeing and personal needs, it is feasible to tour for $170-$340 a month. How can you possibly afford to stay home?

What about the initial cost of your gear? Ease your mind with a few comparisons. The bicycle tourer comes out far ahead of a car camper or recreational vehicle owner in initial outlay, but even when compared with backpacking, bicycling is not expensive. In addition to the high cost of a good pack, lightweight tent and hiking boots, backpacking also means expensive lightweight food for each trip plus transportation to and from the point of departure. Once the initial investment is made in bicycle touring equipment, however, there is little further outlay.

Your investment in camping equipment (depending on your plans) may exceed $200, but the gear is long-lived and touring itself costs little more than daily living expenses. You can do a lot to keep equipment expenditure down by using gear you already have or by renting the more expensive items like sleeping bags and tents. As you gain experience and expertise you can purchase what you need one piece at a time.

More important than acquisition of equipment is acquisition of the skills needed to become a competent cycle camper. Camping requires a degree of forethought and methodology in approach and practice. As you can't expect to be a skilled tennis player your first time on the court, neither can you expect to be an expert camper on your first tour. Even if you have camped in your nonbicycling life, you will find things a little different under cycling circumstances. It is possible to become a skilled camper in one particular environment in a relatively short time, but it can take years to develop the skills necessary to be at home in all circumstances and under all physical conditions. One of the great things about camping is that you can always learn more no matter what the level of your skills. You can learn a lot by reading books about camping, but most skills are developed by doing. Read; try

to find an "old hand" to show you the basics; then go out and do it. You have nothing to lose but lack of experience.

Where to Camp

The choices in a given touring region might range from free public campgrounds to expensive private ones. Public campgrounds are operated by the U.S. Forest Service, the National Park Service and the Bureau of Land Management (BLM). Most have a fee attached, but some are free (especially BLM sites). Services in public campgrounds usually include toilets, tables and fire pits; always check ahead in campground guides to make sure there is water if you need it. Most federal campgrounds are rustic and designed for tent camping, but many new ones are built primarily for recreational vehicles. Frequently these camps are located off paved highways on dirt roads; you might want to take this into consideration when planning your stops.

City and county campgrounds offer facilities similar to those of federal camps, but are located in more urban areas. These, too, generally have low fees. In midwestern America almost every small town has a city park in which you might be able to camp if you ask at nearby houses or at the local police station. Many town and city parks are gathering places for local youths on hot summer evenings; beer drinking and loud music can either delay your bed-

143

time or add to your evening's enjoyment, depending on your preferences.

Private campgrounds are scattered throughout the United States and Europe, especially along major highways. These vary from plush resorts with swimming pools, games, hot showers, laundries, stores and evening entertainment to more spartan types resembling public campgrounds. Many of these private camps are geared to the recreational vehicle and motorized camper; you may find yourself paying $4-$7 for the privilege of pitching your tent. Arguments do no good since you are paying for all of the extra facilities that are not affected by your mode of travel. Noise can be a problem in these camps as vehicles are packed closely together, but if you are in need of showers or laundry facilities, stores or company in the game room, private camps are there for your use.

One of the major advantages of bicycle camping is that you don't really need a campground at all. In many areas, particularly on quieter roads, campgrounds are either nonexistent or so far apart as to be impractical for the cycling tourist's daily use. In much of the United States and Canada where land is public (mostly in the West), you can camp just about anywhere. Water is the main problem but it can be carried with you if you plan ahead. On private land, permission to camp should be obtained with a courteous request to the landowner and a promise not to build a fire or leave trash behind. We have been invited to camp, use well water, and even share a meal with farmers and their families. Appearance and approach have a lot to do with the reception you get.

If you find yourself in a town or city overnight with no camping facilities (or no money for such), other places will sometimes do for quick stopovers. Schools, churchyards and even cemeteries serve if you are observant and careful in your selection. In other words, don't expect to sleep late in a school yard on a weekday morning, don't look for solitude on a Sunday morning camped out in a churchyard, and we personally avoid cemeteries on Halloween night. Any other time a cemetery guarantees you a peaceful sleep among quiet neighbors. Even in large cities, with a poncho or bivouac shelter, there are secluded spots among overgrown vegetation into which you can snuggle for a peaceful night. Unfortunately there is no way to determine sprinkler scheduling; you just have to take your chances on such things.

Selecting a Campsite

In an established campground, you have little control over or need for selecting your own campsite. On your own, however, there are several factors to think about. Water is of primary concern. Every gallon of water you carry weighs over eight pounds, so make your pedaling day as easy as possible. Dry camps are not impossible but a convenient water supply is preferable. If there is no piped or well water available, look for surface supplies — streams, lakes or springs. Assume any surface water is polluted unless proven otherwise. A brook may look pristine yet have a dead horse or sheep herd ¼ mile upstream and out of your sight. Use Halazone or Potable-Aqua tablets when you are not absolutely sure about the water. Diarrhea on a bicycle is a particular kind of hell.

When choosing a campsite don't feel you have to be right next to the water supply, especially in public campgrounds. There is a continual parade to the water source, which destroys any privacy you may be seeking. Camping near a water surface assures you of a damp night. Try to get at least ten feet above the water for maximum dryness. Lakes and streams mean mosquito activity. By locating higher up in open areas you catch any breeze that happens along, which helps keep the bug situation under control.

You might want to settle on a sleeping spot to catch the early-morning sun or to avoid it, depending on your plans for the day. Choose a site that is as level as possible for sleeping — if you have to occupy a slope, place your head up-

hill. Make sure your tent stakes are able to go into the ground before becoming too committed to a particular site. Underlying rock makes tent pitching frustrating if not impossible.

Most people head for the trees when searching out a campsite. Be sure that the trees you sleep under are healthy with no widow-makers (dead limbs) waiting for the next wind to loosen them. We once slept under a large yellow pine tree without a tent only to be jolted awake in the middle of the night when one of its huge cones dropped onto the foot of our sleeping bag. Had it landed on the other end we would have had serious headaches. Look around the area under a tree for debris — it didn't get there by telekinesis. If there is a lot, avoid that area.

Before you start a campfire, make sure it is legal and that the fire danger is low. Look for a source of dead, dry wood close by your campsite. Use nothing but dead wood, preferably that not lying directly on the ground where it has picked up moisture. Always use existing fire rings when possible; if you are the first to camp in an area, make sure no one after you will know you were there. Soak your fire dead out and disperse the rock ring, preferably back to the places the rocks came from.

In established campgrounds select a campsite away from outhouses and set back from major activity points. You have no choice over your neighbors, but people usually congregate as close

145

to each other as possible when camping. If you value privacy, get as far into a lonesome-looking area as you can; usually others will avoid such places if they have a choice.

When camping outside of a campground, find a spot that cannot be seen from the road. Never advertise your presence. The only animal you really have to be wary of is man, yet in over 30 years of camping on three continents we have never had a confrontation or threatening experience with our fellow man or woman. Established campgrounds are possibly more dangerous because of the occasional drunk, traffic hazards and firearms dangers.

Don't ignore the aesthetic considerations of a campsite. How you feel about a particular camp adds to your experience there. No amount of amenities makes up for a feeling of unease or discomfort. On the other hand, a beautiful scene can compensate for deficient camp facilities.

To Tent or Not to Tent

When bicycle touring, as with any overnight outdoor activity, we don't recommend going without some means of providing shelter, whether you use it or not. Don't make a shelter out of native materials; those days are long gone in this overpopulated world of limited resources. Let living things live. Carry your own shelter with you.

Most people associate shelter with tents for some very good reasons. A tent provides shelter from the weather, whether that is dew, wind, rain or snow. It offers protection from insects and flying nuisances such as mosquitoes. It is a place to store gear out of sight while cycling away from camp, and it offers privacy in today's crowded campgrounds. Finally, it gives a degree of mental security as the night shadows fall. Tents make sense, but they are not mandatory due to their high cost and heavy weight for cycle touring.

Tent substitutes are abundant and varied to meet your needs and your pocketbook. Our favorite is the simple backpacking poncho — a rectangular, 54 × 88-inch, 12-ounce piece of waterproof nylon ($20). Wear it as a raincoat (too floppy for cycling), cover your gear and bicycle to keep weather off or pitch it one of many ways to provide yourself with an adequate shelter. Most models have grommets at the corners but we usually add extras around the edges for easier pitching and tying down. All you need is some nylon parachute cord, steel skewer stakes (5 ounces, 75¢ for 8), and some imagination to develop a variety of one-person shelters. As a professional backpacking guide and outfitter in Idaho, Tim used a poncho for his and his clients' principal shelter all summer long in the high Rockies. Its weight, price and versatility are right for cycle camping.

If you want a larger shelter, a nylon tarp serves as well as the smaller poncho. Available in a variety of sizes, we

Poncho pitched as a lean-to (left) and a fly-shelter (right).

like the 9 × 11-foot size best (2 lbs. 2 oz., $37).

The tube tent is a favorite of many campers, although we don't like it. Designed for one or two people, it is made of three-mil polyethylene and is shaped like an open-ended tube (1 lb. 4 oz., $6; 2 lbs., $8). It is fragile. A lot of people leave it when it becomes useless, so it is an all-too-familiar sight half-buried in the dirt around campsites. If you use one, take it with you and dispose of it properly.

The poncho, tarp and tube tent offer adequate protection from weather, but not from mosquitoes. To solve this problem with the poncho, we designed and made a triangular piece of mosquito netting three feet high by four feet across, sewn in a cone shape with a tie

Pitched plastic tube tent.

string at the apex. Tied to the guideline running through the center of the poncho shelter, it hangs down over the head of the sleeping bag. We find it a cheap, lightweight, compact way to repel mosquitoes.

Another tent substitute is the bivouac or bivy bag, a recent innovation in outdoor shelters. This is a close-fitting cover that encloses the sleeper and bag. The bottom is waterproof nylon and the top is Gore-Tex. Even though the sleeper is closely wrapped in the bivy bag, moisture does not collect inside due to the breathable top, yet it is waterproof. Better models come with small mosquito-netted openings for ventilation in fair weather. Tim used a bivy bag made by Blue Puma (1 lb. 9 oz., $79) and reports it to be remarkably effective. Because of its compact size and light weight (just over 1½ lbs.), it is an excellent cycle-camping shelter for one or two persons. Major drawbacks are cost ($50-$100) and lack of internal storage space. It can be a bit tricky getting in and out of as well, especially in pouring rain.

Such tent substitutes make sense for the cycle camper. If you don't want to invest the money in a tent, if you are concerned with keeping weight and bulk to a minimum, or if you limit your touring to dry environments, any of these will make your tour more comfortable and may even extend your touring season by several months.

When one of us tours alone, we don't carry a tent. For two we prefer a

Bivy bag with ground cloth under it.

small one, and when the whole family tours we always use a tent. We compensate for the weight by carrying one sleeping bag for each two persons.

If you decide in favor of tenting, consider these basic points. The primary function of a tent is to keep weather and bugs out, but it must also allow inner moisture to escape or you will be rained on from the inside each morning. Your body gives off a large amount of moisture both day and night. If your tent is totally waterproof, that moisture gathers on the roof and walls. Stay away from all tents that are completely waterproof; even with large window openings for ventilation you will have problems. Cotton tents can be waterproofed yet breathe, but they are too heavy for self-propelled travel.

Most quality tents (with the exception of Cannondale which has a unique double-wall system) have waterproof nylon floors extending partially up the sides with breathable nylon on the top and upper sides. When used with an external fly (roof covering) of waterproof nylon, they will not leak. Internal moisture passes through the roof and walls, yet the fly — pitched a few inches off the tent itself — keeps precipitation out. In anything except dry summer desert conditions, the fly is a necessity.

There are almost unlimited choices in tents. The continual search for the "salable new" has produced about every form imaginable. Many of these new designs are changes rather than improvements. Some are so complicated, requiring so many supporting poles, that it almost takes an M.I.T. graduate to erect them. Try doing it in a 40-mph wind just before a thunderstorm hits. Worse than that, what happens when you lose or break a pole? With many of these models, one missing or broken pole means no tent. Our advice is to stick to tents that require simple, straight poles; the fewer the better. In an emergency you can always make or find a replacement in the woods or at the next hardware store. Many of the newer designs have a large number of seams and panels in the tent fabric. We see these only as more places for the tent to come apart or leak. Keep your gear simple.

When choosing a tent, first decide how much room you require. As space increases, so does weight. Most cyclists feel that the lighter the tent the better, but the first time you spend a couple of days waiting out a storm in a tent designed for pups, your priorities change. Make sure the tent you choose has room for you and your gear. A two-person tent usually suits one with a full complement of gear or two with the bulky gear out in the rain.

When touring with one or both of our children, we use a tent (7 × 7 feet) that has a 6½-foot center pole. This McKinley or Logan style has plenty of space for a family of three or four plus gear. Being able to stand up in it is a nice feature, making the tent excellent for all types of outdoor activity. Two available models are the R.E.I. McKinley II (12 lbs. 4 oz., $361) and Sierra Designs's 3-Man (8 lbs., $250).

For two people, or one space-loving single, better designs are R.E.I.'s Ridge (6 lbs. 10 oz., $160) and Cirque (5 lbs. 12 oz., $120); Sierra Designs's Starflight (4 lbs. 9 oz., $145); Eureka's Catskill (6 lbs., $84) and Mojave (6 lbs., $77); L. L. Bean's Allagash (6 lbs., $71); and Cannondale's Susquehanna (7 lbs. 6 oz., $195). These are samples of the good tents presently available. You generally get what you pay for but don't buy more than you need.

Tents come with their own stakes, but you might want to replace them with seven-to-ten-inch steel or aluminum skewer stakes for lighter weight. They can be easily pushed into most ground types with your hand or foot.

A tent is expensive, but look on it as an investment in a home away from home. The more you do to prolong the life of yours, the happier you will be in the long run. We always use a ground cloth under our tent to ward off dampness and to extend the life of the tent floor. A piece of two-to-four-mil plastic cut the same size as the tent bottom does the job. Mark one side "this side up" and always put it that way under your tent. As the ground cloth wears and becomes unusable, simply replace it with another from your local paint or hardware store; it's better to replace it periodically than your tent's floor.

While at the paint store buy a small (four-to-six-inch) wallpaper paste brush, then cut off the handle. This makes a great brush for keeping the inside of your tent clean; it's smaller and cheaper than a whisk broom. It lasts longer, is lighter, and helps prolong the life of your tent as well as your sanity by keeping sand and pine needles out of your sleeping bag.

Sleeping Bags and Covers

You don't need an expedition-type sleeping bag for bicycle touring unless you plan to ride your bike up Mount McKinley. The tendency is to overbuy. Quality sleeping bags can be had for as little as $35 or as much as $450. With some thought and planning you can end up with just the bag that suits your particular needs without a massive expenditure.

Perhaps no sleeping bag is best for you. You can save cash, weight and bulk by using a small, high-quality quilt or comforter in its place. Since you will be using some sort of pad under you, why bother with a two-layer sleeping system when one top layer will do as well? You get little insulating value from the bottom of a sleeping bag because it is compressed under your body. Keep this option in mind, especially if you are traveling in pairs and want to save the weight and bulk of an extra bag.

If you sleep in pairs and opt for this method as we do, all you need is a good sleeping bag with a full-length zipper or a high-quality quilt or comforter. We have been using this system for years to good advantage. On our family bike tours the children use a Dacron comforter in the same manner; thus we carry only two "sleeping bags" for four people. Even when we lived in the Yukon Territory of northern Canada in a tent for four months, we didn't take to separate bags until the temperature fell below 0°F. at night. Families save a lot with this system. A single twin-size Dacron comforter (67 × 80 inches, 3 lbs. 9 oz., $34) is comfortable for two people down to 40°F. and can be used at home on a bed; twice the use for a reasonable price.

If you need to purchase a sleeping bag, you must decide on the type and the amount of fill in addition to the shape you want. There are three major types of fill: natural waterfowl down (duck or goose), man-made Dacron and Fortrel. Down is the traditional fill with advantages of lighter weight, compactability and breathability, the factor that gives it a large temperature-comfort range. Disadvantages are high cost, difficulty in cleaning and loss of warmth when wet.

Dacron Hollofil II and Fortrel PolarGuard are man-made fibers that are less expensive than down and easier to clean and they maintain a large percentage of their insulating ability when wet. However, they are heavier, less compactable and do not breathe as readily as down. Therefore, they are more restricted in temperature-range performance.

Your choice depends on whether you will be bicycling in cold, damp climates where man-made fibers are a definite safety advantage, or whether you need the greater temperature range of down. Cost might be a factor as well (down is much more expensive). Excellent bags are available with any of these types of fill.

The amount of fill you need is directly related to the minimum temperatures you expect on your tours. Amount of fill equals loft (the height of the bag when fully fluffed on a flat surface as measured from the surface itself to the top of the bag). Loft is the amount of dead-air space that provides insulation to keep you warm. It is only effective when not compressed, so the fill on the bottom of the bag is relatively useless. Practically, then, loft is the total measurement of the bag divided in half.

Loft determines the warmth of the bag. The U.S. Army maintains that the "average" person needs 1.5 inches of loft to be comfortable sleeping at 40°F., 2 inches at 20°F. and 2.5 inches at 0°F. These figures do not take into consideration such factors as windchill, type of shelter, and individual metabolism, which vary widely. Use them as a guide only. Generally, for a three-season bag (comfort to 20°F.) look for 2-2½ pounds of down, or 2¼-3 pounds of man-made fiber. The temperature range of a bag depends on the elements of loft and breathability coupled with quality construction and shape.

Of the three basic shapes of sleeping bags — semirectangular (sometimes called semimummy), rectangular and mummy — the mummy is most efficient. At 40°F. you lose up to half of your body heat through your head alone. At 5°F. this figure increases to three-quarters. The mummy bag with its built-in head cover allows a sleeper to draw up the bag so only the nose and mouth are exposed. Its narrow shape is more efficient because of less surface area for heat transference. Mummy bags take a little getting used to at first but most people stop fighting them after two or three nights. It helps to think of a mummy bag as a thick skin that tosses and turns with you rather than a shell inside of which you attempt to turn.

Semirectangular bags are larger

than the mummy style; some even have a head covering. Above 45°F. you rarely need a head cover, and if you anticipate temperatures no lower than freezing (32°F.) a knit hat serves as well. Advantages of a semirectangular bag are added comfort due to extra leg room and the bag can be opened for use as a comforter if it has a full-length zipper. The third kind — full-size rectangular bags — are comfortable and capable of making excellent comforters, but we do not recommend them for cycle touring due to excessive weight and bulk in areas not necessary for body comfort.

If you have a firm idea as to what you want in a sleeping cover and you deal with a reputable dealer or mail-order house, you won't go far wrong. Beware of the gung ho salesman who wants to outfit you for an expedition to the Himalayas. Buy the best quality you can, but don't end up with a bag that is too hot for 90 percent of the places where you will be using it. For much of the United States, in the warmer half of the year, a bag good to 40°F. is sufficient if you are using a tent. On those few nights that approach freezing, a wool-knit hat and a layer of dry clothing worn to bed will give adequate protection if not comfort.

A good sleeping bag should last a lifetime if taken care of. Use a heavy-duty nylon stuff bag to carry it. Line this with a plastic bag, then stuff — don't roll — your bag into it. No stuff bag is waterproof after it has been punctured with thousands of needle holes. You can trust seam sealant and hope the top clo-sure is away from the blast of the rain, or you can use an inner plastic bag and be assured of having a dry sleeping bag at the end of the day.

When not touring, air your bag completely and store it loosely in a dry place in a large pillowcase. If you leave it tightly compacted in the stuff bag, it will slowly lose its ability to spring back to maximum loft.

On tour, especially on cold nights, remove your bag from the stuff bag and fluff it up an hour or two before bedtime. This allows the fill to reach its maximum loft before you crawl in. If the dawn is bright and dry, open the bag to air in the sun for awhile to get rid of trapped body moisture that accumulates during the night.

To obtain maximum life expectancy from your bag, add a liner that can be removed for laundering. Glenda lined all of our bags using cotton/polyester flannel sheeting tied in with bias-tape ties. Since the liner can be untied and removed for cleaning, the bag itself rarely needs laundering — possibly the hardest wear a sleeping bag can get. The sheet adds a little weight and bulk, but fits into a regular-size nylon stuff bag and adds a bit of warmth on cold nights. It is especially nice to slide bare into warm flannel instead of icy nylon.

Sleeping Pads

The pad under you is more important than the cover over you when it comes to insulation and warmth. A sleeping pad performs two functions; first, it cushions you from the hard ground. You really appreciate this after a long hard day on a bicycle seat, unless you are one of those fortunate few who can sleep soundly on a bed of rocks. Second, the pad acts as insulation between you and the cold ground. The bottom loft in your sleeping bag compresses to a useless amount under the weight of your body, so the thickness of the sleeping pad is critical in keeping your body heat from being transferred into the ground.

Sleeping pads come in three-quarter lengths (about 42-56 in.) and full lengths (72 in.). Widths vary from 20 to 24 inches. The full-length pad is more comfortable, of course, but heavier and more bulky. The three-quarter length is just as comfortable under the main part of the body; extra clothing or jackets can be used under the lower legs for insulation and comfort.

For overall comfort, an air mattress is hard to beat, but it provides little if any insulating value due to moving air in it. The air mattress is great for summer conditions, but is uncomfortable below 45 or 50°F. Besides providing comfort, the air mattress compacts nicely, a decided advantage for bike touring. The best air mattress we have found is Air Lift (small — 1 lb. 5 oz., $20.50; large — 2 lbs. 7 oz., $29.50) consisting of separate, replaceable tubes in a nylon cover.

Ensolite (small — 1 lb. 6 oz., $7.50; large — 1 lb. 13 oz., $12.75) and Blue-Foam (small — 6 oz., $4.75) represent the closed-cell type of sleeping pad so popular today. Each cell is enclosed so that small dead-air spaces trap and hold the air. It will not absorb water so no protective covering is needed. These pads are very light, fairly compact, rugged and excellent insulators, but they leave a lot to be desired in comfort. The most common and useful thickness ($\frac{3}{8}$ in.) just barely fools your bones into thinking they are not on the cold, hard ground.

More comfortable is the open-cell pad constructed of urethane foam. This type does not insulate as well as the closed-cell type, and will absorb water. It is bulkier with a common thickness of $1\frac{1}{2}$ inches. Most come with protective covers such as those sold by R.E.I. (small — 1 lb. 14 oz., $14; large — 2 lbs. 12 oz., $18.50).

A new pad on the market offers the tourist the best of both worlds. Enclosed in a nylon cover, it is a sandwich of $1\frac{1}{4}$-inch open-cell foam with $\frac{1}{4}$-inch closed-cell foam. Even with its nylon cover, it should be carried on your bike in a waterproof plastic or nylon sack. This is an excellent product for the person who wants both insulation and comfort. The EMS Super Pad comes in small (1 lb. 10 oz., $15) and large (2 lbs. 14 oz., $19.50) sizes.

Which sleeping pad you prefer depends on your attitudes toward bulk, weight, comfort, durability and size. Whichever you choose, do use one. The bad old days of sleeping on the bare ground are gone forever. A modest expenditure for a good sleeping system will save you the money you might have spent for motels rather than facing another miserable night on the cold ground.

A ground cloth is an integral part of your sleeping system. If you are tenting, you are already aware of its advantages in preserving the tent floor and keeping moisture out. Even if you are using a poncho or tarp shelter (especially if you are using these) the ground cloth is a necessary item. It keeps moisture and dirt off your sleeping pad and cover, adding years of life to each. For maximum efficiency it should be a foot larger in length and width than your pad. The lightest and most durable ground cloth is made of coated nylon taffeta available for $3.50 a yard in a 55-inch width. A less expensive alternative is two- to four-mil polyethylene, which can easily be replaced as it wears out.

Mark your ground cloth on one side to insure that all the tree sap and gunk is on the bottom every time you use it. A nylon ground cloth doubles as a tablecloth or picnic ground cover for maximum usage.

The most complete, high-quality sleeping system can be enhanced by a few maneuvers as you set up camp and prepare for your night's sleep. Try to find as level a sleep site as possible and remove any small stones, sticks, pop-up tabs and bottle caps. Spread your ground cloth, then lie on it for a minute to check for anything missed or an undetected slant. If a slope is unavoidable, put your head uphill. It is better to take

care of these site-selection problems while still light when you are functioning with daytime perception. Struggling around at midnight to dislodge a rock under your shoulder is no fun.

If the night appears to be cold or your bag is thin from a long period of compression, open it and fluff well at least an hour before bedtime. Sleeping bare is probably the most comfortable, unconfining and relaxing way to sleep, but if you insist on clothing, make sure it is absolutely dry. Don't sleep in any clothing you cycled in that day as body moisture trapped in your clothes means a colder night. Depending on your tolerance and the minimum temperature you expect, add a knit hat and dry socks for maximum comfort.

A jacket or spare clothing inside your clothing bag serves as a pillow; add more clothing under your legs if the sleeping pad is short. For middle-of-the-night sanity, always put your light, watch and water bottle in the same easily accessible place.

Bumps in the Night

For those new to camping, the first few nights may be a bit unnerving. Most of us live very sheltered existences, with little experience in the normal nocturnal sounds of the wild. There is a whole world of little animals out there who do all their business in the night. They will not harm you but tend to stumble around a bit. We have had mice unwittingly race across us, and Glenda once had a raccoon walk lazily over her in her sleeping bag. Skunks and raccoons are common night neighbors. The only thing you have to fear is your own panic. Lie still and you might be entertained; probably you will be left with a humorous story to tell around the next campfire.

Other nighttime sounds are falling limbs, pinecones, and rocks and the wind whispering through treetops. Owls are famous for peopling the night with spooky sounds; learn to recognize them for what they are and your imagination has that much less to feed on. Aside from bears — and they're mostly in national parks where they have lost their fear of man — there is nothing that will do you any real harm. Make sure your food is suspended out of harm's way between two trees (not over your head) and you should pass the night well.

Sleeping out of doors is one of the most pleasant experiences imaginable, especially when you have taken the necessary steps to insure a comfortable bed. The first several nights you may be a little stiff and sore from cycling all day and sleeping in an unfamiliar bed. All of that passes with time and experience.

Food Preparation

Bicycle camping does not necessarily mean preparing your own meals.

If you don't enjoy doing it or don't want to carry the extra equipment, there is only money between you and taking all your meals in restaurants. Of course you must then cycle in places where there are restaurants that offer the type of food that both agrees with you and favors your cycling activity.

Food preparation is a normal, even enjoyable procedure for most cycle campers. In most areas of North America and Europe you are never more than two days from a supply point (grocery store) so it is not necessary to carry large amounts of food. The food you buy need not be dehydrated or of special preparation, so you save money while enjoying fresh, familiar food. Frequently you can purchase your dinner and breakfast supplies toward the end of your cycling day so you do not have to carry them any great distance.

Never be totally dependent on a store being open. We always carry one compact, dehydrated emergency meal in case we don't make it to the next town or the store is closed when we get there. We have come close, but have never yet used it.

Preparing your own food does not always mean cooking. During the hot summer months when most cycle touring takes place, it is easy to completely forgo cooking. When touring in summer we rarely cook since we crave cold foods and drinks. Read more about what to eat in chapter thirteen.

Going without a stove, pots and fuel

can save up to three or more pounds and a lot of bulk besides. This is tempting given the general availability of food on most tours. There are, however, two situations where you should cook; when temperatures are low so that you want and need warm food, and in Third World nations where food and water might be questionable. Even in the summer, hot food is a priority item in high-altitude touring.

If you decide not to cook, your only needs are eating utensils, tools for cutting and opening, and a means of carrying fresh food. Cooking requires a decision to either carry a small pressure stove or opt for open fires.

Open-Fire Cooking

The traditional method of camp cooking is over an open campfire. Many people don't feel as though they are camping unless they breathe in a little wood smoke. Aside from a romantic aspect, an open fire saves having to carry a stove, and you can use more than one pot at a time. On the other hand, open-fire cooking requires a degree of skill not common in our overly processed society. It takes more time to gather wood, build the fire, wait for a bed of coals, prepare the meal, clean the pots and extinguish the fire. You can get pretty grubby from that romantic aroma. The biggest drawback is that open fires are restricted or prohibited in many

areas, with good reason. Fire permits are frequently required, and they are rare landowners who permit you to build a fire on their property. Overpopulation and environmental considerations work against your getting wood in the first place, unless you buy it in organized campgrounds. No matter how aesthetically pleasing the fireside, denuded trees, campfire-started wildfires and old fire pits that mar the landscape all work to end the age of the open fire.

We are not anticampfire, having spent many memorable evenings with wood fires either in the open or in portable wood stoves. But for the camping cyclist primarily restricted to heavily traveled paved roads, the campfire is not usually a practical means of food preparation. If you do use a fire, make sure it is both legal and safe for the area you are in. Try to use already established fire rings or pits rather than building a new one. Clear at least a ten-foot circle around your fire down to mineral earth (no humus, dry leaves, sticks and grass). Gather only dead, downed wood that has not picked up moisture from the ground. Keep your fire small using pieces of fuel that will completely burn up. Carry and use a small, stainless steel backpacking grate (3.5 oz., 5 × 15 inches, $5) to make your cooking easier and more efficient. Carry your pots in bags to keep from blackening the rest of your equipment. If you prefer to clean the outside of your pots each time, coat them with soap before using on the fire; the black comes off much more easily. Most important, make sure your fire is completely out by drowning it with water until you can stir the ashes with your bare hand. Fire can burn deep into some richly organic soils only to erupt days later into a wildfire.

Stoves

The so-called "backpacker" stove is an alternative to the open fire. It is small, fast, efficient, clean and relatively easy to use. It poses no danger to the environment and leaves nothing behind. On the minus side for the cycle tourist are its bulk and weight (1-2 lbs.), and the fact that on longer trips you must also carry extra fuel. These stoves are noisy, with no comparison to the quiet romance of the open fire. And they are not cheap. A good stove will cost you anywhere from $25 to $50, although the investment is small considering its long life span.

Before you attempt to choose a stove to tour with, you must decide what type of fuel you prefer. Your choices are white gas, kerosene and butane. White gas (Blazo, Coleman fuel, Camplite, Campstove fuel) was once available in any quantity at most gas stations. It is now almost impossible to find so you must purchase brand-name fuels in one-gallon cans at outrageous prices. That size is impractical for cycle tour-

ing, so you must carry small containers from home or use unleaded gasoline from service stations. Unleaded gas works, but over an extended period will plug your stove.

In spite of cost and quantity difficulties, white gas is highly efficient, generally available throughout the United States and Canada, and clean. It readily evaporates if spilled and no special starter fuel is needed to prime the stove, although many require priming with white gas, which can be a tricky procedure. Highly flammable, it needs to be used with caution. White gas can be impossible to find in many other countries; in Europe ask for naphtha and hope for the best.

Among the better white-gas stoves are Svea 123R (1 lb. 2 oz., $29), Optimus 8R (1 lb. 7 oz., $33), and Coleman Peak 1 (2 lbs., $28.50).

Kerosene (paraffin in the United Kingdom, *petroleo* in Latin America) is available all over the world. The kerosene stove is practical for the bicycle tourer with expansive plans. If you can't get kerosene for some reason, you can use diesel fuel, stove oil or home heating oil. Kerosene is a relatively safe fuel in that it must be heated before it will ignite; if you spill some you have a mess but no real danger. Extremely efficient, it is cheap to use.

Problems with kerosene relate to its difficulty to light. It requires special priming fuels; alcohol is the most common and is available at drugstores in most countries. Tubes of jellied alcohol are available, which are more convenient for the cyclist to carry. In a pinch, you can use gasoline to prime. Kerosene is smelly, dirty and won't evaporate when you spill it. Two of the best kerosene stoves are the Optimus 45 (2 lbs. 7 oz., $40) and Optimus 00 (1 lb. 11 oz., $37).

The third common stove fuel is butane. It is available in many forms but for cycle touring, the disposable cartridge type is most practical. Butane is fast, simple to use since it requires no priming or preheating, and delightfully quiet.

Disadvantages are lack of efficiency compared with white gas or kerosene and dependence on expensive, difficult-to-find cartridges. In the United States and Canada replacements can be purchased at outdoor or sporting goods stores, while in Europe they are available at many campgrounds and tourist-type stores. As for the rest of the world, good luck. Another difficulty, especially for the cycle tourist, is that the cartridge must remain attached to the stove until emptied, a bulky requirement. When empty, the cartridges stink unless you tape over the hole; so they

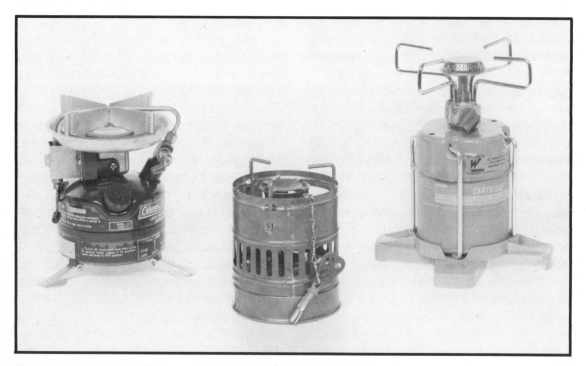

Three popular stoves: Coleman Peak, Svea 123 and GAZ Bleuet S-200.

need to be disposed of properly and quickly. Good butane stoves include the GAZ Bleuet S-200 (1 lb. 13 oz., $12) and the GAZ Globetrotter (1 lb., $19.50). Cartridges for the S-200 weigh 11 ounces each and cost about $1.35; for the Globetrotter the cost is $1.19 and cartridges weigh 6 ounces each.

The fuel type you choose depends on the extent of bicycle touring you anticipate as well as your own preferences in handling ease. Both white gas and kerosene stoves require attention to detail and some experience in use — best gained in noncritical situations such as camping in your own backyard. If you want simplicity and don't mind the shortcomings, pick a butane-burning stove. We use a Svea 123 (white gas) stove for tours of no more than a week or two in the United States and Canada. For longer than that, or outside those two countries, we use the Optimus 00 kerosene model due to its efficiency and more easily obtainable fuel.

Good operating techniques ease your job no matter which stove you use. Place the stove on a level, stable spot (not in the tent) where it is sheltered from the wind as much as possible. Have your food ready to go before you light the stove; always use a lid for quicker, more efficient heating. When using white gas or kerosene, strain all questionable fuel through a rag or Coleman filter funnel (1 oz., $1.50) as you fill the stove to prevent problems halfway through the stew.

Prime white-gas stoves using a three-inch section of plastic straw (with your finger over one end to provide suction) or an eyedropper to lift the fuel from the tank into the primer cup. Always tighten the tank filler cap before lighting, and never refill a hot stove. In very cold conditions insulate white-gas and butane stoves from cold ground or snow.

Extra fuel for a butane stove means carrying as many cartridges as you need or touring where they are readily available. With white gas or kerosene, extra fuel should be carried in a strong, leakproof metal container. This can be carried in one of your water-bottle cages if it fits properly; many cyclists carry one attached to the underside of the down tube, so it can't harm other gear if the container leaks. You can carry kerosene in a good-quality water bottle. Be sure it is well marked so there is no possibility of confusion with bottles containing water or drinkable liquids. Sigg makes an excellent, strong, round spun-aluminum fuel bottle with a good gasket and tight lid that is virtually leakproof. Of the three sizes — ½ pint (2 oz., $4), 1 pint (4 oz., $4.50), and 1 quart (5.5 oz., $5) — the pint best fits into a water-bottle cage. Fuel can be carried in your panniers, but put the container in a plastic bag first in case the impossible leak occurs.

An excellent accessory for the Sigg fuel bottle is a pouring cap (1 oz., $1.50) to use when you fill your stove. It is easy

Sigg Tourist Cook Kit (and Sigg fuel bottle) assembled with a Svea 123 stove and ready for use.

to control the flow so you will be able to dispense with a funnel if your fuel is clean.

Cookware

How much do you plan to cook and for how large a group? Some people can get by with a number-two tomato can and a spoon (Tim), while others seem to need a full field kitchen (Glenda). Read through chapter thirteen, "Food for Touring," before making your final decisions on cookware and utensils. It might change, or at least define, your ideas on this subject.

A basic kit for two to four people is a set of two nesting aluminum pots with lids. Your stove should fit into the smaller pot for maximum compactness. Handles that can be removed or folded into the unit are best. Pots without handles can be lifted with a pliers device called a pot gripper (2 oz., $1.25).

The outfit we use most and like best for one to five people is the Sigg Tourist Cook Kit (1 lb. 8 oz., $25). This unit has two pans (3½ pt. and 2½ pt.), a lid that serves better as a pot than a skillet, a stove base (for the Svea 123), a wind protector and a pot gripper. The whole thing nests into a unit only 4¾ × 8¼ inches. The Optimus 00 kerosene stove fits into the basic cooking pots when the wind screen and Svea stove base are removed. (They are not needed for the Optimus 00.) You can purchase separately 6¼-inch aluminum Sigg plates (2 oz., $1.50), which nest into the Tourist Kit. If you like frying foods, carry along a Teflon-coated aluminum frying pan with holding handle (12 oz., $5.50).

When cycling with a group of six or more, you need two Tourist Cookers or a pot large enough to hold the whole unit. Your choice in cooking sets is endless, including the possibility of buying pots separately to fit your individual needs. For cycle camping use nesting units that incorporate your stove for maximum compactibility.

On long tours with large groups, especially when touring in isolated areas where prepared food is hard to get, the Optimus Mini-Oven (15 oz., $15) comes into its own. This sits on top of most small stoves and lets you cook up goodies such as bread, biscuits, pies and even cakes. Carrying along the basic ingredients is far easier than the completed product.

Another great cooking aid (mostly for large groups due to its size and weight) is the English-made Skyline four-quart pressure cooker (2 lbs. 13 oz., $34.50). It is invaluable for quick cooking, especially at high altitudes. It enables you to include many grains and cereals in your cycling diet, which normally require too much time and fuel to be practical for camping. Saving fuel helps make up for added weight.

Your choice in cups and plates is almost limitless. Ever popular are stacking plastic mugs and the ubiquitous stainless steel Sierra cup (3 oz., $2). Stainless steel, unlike aluminum, won't burn your lips when filled with hot fluid. We frequently use cups instead of plates, since food comes off the stove in single courses and cups are much easier to handle than hot aluminum plates. When touring with the children Glenda prefers deep, stacking plastic mugs, as food — especially liquids — is less likely to slosh around than with the shallow Sierra cups.

Any utensils will do although many prefer the light, stainless steel variety that clip together (3 oz., $1.50). Don't forget a sharp, simple camp knife. You don't need a ten-inch "macho" survival weapon. While Tim was guiding in Idaho, he discovered that the biggest greenhorns always seemed to have the biggest knives. All you need is a sheath or folding knife with a four- or five-inch blade. Most wooden-handled boning knives available in hardware stores are fine. L.L. Bean sells an inexpensive, high-quality camp knife with sheath (Bean's trout knife, 4 oz., $5). We used a

folding knife for a while but got tired of cleaning cantaloupe seeds and fish scales out of the handle groove. Except for small tasks, multiple-blade knives are useless around the kitchen.

On longer trips you will have to have some means of keeping your knife sharp. More expensive, high-carbon steel knives require expensive stones or steels for sharpening, but cheap knives are sharpened easily (and frequently) with a small whetstone or sharpening steel. We like Herter's convenient five-inch sharpening steel for all-around camp use ($2.75).

Don't forget a can opener. Probably the greatest material contribution to civilization made by the armed forces has been the tiny GI or P-38 can opener (0.2 oz., 25¢). Tie a piece of red cord to it as it is forever turning up lost.

A handy, specialized kitchen item necessary in desert areas is a folding water bottle. The best one we have found is Swedish-made, soft plastic with built-in wooden handles at each end. It holds 2½ gallons, has a spigot and can be rolled up into a compact bundle. We carry one on many of our tours; it refuses to wear out. Tim has rigged up a portable shower by attaching a water sprinkler to a piece of flexible plastic tubing, which fits tightly onto the spigot. When we arrive in camp early, we fill the bag, hang it in the sun to take the chill off the water and soon enjoy a makeshift shower.

Unfortunately, we know of no present source for these Swedish bags, but check around. Other varieties of folding plastic bottles are readily available (2½ gal., 4 oz., $1.50). If you don't carry an extra water container, yet get caught needing one partway through your tour, use a bleach bottle from the trash at a laundry. It cleans up easily, is reliable and free.

One last item to store with your kitchen gear is a supply of garbage bags. Save plastic bread sacks or produce bags for this purpose, or you can always use paper grocery bags as you buy food along the way. Carry your trash with you until you find a proper receptacle.

Packing Up

There it sits. All that stuff you are planning to take along on your tour. How are you ever going to get it all onto your bicycle? If you have planned carefully and are taking only what you know you will need, rather than what you think you will need, you should be OK. If the pile still looks impossible, go through it all separating those items you will be using every day or must have in certain situations. That extra-large cooking pot, the pajamas, the full-size bath towel — essential or just nice to have? If necessary, make two piles; those things you absolutely can't do without and those things you think are important to have along. If it all ends up in the first pile and it is still too much, you have a problem. Better take along a spartan buddy on a big bike. Check your equipment against the lists for various types of tours in Appendix A. These are not the final word, but what you have should resemble the suggested list.

For weekend motel touring, you can probably get all of your necessary items into a stuff bag that you can tie onto the top of the rear rack. A 10 × 20-inch stuff bag (3 oz., $5.50) is the least-expensive way to carry gear on short trips, or if you have a handlebar bag and seat bag you can put your gear into them.

For cycle camping, packing is a bit more complex. Organize your equipment into functional groups — kitchen, sleeping, shelter, clothing, recording (camera, note pads) and miscellaneous. Give some thought as to how and when you will be using various items and separate them accordingly.

To keep things both dry and organized, we use individual bags Glenda sews up from coated nylon taffeta material (55 in. wide, 2.7 oz., $3.50 yd.). Light, strong and waterproof, the material comes in a variety of colors, which permits easier identification either by different categories or by different members of the family or group. Digging through panniers at dusk when everything is in identical blue bags can be upsetting. You could number or label bags if you prefer one color.

We have clothing and toiletries bags for each family member, and separate bags for tools, shower shoes (usually wet and muddy), washcloths (also wet), gorp, writing materials, toys and food staples. We go bananas over bags.

Once everything is categorized and packed in whatever individual manner you prefer, decide what you want in your handlebar bag. Reserve it for small items you use frequently or need to find easily. Our handlebar bags carry camera gear, glasses, sunscreen, lip cream, wallet, notebook, pencil, handkerchief, snack food, frequently used tools and any other personal necessities. Once your handlebar bag gear is separated, weigh it with the bag — then weigh your remaining gear. The front load should be approximately 20-30 percent of your total gear load. Do some juggling if necessary to stay within this range. If you are using front panniers, try different equipment up front until you arrive at the best weight for the handling qualities of your own bicycle.

Remaining gear goes into the rear panniers. First decide on what you want and need in any outside pockets. These are things you need to get to often or fast such as extra water, lock and cable, rain gear, extra food (snack or lunch), and perhaps a jacket. When loading the main compartment, keep heavy items on the bottom. Tools, stove, cooking gear, air mattress and staple foods are best here. Put lighter items such as clothing and toilet articles on top.

Pack each pannier set (front or rear) evenly. One side should be within one or two pounds of the other for best-possible riding characteristics. Once

you have an evenly spaced load, maintain it — and your sanity while on the road — by always putting everything back the same way each time you load up. If you do this initial packing at home with access to a scale, and then stick to your arrangement while on the road, you ease your passage as well as insure a smooth-handling loaded touring bike.

Once the panniers and handlebar bag are full, it is time to strap on the sleeping bag, tent and sleeping pad. These travel best sideways across the top of the rear rack if your panniers permit this arrangement. With front panniers and rack a small tent or sleeping bag can travel up front, but usually everything in this category goes to the

A good example of a poorly loaded touring bike with too much weight for back, oversize equipment and panniers too far behind axles. Straps are a more secure tie-down than Bungee cords.

163

rear. Put the heaviest item forward next to the seatpost, being very careful that it does not interfere with the rear brake even if the load shifts. Shift the load as far forward as possible since a heavy load to the rear can cause fishtailing.

Elastic stretch (Bungee) cords are popular tie-downs but we don't like them. Sometimes these cords are not stretched enough to put adequate pressure on the load or to keep them from coming unhooked. If they do come loose or one time you forget to hook them, the hook will grab onto the spokes. Then you have real problems. Many accidents occur on loaded touring bicycles when objects become entangled in the wheels. We prefer ¾- or 1-inch nylon straps with secure buckles. Use the kind that can be adjusted for length, fasten them securely, and you won't have to worry about shifting loads or spoke entanglement. Interlace the straps (two or three) through the

164

rack platform and on either side, place your baggage on the rack, then cinch it all down firmly.

When everything is carefully and thoughtfully loaded on your bike, check all attachments one more time before taking off on a trial run. Riding a fully loaded touring bike is a lot different from jamming around unloaded. It takes you longer to start and stop, not to mention the extra instability due to the heavier, higher load. Go slow to get the feel of things, staying out of traffic or other scary situations. Ride as much as possible with your bike fully loaded before setting out on a long tour. You will be doing your body a favor and you will have time to correct any problems before you get away from home.

Plan ahead, allow yourself plenty of practice time, and the day will soon come when you roll out of your driveway completely self-contained, self-propelled and self-confident. There is nothing between you and the world but miles.

Chapter Ten
A Typical Touring Day

Imagine yourself already on the road, let's say 14 days into a month-long tour of the backcountry of Utah and western Colorado. You are touring alone, camping along the way with occasional stops in motels, completely self-contained with your camping and touring gear in rear panniers and a handlebar bag.

The buzz of your alarm (travel clock or wristwatch) shatters the silence of your still-dark tent; you turn it off, groaning at the 4:30 A.M. hour. Just as you settle back into your sleeping bag for 40 winks, you remember where you are and why you must be on the road so early. It is the last of the desert but temperatures for this July day are predicted to reach 100°F. You have many miles to go before that happens, a lot of them in the higher elevations and steeper roads of the western Rockies. Adrenalin

sends you out of your bag, bike light in hand, to search for your clothes. As you feel the cool morning air of the high desert just before leaving the tent, you grab your warm-up jacket.

Emerging into the predawn darkness, you pull out your sleeping bag and lay it over the top of the tent to air in the low humidity of the desert. You remember tours in the Midwest and East where you had to air it inside the tent because everything outside was soaked with dew. This brings your first smile of the day and renews your love of desert touring.

Breakfast begins with a bowl of cereal moistened with powdered milk or the last of the fresh milk you purchased the night before. A slice of whole wheat bread spread with peanut butter is either topped with or accompanied by a banana, the last of several you bought at a fruit stand two days ago. You make a mental note to buy more this evening. You decide against starting up the pressure stove for your usual cup of hot herb tea with honey due to the rapidly increasing color in the eastern horizon.

You watch the few, temporary clouds turn from deep purple to pink with silver trim as the still-sunken sun begins its influence on your half of the world. The morning silence is punctured by the chirping of a cricket nearby and the distant, soft hooting of an owl as he turns loose of the night so your day can begin. You break the moment to gather your cup, spoon and knife — the only dishes to clean after your simple breakfast.

One of the biggest rewards of bicycle touring is your ability to be independent and self-sufficient. All the supplies at this typical campsite can be readily loaded aboard the bike and transported as far as you care to go.

Once in motion, you put away your kitchenware, stuff the now-dry sleeping bag into its sack and roll up your sleeping pad. While inside the tent, you gather up the paraphernalia of the night — map, book, light, watch and extra water bottle. Once the loaded panniers are outside the tent, you sweep it out, drop it and roll it up. The ground cloth needs to be shaken and turned over a bush to dry; even in the desert it picks up moisture from the ground, blocking it from entry through the tent floor. At this point you welcome the call of nature. You grab your trowel and toilet paper, going off to find a spot that is no good for anything else (not in the middle of a potential campsite, picnic area or trail). After making use of the 6- to 12-inch hole you dug, you cover it with the original dirt and place a good-size rock on top to discourage reexcavation by desert animals.

On returning to camp, it is time to check your bike for the day's journey before loading it up with gear. After checking the tire pressure with your gauge, you pinch the spokes in pairs all around to check for loose ones, then spin each wheel while observing its passage past the brake pads to check for trueness. Finally, you run your fingers lightly over the tires for imbedded objects and check the functioning of the brakes.

By now the ground cloth should be dry (if not, fold the wet side into itself) so it can be folded and slipped into the tent bag along with the stakes, brush, fly and tent itself. After checking around for loose items, you hook the panniers and handlebar bag to your bike, making sure everything is snug and properly hooked. You strap the tent, sleeping bag and pad on top of the load, again taking care that everything is well cinched down with no loose ends. Then you put the snack food for the day into the handlebar bag for easy access. After filling your water bottles from the folding water jug, you strap it across the top of the load on the rear rack, noting that there is only about a half-gallon left. Since there is a town about 35 miles ahead, you are not concerned. This should be your last "dry" camp as you will be in the mountains tonight.

One last look around camp reveals yesterday's socks hanging on a bush; you spook a white-footed mouse as you grab them and stuff them into your panniers. It's a good thing you can get into them easily even with everything already loaded on top. The mouse eyes you suspiciously from under another bush as you begin a few stretching and twisting exercises. You have completely lost the stiffness and aches of the first week out, and your body quickly responds to your exercise routine. Warmed up, you walk your bike back along the almost invisible dirt trail you followed about ¼ mile from the highway around a small hill to the quiet, secluded spot where you spent the night. Out of sight from the road, you were careful not to camp in the wash just a little farther on. Dry now, its steep banks attest to the torrents of water that have poured down it in past flash floods. It could flood even though not a drop of rain is falling for miles around. It drains a small range of mountains in the distance; a good rain there (out of your sight) might mean a flash flood here. Flash floods cause more deaths in the United States than any other weather-related phenomenon, including tornadoes and hurricanes.

The eastern sky is clear and bright as you reach the highway. You are glad you passed up that other camp at the base of yesterday's last hill; morning muscles need a warm-up on the bike before attempting anything really strenuous. You mount your bike by straddling it first, putting one foot into its toe clip, pushing off, then placing the other foot in its clip as you coast the first few yards. Fleeting pain registers from your butt as it settles into position, but the ache lessens as your whole body adapts to its familiar cycling pose. Spinning (pedaling rapidly) in your lower gears helps get your muscles warmed up and accustomed to their task for the day.

You are all alone on the highway during this very special, presun period except for an occasional rabbit or tortoise that chooses to cross the road ahead of you. Suddenly you spot a coyote. He freezes in disbelief as he tries to interpret your intrusion into his world. You slow to a halt, then stand absolutely still until he tires of the game and lumbers off to see what unsuspecting prey

he might find for an early breakfast. You use this opportunity to remove your warm-up jacket, placing it in the outside pocket of a rear pannier. Muscles are warmed up now and the coyote has given you the second smile of the day.

Back on the bike, your cadence is smooth as you approach the first hill of the morning. Gearing down, you grip the bars and put your legs to the test. The grade increases but you match it with your gears, suddenly finding yourself at the top breathing hard but not overly tired. You are on a plateau with the sun just peeking over the horizon up ahead. Time to stop for sunscreen, lip cream and a drink of water and to attach your helmet visor since the sun will be hitting you directly in the eyes for an hour or so.

On the go again, traffic has increased with daylight. You find yourself checking frequently in your rearview mirror and relying more on your ears to let you know what is happening behind you. There is about a foot of good pavement to the right side of the fog line; you know you might need it if crowded from the rear. When a big, semitrailer rig or bus approaches you drop to the down position on the handlebars and hang on to keep from being bumped around by the slipstream; that shoulder looks pretty good to you. If the road is narrower or another vehicle is approaching head-on so the vehicle to your rear can't give you any room (otherwise most truckers and bus drivers will, most RV drivers won't), it is best to stop com-

169

pletely and straddle your bike until the danger passes.

Fast-moving, large vehicles kick up quite a slipstream, but it is worse when the wind is blowing. If the wind is coming from your left or ahead, an approaching truck breaks its relatively steady pressure as well as tossing you around in its own turbulence. If the wind comes from the rear or your right, the shake-up won't be as severe since the wind remains constant. A lot depends on the strength of the wind, the speed of the truck and the lay of the road. No matter what, if there doesn't seem to be enough road for the two of you, stop to allow the vehicle to pass; it's the polite thing to do. If there is room for the vehicle to go around, give yourself enough road space to maneuver in case of turbulence. Don't ride on the very edge of the pavement; you are inviting the vehicle to edge by without passing properly. One slip of the wheel and you will be in the ditch on your head (helmeted, of course).

An hour has passed since you mounted up; it is time to take a break. You look for a spot where you can see both directions down the road, pulling off the highway completely if possible. The slipstream of a truck can knock over a bike parked on the shoulder whether it is leaning on a post or a kickstand. You always try to park your bike standing up, either on its kickstand or leaning (carefully) against something solid. Laying a loaded, lightweight touring bike continually on its side subjects

it to unnecessary strain and abuse.

A 10-minute break every hour helps you maintain a good touring pace. You resist the temptation to flop on the ground; walking around while you eat and drink helps keep your muscles loose and dries your shorts faster. Even if you don't feel particularly thirsty, you drink something. As the day proceeds to warm up (you, too) you drink every 15 minutes or so to insure adequate hydration. Don't trust thirst as an indicator of need.

On the road again, you see a cattle guard ahead. Frequently found in the West, they are pits covered with closely spaced steel pipes. Livestock will not cross them so they serve as fences across the highways. It is best to stop, dismount and walk across. Cattle guards are hard on your wheels and dangerous to your health if you slip while crossing. If you insist on riding over them, cross perpendicular to the pipes, not on a diagonal. The same goes for railroad tracks. Both of these are dangerous situations for cyclists; we speak from painful experience.

As the morning progresses with a cooling breeze from your own momentum in your face, you approach a small town — one where you are picking up mail sent in care of General Delivery. Your friends and relatives have been cautioned to put "Please Hold for Bicycle Tourist" on all mail so it won't be returned (hopefully) as required after a two-week waiting period in case you are delayed. You are also expecting a tire from your local bike shop since the one you are riding on has a nasty cut and there are no shops on your route. In the post office, you pick up letters from home, new maps for the section ahead on your journey (you left these prepackaged to be mailed by people back home on a set schedule), an unexpected box of homemade cookies, and some friendly words from the postmaster who has been wondering who you were and what you would be like. The tire arrived too, so you are all set for the next leg of your trip. This town was chosen as a mail drop because it was located on the route you were most likely to take, yet it was close to an alternative route you were thinking about. Before you leave the post office, you mail a postcard home notifying folks of the next mail drop if they don't already know it.

The clock on the post office wall says it is only 10:30 A.M., so you decide to push on the next 18 miles to a larger town before it gets much hotter. You plan to change your tire during the afternoon break. A fruit stand just on the edge of town speeds you on your way with fresh fruit for now and a little in your pack for later. The proprietor lets you fill your water bottles there too and you still have the half-gallon in the folding jug for emergencies. There will be no water until the next town.

The 18 miles pass quickly except for one section that has been freshly tarred. It is common for highway departments to put down fresh oil with a layer of sand and gravel for cars to pack down. Works fine for them but it is murder on a bicycle. So you dismount and walk your bike on the dirt shoulder; better than riding through that messy, gooey stuff. A few cars honk as they pass; you recognize some people from the fruit stand as they wave. You are feeling good, physically alive, and one with blue sky and wide horizons. You can hardly tell where your own body leaves off and the scenery begins.

Toward the end of the 18 miles you begin to feel the heat, approaching 100°F. now, and you know it is time to get off the road through the middle of the day. There is no longer a breeze as you match the speed of the wind to your rear so you feel like you are pedaling in a dry sauna. As your thoughts turn to shade trees and swimming pools, you spot the next town just ahead. Larger than the last, it is still small enough to cruise around easily on your bike for a quick reconnaissance. Is there a shady park? A coin laundry? Maybe showers at a truck stop, at the laundry or at a public swimming pool? Sometimes independent motels will let you shower for a small fee during the quiet daytime hours. You take a good look around since you plan to be here three to four hours. A stop at the chamber of commerce building tells you there is both a coin laundry and a swimming pool, the latter in a big, shady park. The town planner comes out to shake hands and discuss bike touring in general, his town in particular. He likes your idea of developing a list of families who would

171

be interested in putting up bicyclists overnight to keep on file at the chamber of commerce.

Laundry first, fun later. In the laundry rest room you change into your swim trunks or clean clothing if you have any at that point. (Glenda uses our lightweight tablecloth as a sarong while everything else is in the wash.) Laundry times can be filled with letter writing, journalizing, map study or catching up on the newspaper. You might simply sit and watch your clothes going around without you.

Once the laundry is done, a rumble in your stomach sends you cycling to a grocery store to pick up lunch and a can of frozen orange juice concentrate to mix in your water bottles. With a pinch of salt it is a cheap, comparable substitute for more expensive athletic drinks, which can be impossible to find in many small towns.

Now to the park to relax, eat, swim and shower. Be sure to take in everything you will need if the pool is in the usual fenced enclosure. Lock your bike to the fence or some other permanent object within view. This pool lets you exit and reenter for a single fee so you take a quick, refreshing plunge, then retire outside near your bike for a nap under a shade tree. You continually sip orange juice and water throughout the afternoon to maintain your liquid and electrolyte levels.

After your nap you decide to change your tire, clean up your bike and oil the chain. With a small, damp rag you start at the top and work your way down, all the while looking for any problems that might need your attention. Then you use your cutoff, one-inch paintbrush to clean off the cluster. With the newspaper you were reading earlier (or one appropriated from a trash can) you shield your bike as you spray and wipe down your chain. As you lock up the bike again after putting away your tools, there is time for another swim and a good, soap-down shower before stepping into your clean clothes.

By now it is 4:00 P.M., the worst of the day's heat is over. It is still in the high 90s but you feel strong and refreshed from your long stop as you pack up to hit the road once more. The next town is 20 miles away, but you have checked with at least two people who say the market there is open until 9:00 P.M. You decide to wait until then to buy your food for dinner, breakfast and tomorrow's snacks.

Outside of town you begin to climb more rapidly on approaching the mountains. Passes are higher with shorter downhill jaunts in between. Small subsistence ranches fill valleys as the uninhabited desert gives way to marginal farmland. Gone are the red rock mesas and buttes of the desert, which filled your days with deep shadows and gaunt shapes testifying to an eon of wind and water working on unprotected land. You miss them in a way, as though friends have been left behind. But lonely ranches fill the void where farm families sometimes wave to you from front porches in this late afternoon.

About a third of the way up a particularly steep climb, a dog comes racing out from a ranch barking every inch of the way. Most dogs you encounter have limited territorial bounds, usually stopping at the road. You automatically check for your small spray can of Halt dog repellent mounted on the handlebar stem — it's the same as mailmen use — and find it reassuringly in place. Some of your cycling friends use their pumps as weapons against dogs, but you think that is too dangerous for both you and the animal. Instead, you always attempt to outrun them unless you get caught laboring up a grade like this one.

Oh, oh. He is a big one and still coming fast. You shout a firm, authoritative "No!" but Dummy doesn't even check his pace. Concentrating on controlling your bike and watching the road, you wait for him to cross the point of no return onto the highway, then taking aim, you let loose a stream of Halt as he gets about ten feet from your leg. Dummy acts like he hit a brick wall, tumbling head over heels and coming up pawing frantically at his nose. You are forgotten as he tries to get at the offending material. Halt is only red pepper and wears off quickly, therefore harmless to the dog, but there is no doubt about its effectiveness if your aim is good. You love dogs in general, but you know that you have not only saved your own skin, but that this might deter the dog from future encounters that could end his life

under the tires of a nonforgiving truck. That wouldn't wear off. You hope he has learned a lesson; one good thing, you certainly got to the top of that hill in record time.

At the top of one particularly grueling ascent, there lies before you a long, steep, winding downgrade of two miles or more into a major river valley. It's a good time to take a break to allow the sweat of the last climb to evaporate before the long, cooling descent. While you drink and eat a snack, you walk around your bike checking to make sure there will be no surprises as you sail down at high speed. Brakes, tires, spokes, cables and gears are all in order. You also check the rack and rear load to make sure it is still tightly cinched and secure. Back on your bike, you wait for a long break in the traffic before pulling out onto the road.

You move into the drop position for maximum control with sure access to the brakes. As the landscape sails by at increasing speed, you apply the brakes in short blasts — the rear just a fraction before the front. Using both brakes, you apply a little more pressure to the front as that takes the brunt of the weight, but the back brake is equally important in acting as a drag to keep the rear down. Since it is still pretty hot, especially the road surface, you stop halfway down to check for overheated rims. There isn't much danger since you are riding with clincher tires instead of tubulars, but caution is needed since the rim could conceivably heat up enough to blow the tube. Braking friction can soften the glue on tubulars enough that they could roll off the wheel at the worst possible time. Either way, it is best to stop partway through a long descent with a heavily loaded bike to check the rims. If they are too hot to touch, wait for them to cool somewhat as you enjoy the view, take some pictures or have a drink.

Back on the road you are careful to ride a little farther out than normal to avoid loose gravel or other hazards that might be difficult to negotiate at this speed. You feel comfortable in the normal path of the right wheel of automobiles, away from the dangerous oil slick between the wheel tracks. On hot days such as this one, or when the road is wet, this oil track becomes a real hazard — especially to a loaded bicycle traveling downhill at high speeds. Because you are aware of the hazards, are prepared for anything, and know that you and your bicycle are in top condition, you thoroughly enjoy this long, downhill run with no mishaps.

Since you do not yield to the temptation to let all systems go in a totally out-of-control, breakneck descent, you pedal most of the way downhill in your highest gear, keeping your leg muscles warmed up and preventing cramps from windchill on overheated perspiration-soaked legs. Sometimes pedaling is more of a spinning exercise but it serves the purpose.

What a great ride! At the bottom the road turns to follow the river gradually upstream into the mountains that begin to close in on all sides. You have truly left the desert now and are in the Rockies. Your eyes welcome the darkening, descending line of green timber, which seems almost to rush into the river valley as you climb steadily higher. During a rest stop you check your map and see that the town where you will be buying dinner is just up the road, possibly two or three miles away. You hope to camp at a forest service campground 11 miles beyond the town. If you don't make it that far, there is plenty of open country in which to camp. But it is only 6:00 P.M. and doesn't get dark until a little after 9:00 P.M.; you figure you will be setting up camp around 7:30 P.M. with plenty of daylight left.

As you roll into the sleepy little river town, you locate the market on Main Street. It is no supermarket but will surely have what you need since you are not relying on hard-to-find, specialized lightweight foods. You lock your bike in front of the store near a window but out of everyone's way. Just in time you remember to remove your helmet, sunglasses and rearview mirror, smiling as you recall the startled look on the storekeeper's face at that tiny town in Utah last week when you forgot to do that. He must have thought you to be from the moon. Your handlebar bag comes off quickly to accompany you into the store since you will need your list, pen, traveler's checks and ID for this "serious" shopping trip.

The store is busier than you expected with people gathered around the bulletin board reading about local happenings and others gathered around the cooler drinking Cokes. They are friendly and some who saw you ride up ask where you are going and where you come from. They are surprised that you have been on the road two weeks, averaging 70 miles a day. One old rancher tells you about the high mountains up ahead and offers to take you over the pass to spend the night on his ranch in the next valley. Tempted, you think about it, then decline his offer, trying to make him understand that you are doing just what you want to be doing by choice. That is what cycle touring is all about. He smiles, shakes his head, and says he is jealous of your freedom and wishes he were "young again." You tell him about your 66-year-old touring partner in the Appalachians last year. He laughs and says maybe he'll take up doing what you're doing then, in his "old age."

You fill your grocery cart with food for dinner, breakfast and snacks tomorrow. The thought of fresh lettuce, orange juice and cold yogurt prods your appetite as you pay for your purchases and load them all into your panniers with a loaf of bread riding temporarily on your back in the canvas book bag you carry along just for such overloads. You filled your water bottles but know from your campground guide that there is water at your evening's destination. You have emptied the folding water jug since you will be following a stream all the way and have water-purification tablets in case you don't get to the campground tonight.

The road gets really steep as you begin to feel the day's mileage in general weariness. You are thankful when you pass the national forest entry sign; your camp is not far now. The road narrows as it winds upward. You force yourself to concentrate on what is ahead and what you can see in your rearview mirror. Drivers, especially if they are from out of state and not accustomed to driving in the mountains, tend to panic a little on narrow, winding roads. You, on your fully loaded bicycle, are not one of the sights they expect to see around the next curve.

Just then you spot a huge motor home rounding the curve behind you. Glancing ahead you see nothing but traffic; he won't be able to pull around you and he doesn't seem to be slowing up at all. There would be room for him to pass except for the mirror that sticks two feet out into your space. You know he must be unaware of the danger it represents for you as he is not attempting to slow his speed at all. Since what little shoulder there was disappeared about a mile back, you immediately pull off onto the dirt edge and wait for him to pass. The driver waves at you in a friendly fashion, seemingly unaware of your panic.

Your knees are a little shaky as you get back on the road and push pedals again. With more than the usual relief, you enter the turnoff to the campground, a small forest service sign at a

175

Some cyclists prefer to travel alone because they feel it permits greater independence and mobility.

dirt road going into the woods at the right. It is an older campground with small spaces pleasantly tucked into the forest — a tenter's paradise. There are only a few other campers spread throughout the 11 sites you have to choose from. Finding a fairly isolated spot away from the outhouse, you pedal back to the entrance and deposit your two dollars at the self-service permit station.

With an hour or so of daylight left, you pitch your tent, fluff your sleeping bag since it will be much cooler tonight than you are accustomed to, and prepare dinner. As you sip the chicken bouillon you prepared in water boiled while setting up the tent, you fix a salad with fresh green lettuce and ripe tomatoes. When it is ready you start the pasta cooking for macaroni and cheese, your main carbohydrate for the

176

evening. Dessert is a big cup of yogurt as you lean against a ponderosa pine watching the sun's last display of color in the west. Food never tasted as good.

A final batch of water warmed on your stove goes to do up your few dishes with enough left over for a sponge bath as you change into warmer clothing for the evening. Although it isn't really cold, you have been so long in the desert that the mountain air at 6,000 feet seems to have a chill to it. There will be no difficulty sleeping to-night.

As you finish up your chores, some of your camping neighbors walk by and stop to talk. They are curious about your mode of transportation and seem a little amazed at your lack of gear. When they ask how far you came today, you realize that you don't know so you get out the map to check. It turns out to have been an 84-mile day, really good for the amount that was in the mountains. They laugh because they have come that far in their car since midafternoon. But this day will stand out in your life as special, filled with sights, sounds, smells and experiences that will make you forever feel a part of this piece of the world. For them, it was just another long day behind the wheel on the way to somewhere else.

The couple, somewhere in their mid-thirties, say that they would like to try what you are doing sometime but don't think they could make it. You try to convey to them your belief that anyone who is physically capable can travel long distances by bicycle if he really wants to. It has been done by the deaf, the blind, and even by people with only one leg. The secret is in a heart and mind that are curious about the world, and flexibility enough to fit in just about anything that comes along. But their questions center on the kind of bike you have, what sort of camping equipment you use and how extensive has been your physical conditioning. All of those things are elements, but they are not what is important. You tell them instead that yes, you are organized and yes, you need to be aware of the difficulties, but most of all you need to be loose enough to accept unforeseen circumstances such as breakdowns, detours, and an outstanding sight-to-see as additions to your tour, not interruptions. Bicycle touring itself becomes the whole experience; everything else — including getting where you are going — is just a small part of the larger whole.

You smile to yourself remembering your first tour. You had eight days, yet came home four days early after several mechanical breakdowns and missing a bus when it became apparent that you wouldn't be able to complete the tour as you planned it. Now, you would simply change your plans accordingly and spend all eight days on the road, even if it wasn't the "original" road. Any road will do; it is the traveling on it that counts.

Your guests wander away, convinced that they really would like to take a bike tour if only . . . But perhaps meeting you has broadened their horizons to the point that one day they will match their wishes to wheels.

It is completely dark now with stars as your rooftop companions. You take your panniers into the tent after locking and covering your bike. There will be dew in the morning, the desert seems a long-ago memory. You put your bike light, water bottle and wristwatch next to the head of your sleeping bag. You won't need an alarm in the morning to beat the heat of the day. As you lie in bed you can hear all sorts of night noises as the world outside your tent passes into the care of the nocturnal. You hope their night is as fruitful and happy as your day has been.

Chapter Eleven
Touring with People

If you would rather not strike out on your own right away, or if you are tired of touring alone and want some company, try a group tour. You don't have to be an expert or even an intermediate rider to enjoy a tour if you are careful to match your ability to the group's. People on bicycles seem to us to be an especially nice assortment; politics, religion, occupations and interests vary as much as with any combination of folks — but there is a unifying force in traveling by two wheels and human power that transcends differences. A group bicycle tour can be one of the outstanding events in your life.

Choosing a bicycle-tour group is a little like getting married; you never really know what you are getting into until it is too late to get out of it. Cyclists seek touring companions for a variety of reasons; some want company — a friendly face across the handlebars and at the dinner table — while some need the identity and anonymity of a group to get away from themselves for a bit. Groups offer practical services such as mechanics, meals and gear toting besides handling details of transportation and accommodation. A few join groups to find an echo chamber for their egos; these are the ones who have been everywhere and done everything, and are all too willing to tell you about it.

If you join a group with your eyes open and a willingness to give as much as you get, your chances of having a pleasant tour are good. Much of your happiness and satisfaction depends on your own attitudes and flexibility but a lot depends on the group. How can you find the right tour group?

Touring in a group offers advantages of company, support and conversation. And by employing the technique of drafting, riding in a pace line behind each other, group touring makes the cycling easier.

Finding Your Group

There are many groups from which to choose, more than ever before thanks to the widening interest in using bicycles for recreational travel. Consult Appendix D for a list of some of the groups available. But which one is right for you? To find out look at the group carefully and ask questions.

Commercial groups are in it for a profit, giving you certain services for a fee. They range from the slick-brochure type offering a multitude of tours with a wide variety of dates to choose from down to the small operator who has one or two tours a year and will send you mimeographed information if you send a return envelope. The former is not necessarily good nor is the latter bad; investigate each carefully.

Nonprofit touring groups are sometimes hard to distinguish from the commercial type. Their nonprofit classification is usually due to educational activities that exempt them from tax-paying status. Most such groups offer a good program with dedicated staff, some paid and some voluntary. The education, however, can be the school-of-hard-knocks variety. Be careful in your selection and be prepared for anything.

You might select your touring companions from a club or group that has some common interest such as religion or occupation. Such groups range from superorganized with complete tour packages to just a bunch from the neighborhood who decide to ride together for a specific trip. Bicycle clubs and organizations frequently have tour schedules that you might find appealing and suitable to your schedule and finances. Write the League of American

Wheelmen (address in Appendix E) for cycling clubs in your area.

When you find a group that interests you, first determine if they cater to a particular age group, income or ability level. If roughing it is your thing, you probably wouldn't be happy riding with a group of elderly professional people who travel with nothing heavier than a credit card. On the other hand, if your idea of roughing it is having to carry your own toothbrush then you certainly don't want to join up with a group spending 14 days camping in the Ozarks. Write to the tour group for information on ridership if you can't find out through other sources. Make sure you know what they expect in riding ability. Ask what will be the longest day traveled. Don't accept daily averages as the whole picture. Three groups might all average 50 miles per day; one travels 100 miles one day and rests the next, another might actually come close to the advertised average, and the third may have two days at 30 miles each and one at 90 miles, which also averages out to 50 miles per day.

Choose a group that is going where you want to go. If you have no interest in tennis and antique shopping, don't join a tour that allows up to half of each day for those activities. If your idea of heaven is a leisurely tour of California's wine country with lots of time for exploring and tasting, make sure the tour you join sees things the same way you do. Decide whether where you go is more important than with whom you go. Don't

Many cyclists of varying abilities, including the couple in this photograph, find sufficient challenge in group tours (listed in Appendix D).

get so picky that you eliminate the element of serendipity — the aptitude for making accidental fortunate discoveries. That quality is basic to bicycle touring anywhere with anyone.

181

Match your tour group to your pocketbook. Some provide total care for a lump sum, paid in advance. Others provide only guide service with a pay-as-you-go system for participants. Either way, be aware of the total cost including transportation to and from the touring area, incidentals, meals not included and entertainment. Don't let financial shock spoil an otherwise delightful trip.

How does the group handle transportation to and from the tour site as well as any midtour transport that may be necessary? The tour may seem like a dream trip but getting there and back again can tax your resources, time and patience beyond the worth of the trip itself. Make sure you know what part of bike transport is up to you and what part is taken care of by the group long enough in advance so that you can include it in your planning; for example, do you need to get a bike box or pack your bike some special way?

Finally, if you are restricted in when and how much time you can devote to a tour, make sure the group plan fits your schedule. Bicycle travel is an inexact science (one of its most appealing aspects, we think), so to be realistic always leave yourself a day or two at the end for the unforeseen.

What to Expect

Once you decide on a certain group, or perhaps even before making the final decision, there are a number of questions you should answer before actually loading up. Write if there is time, telephone if not, but get someone to hear you out and give you straight information or at least a healthy "I don't know." Don't be afraid to ask questions. If you can, talk with someone who has been with the group (if it is unknown to you personally) on that or a similar trip. If everything was roses, ask them what they liked least about the tour. Generally, here are some other things you should know before departure.

How and where will you sleep? Is it camping, motels, inns, a combination or a variety of "public" facilities? You need to know this so you can plan your gear, of course, but you should also have some idea so you can psych your body for what is ahead. Rest is as important to you as good food when touring by bicycle; make sure you know what you can expect in general.

What about meals? Will you be eating out, supplementing in the grocery store, preparing your own, or do you have a choice? Must you always eat with the group? Is cooking shared or shirked? Do you have special dietary needs? Even if it is not so normally, food becomes a very important item in your life on a bicycle tour. One tour we led was a "bring your own food" camp-out. We stressed the hunger factor well in advance but several people brought minimal amounts of food for various reasons. We ended up spending the evening cycling ten miles farther to a

The Bikecentennial organization in Missoula, Montana, offers some of the best organized and interesting tours in the country. This organization, which initiated the cross-country ride to celebrate the 1976 Bicentennial, has considerable experience in leading bicycle tours.

restaurant and grocery store where everyone happily spent several hours eating.

What about the leaders? How many are there for how many riders? Are they paid or volunteer; do you care? What is their experience and background? Group leadership experience is prob-

ably more important than actual bicycling experience, although you should be able to expect that the leaders have at least performed the equivalent of the trip. Are the leaders trained in first aid and do they know emergency procedures? If not, perhaps you should.

How does the group ride? Some split up into very small groups of perhaps two or three for the day, meeting at designated points along the way. Others ride in huge gaggles of 20 to 40 and should be avoided if possible. Some allow total freedom during the day to ride as fast or as slow as you wish so long as you show up at night where the group sleeps over. Be sure you know the route and stopping place before you set out if such is the case. You will need to be mechanically self-sufficient or at least be able to notify someone if you are delayed. However the group rides, for your part insist on riding single file. Use off-bike time for visiting unless you are on a no-traffic roadway or bikeway. In groups it is too easy to let conversation overshadow the fact that you are operating a vehicle on the public roadway with all the responsibilities of doing so.

Will you carry all of your gear or is there a "sag wagon?" If there is one, it may go on ahead to each stopover or it may follow behind as a sweeper to help with any troubles along the way. It may only carry gear or it may provide mechanical assistance as well with spare parts, tires, tubes, and so on. Is it part of your group duty to drive the sag wagon one day or more? Can you rely on it if you get sick, injured or just pooped along the way?

How safety conscious is the group? What is done to increase visibility or is it the individual's responsibility? Some groups provide bright flags and vests to both identify the group and increase its visibility. Others frown on such things as unprofessional and somehow degrading. What about helmets? No group we know provides them but neither should a group discourage them; some even require their use.

What about mechanical aid? Is everyone in the group on his or her own? If so, you will need to outfit yourself with tools and know how to use them (see chapter fourteen). Most groups have mechanically skilled people somewhere in their ranks, but that doesn't mean they will be around when you break down; they might be ten miles ahead. If repair facilities are in the sag wagon, make sure you are riding with someone who can go off for help unless it remains in the rear. The best bet is to have your own repair kit and pump so you can get yourself back on the road.

Will you be renting a bike or providing your own? Know what is required. Some groups accept single- and 3-speeds, others require 10-speeds. If you rent, do they have the right-size frame for you? Know your size and make sure ahead of time that it is available. Don't make do with an ill-fitting bicycle. If you rent, can you bring along your own saddle (if you have one well broken in)? It

can help soothe the most savage rental beast.

Finally, what if . . ? Ask a few questions like what if you get sick? What if there is a last-minute emergency and you can't make it? Do you get a refund in part or whole? Be fair to the group — many work on tight schedules and budgets, which don't leave much room for last-minute cancellations. Give plenty of notice if you must drop out and, if you can't, don't expect full return of your money. If you get sick or hurt, who is responsible financially for medical aid and transportation if it is necessary? Find out about insurance coverage for the group. You will probably be asked to sign some sort of waiver to hold the group and its leaders not responsible in case of injury. Take it seriously and check out your own insurance coverage while bicycling.

What Not to Expect

Don't expect your touring group to be all things to all people. It is most likely no more than a loosely knit group of people who will be sharing an exciting and pleasant experience with you for a set period of time. They cannot solve your problems; you must do that. At the most they can provide a new perspective and some friends that you didn't have before, along with a lot of memories — mostly good ones we hope.

Don't expect to be entertained. You

get out of a group what you put into it, sometimes less, sometimes more. At times a group automatically clicks so there is a special something about it, an identity of its own made up individually but given a life beyond the sum of its parts. That is the good kind. There are also groups that become wailing walls for lost hopes and scapegoats for disillusionment. Whether due to poor planning, bad weather or just the vagaries of the road, the group turns on itself and breaks apart into sullen sectors of accused and accusers. That is the bad kind.

Don't expect everything to go as planned or announced. There will be changes, breakdowns, diversions; all the things that can happen to an individual touring multiplied by however many are in your group. Don't expect to have all the fun and shift the down times onto someone else. As in a marriage, you are with the group for richer and poorer, otherwise you shouldn't be there at all. Adaptability and flexibility, the two qualities that insure the success of an individual tour, work as well when touring with others. You may need them even more, since there is a greater possibility of problems due to sheer numbers.

Don't expect anyone to wait on you either on the road or at the table. It sounds harsh but if you can comfortably cycle only a maximum of 30 miles a day you have no business joining a tour group that expects to do 60-80 miles per day. You will only frustrate yourself and perhaps jeopardize the tour for oth-

ers. There are enough groups of varied ability that you can find one to suit your speed and temperament. It can be just as frustrating to feel like cycling 80 miles a day yet be in a group that tours 20 miles, then spends the rest of the day in the pool or around the town. Most groups will accept anyone who will pay the price; it is up to you to see that you are paced with the pedalers.

Don't assume much of anything. Don't assume someone else will have a first-aid kit, don't assume someone else will have a pump, don't assume anyone knows how to repair a spoke, don't assume everyone will wait while you take pictures of wild flowers, and don't assume you will feel marvelous every single day. Most of all, don't assume the group is organized or well thought out. Hope that it is, but don't assume so. Assume only that you will get along well because you are prepared for anything and that just about anything is apt to happen. One other assumption is permitted; assume you are really going to enjoy the trip.

Getting Ready

Preparing for a group tour is not much different from preparing for an individual tour; at least it shouldn't be. Too frequently a person relies on a group to fill gaps in knowledge, skills and gear. It is much better to join a group for companionship, fun and new viewpoints than out of need and dependence. First, you would be assuming expertise where it might not exist; second, you would be contracting for a service not actually part of the package. Exceptions to this are tour organizations that advertise to teach and extend bicycle skills. Such teaching tour groups are a real aid to the beginner who wants to head out but needs help, and to the more experienced rider who wants to extend the range of his or her knowledge. Our experience in leading this kind of group has been enjoyable and especially gratifying.

If at all possible, meet with your tour group ahead of time both to get acquainted and to assess expectations. If you haven't done so already, get answers to the questions above and any others that directly concern you. If there is to be a division of labors, this is the time to volunteer in areas where you have competence and to be honest about those areas where you don't. If you hate preparing meals, admit it. Perhaps you can trade off with someone else who feels just as strongly about something you don't mind doing.

Make sure your gear and your bicycle are in top condition. If you master the contents of this book, you should be in pretty good shape. Just don't expect to do last-minute maintenance your first night on the road. You may not get that far and, if you do, you will certainly have better things to do than work on your bike.

Be as self-contained as possible, even if you are going unladen, with a sag wagon to carry your gear. Self-containment is an attitude as well as a state of being and can be as important a piece of equipment as a patch kit or a sleeping bag. Be physically prepared for the tour as well. Get in shape ahead of time so you can spend all of your energies on enjoying and getting to know your tour mates rather than on agonizing over sore muscles and exhaustion. You owe it to yourself and your tour group to be in shape for the trip ahead of time (see chapter twelve).

On the Road

Just before leaving your house, look around to make a final check. Do this especially if you are very excited about the trip. On one of our tours one of the young men showed up after an 85-mile automobile trip from his home and unloaded his bike only to find that in his excitement he had left the entire front wheel at home. Don't ask us how, he just did. Fortunately we had an extra wheel that saved his tour.

Show up on time, better yet — be a little early. It is hard on yourself to be late and hard on everyone who has to wait for you. Allow time for last-minute delays, traffic, gas lines, ticket counters, baggage checks, lost items, having to return for something forgotten and anything else that comes along. Give yourself enough time and you won't be nervous or in panic.

Once at the starting point, you are

186

part of the group. Now is not the time to suddenly exercise your independence. You have joined by choice and you should work at being a member of the tour group. Don't get ahead or stay behind to shop, eat, sleep or meditate. If you must deviate from the group, let the leader know where and when you can be expected to return.

As you ride, watch the rider ahead of you for sudden stops and leave enough room to maneuver. Let a rider know you are passing if it is necessary to do so by calling out "passing on your left" and waiting a minute to be sure you were heard. Don't pass on the right as you will be forcing the other rider out into the road. Follow the rules of the road: stop at all stop signs, signal intentions (it's the law), ride on the right and yield to pedestrians. When you spot obstacles such as glass, potholes, gravel or automobile parts let the rider immediately behind you know by calling it out or signaling with your hand. Don't daydream or get so engrossed in conversation that you become oblivious to the road or to the traffic, even if there is very little. At rest stops, park your bike — along with the others — completely off the road and out of anyone's way. No restaurant or shop owner wants 20 bicycles blocking the entryway no matter how much money you are spending there.

If you are especially competent, watch out for the less-experienced members of the group. They will appreciate your attention and you will be helping them to enjoy bike touring just that much more. You might be able to prevent an accident or injury that would be detrimental to the entire group.

Try to give something special to the group from your talents. Maybe you can cook, sing, patch a tire in two minutes or make jokes on cold, rainy days. A harmonica does wonders when a group is huddled together under a tarp waiting for the rain to stop. On one tour we remember, one of the girls was totally inexperienced and really beyond her level physically. Yet she could listen with a passion. She paid rapt attention to anyone who was talking, asked intelligent questions and remembered what was said; she made each of us feel truly important, wise and unique. That is as much a talent as playing an instrument or cooking an omelet.

When things go wrong, the leader usually gets the blame and the group sometimes splits into those for and those against the establishment. Try to stay out of such wrangling; be reasonable and rational. Some things just can't be helped and complaining certainly doesn't solve anything. Instead see if there is something you can do to help smooth things. Recognize bitching for the useless exercise it is and help to redirect the complainant's energies into constructive directions. The leader is there by appointment, not by election — mutiny serves no one.

In any group, personality conflicts occur. Avoidance works better than trying to make someone over who sees no

187

need for change. You joined for the tour itself; no one promised perfect partners. A smile works wonders; common courtesy is hard to rebuff.

Bicycle touring together is a beautiful way of turning strangers into friends. Once you have conquered a mountain pass, a desert or a continent together, little else matters. You may then go separate ways but you will always be connected in time and space by your turning wheels. What better way to build a friendship? A good touring group fosters companionship, community and communion. We hope you find just such a group.

Touring with Your Family

The fact that you all know each other is a primary advantage in touring with your family; it can also be a primary disadvantage. While a family bicycle tour can be a rewarding, loving, exciting experience, it is no place to look for miracles in a family that is having problems. The best guide as to whether you should try bicycle touring as a family (assuming everyone likes the idea in the first place) is if you enjoy being at home together. If so then you will enjoy being on tour together; simple but basic.

When touring with your family, choose a route and destination that interests every member. Each section doesn't have to appeal to each person,

but make sure there is something to interest everyone often enough to be an incentive. We like historical trails, towns and regions that give a fourth dimension to touring, sort of one step beyond now. But our children don't yet appreciate history much beyond tales of cowboys, Indians and outlaws, so we try to get some of that in our historical meanderings as well. Boot Hill and the Oregon Trail have felt the touch of their wheels and heard their excited questions. Amusement parks fit well into a family tour as do ice cream parlors occasionally and circuses. Don't forget the appeal of a motel TV on the night of a favorite program. An overnight bike tour to a baseball game, county fair or swimming beach is sure to excite the children and refresh the parents; what better way to teach them that getting somewhere can be half the fun?

Don't try to pedal farther than you can comfortably travel as a family, whether that is 10 miles or 80. You are only as strong as the weakest person in your family, so plan tours with that person uppermost in mind. Never abandon one rider to the rear — it can be a frustrating, devastating experience for that person. We once rode with a group that was considerate enough to always wait for the rear rider, even when that meant taking a 15-minute break by the roadside, but as soon as the rear rider caught up, the group would mount up and move on, never giving that rider a chance to rest and feel part of the ride. We found out much later that if Glenda hadn't stayed behind with the person, she would have given up on bike riding entirely. As it is, years later she is still enjoying touring and keeping up with everyone too, we might add.

Especially with children, pace the day so there are breaks for noncycling activities. As little as ten minutes an hour taken out to look at wild flowers, pet farm animals or toss rocks into a stream can turn a reluctant pedaler into an enthusiastic tourer. We are not above bribery when it comes to moving our kids down the road, especially if we know it is a particularly boring section of a tour for them. Being able to order anything on a menu (careful where you go if your budget looks like ours), an afternoon given over to the delights of a library, and even — if the going is really rough — the promise of a malted milk or chocolate sundae have all been known to push our children a few miles farther than they thought they could go. Know when your family partners are lagging due to boredom rather than exhaustion or physical problems. Hypothermia (see chapter twelve) can sound like whining or even boredom if you are not aware of what is happening in someone else's sphere. Knowing each other helps out here.

Allow enough time to get where you are going and still enjoy getting there. No one likes being constantly prodded to move faster, especially most children and one mother we know. If pacing is a big problem, load the fastest rider with the most gear and let the slowest ride

empty. Some equalizing can be done through gearing also if you have ridden together enough to know what needs to be done.

Don't assume the children will be the slowest. On many mountain roads we don't particularly like to recall, Kirsten raced ahead of us to the top while we walked at a decidedly middle-aged pace. She actually had more trouble keeping pace with us cross-country on the flats because of her smaller wheels and lower high gear. Long, steady climbs can be especially tiring and discouraging to smaller children. Take a break partway up if necessary.

When touring with your family, don't set rigid destinations for each day on the road. Be flexible. Perhaps those words should be at the head of each chapter in this book; but given your flexible attitude disaster can be disarmed, delay can become delight and detour can turn into diversion. As if all that isn't enough, flexibility just might save your tour. If some of the family don't feel like riding on a particular day, don't. The fun of bicycle touring is both in being where you are and how you got there. Where you are going means nothing until you get there; don't let it become more important than that.

For some excellent tips on touring long distances with children, see Tony and Robbie Fanning's article "Taking the Kids Along" in the June 1979 issue of *Bicycling* magazine. They emphasize the value of including children in the planning stages of a tour, letting them

189

feel an integral and important part before you ever set foot to pedal. We concur and recommend this approach as we have used it with our children successfully many times.

Young children tend to do what you expect of them. If you expect whining, boredom and complaining, that is usually what you get. If you expect happiness, some excitement and enthusiasm, you usually get that too. A hug and a smile are an unbeatable combination for biking blues in a family. Come to think of it, a hug and a smile fit nicely into any touring group. When it comes right down to it, people are people anywhere; it only seems that people on bicycles are something extra special. Then again, maybe they are.

Chapter Twelve
Physical Conditioning

Going on tour without being in reasonable physical condition is like surfing without knowing how to swim. You can do it, but you miss a lot of the pleasure and you are taking a chance with your well-being. Adequate physical preparation before undertaking any strenuous sport means the difference between being comfortable enough to enjoy what you are doing and being so miserable as to discourage keeping up with the activity.

Bicycling is unique in that you begin to participate immediately, no matter what your level of physical condition. Even if you start in poor shape, with patience and determination you can work your way toward excellent physical condition while enjoying bicycling from the very beginning. The key is to approach it slowly and methodically. Never set out on a long tour figuring you will get in condition on the way. It might happen given an unlimited amount of time for a very relaxed tour, but it rarely comes that way. Conditioning happens over several hours a week spread out to give the body time to adjust to new expectations. This is best accomplished before going on a long tour where you will want to spend many hours on your bike with off-hours doing things other than lying around groaning.

Physical fitness for bicycle touring means two things: heart and lungs that work at maximum efficiency (cardiovascular conditioning), and muscles that are strong, efficient and capable of performing day after day without strain or trauma (muscular conditioning). Both types of fitness, although not mutually exclusive, are requisites of long-distance touring.

Bicycle touring as a relatively simple, noncompetitive activity does not require the physical conditioning needed for strenuous, competitive athletic events. But sadly, many Americans are more sports minded than physically active; passive spectators rather than active participants. The facts speak for themselves: "850,000 Americans die each year from heart and blood vessel disease and . . . 50 percent of all deaths are related to cardiovascular illness. . . . 15 million Americans are obese to an extent which seriously raises their risk of ill health." (From *Dietary Goals for the United States,* 2d edition, U.S. Government Printing Office.)

Proper, regular exercise will not make you immune to ill health, but coupled with good dietary habits and sound genetic structure it can go a long way to insure that you will enjoy your full potential for an active life. Whether you see bicycle touring as a means toward physical fitness or whether physical fitness is only an integral part of the joy of bicycle touring, you owe it to yourself and your loved ones to get into good condition and maintain it as a normal part of your life-style.

Taking pulse with Harvard Step Test. This test measures cardiovascular condition.

Determine Your Present Condition

Knowing where you are now acts both as a base from which you can measure your progress, and as an incentive to begin. Before initiating a program of conditioning, visit your doctor for a complete physical exam, including a stress electrocardiogram (EKG) if possible. This is particularly important if you are over 30 years of age and have not exercised regularly. Your doctor, especially if he or she is knowledgeable in sports medicine, should check for organic conditions that might affect your exercise capacity and, hopefully, encourage you to begin. If your doctor is uninterested or negative about the benefits of exercise, perhaps it is a good time to find a new doctor for your new life.

If you are unable to obtain or afford a stress EKG, there is a simple test called the Harvard Step Test that you can perform yourself or in conjunction with your doctor. It provides a basic evaluation of your physical condition but does not indicate abnormalities or limitations in your cardiovascular system. Repeat the test throughout your conditioning program to document your progress.

With a clean bill of health from your doctor, you may take this test anywhere with one person to aid you. You will need a bench, stool, sturdy table or something strong of the proper height onto which you can step. The step's height depends on your own height as follows:

If you are	the platform should be
under 5' 0"	12"
5' 0" to 5' 3"	14"
5' 4" to 5' 9"	16"
5' 10" to 6' 0"	18"
6' 1" or over	20"

You will be stepping from the floor to the platform with both feet, then back to the floor again at the rate of 30 times per minute while someone times with a stopwatch or a watch that has a second hand. Before beginning the test, practice a bit to develop the pace; a step up and back down in two-second intervals is about right. Have your assistant monitor your pace throughout the test.

Once you have a feeling for the pace, rest a bit, then begin the test.

Step onto the platform at the established rate for a total of four minutes, or as close to it as you can get. If you can't make it for the full four minutes, be sure to have your assistant write down the exact length of time you maintained the pace.

At the end of 4 minutes or whenever you must stop, sit down immediately to rest. Take your pulse at the end of 1 full minute of rest, counting heartbeats for a full 30-second period (using the carotid artery in the neck just to the side of the larynx for best results). Have your assistant write down your 30-second count, then repeat at 2 minutes, and again after 3 minutes from completion of the stepping. Take the sum of the three pulse counts, multiply by 2, divide that number into the total number of seconds you were able to perform (240 if you completed 4 minutes) and multiply by 100. The formula looks like this:

$$\frac{\text{seconds of performance} \times 100}{\text{sum of pulse counts} \times 2} = \text{Recovery Index (RI)}$$

If your RI is 60 or less you are in poor condition; 61-70 is fair; 71-80 is good; 81-90 is very good; and 91 or over is excellent. Please note that this test does not take age into consideration. Your maximum cardiovascular potential is reached by about age 20, declining to about 70 percent by age 65. Muscular strength is usually at a maximum in the mid-20s, declining to about 80 percent by age 65. If you are over 30, take this into consideration.

Do not be concerned about where

you place right now. It is only a starting point. In fact, the worse your initial condition, the greater the results you can expect. Use your RI as a basis for comparison while you progress through your conditioning program.

Your resting pulse rate is another indicator of physical condition, one which you can easily monitor. The pulse rate drops with conditioning, reflecting increased capacity of the heart to perform more efficiently. You will notice this just a few weeks into a training program, but you will also see a gain in pulse rate if you stop exercising for as little as two or three weeks. For this reason, pulse rate is an accurate and quickly determined indicator of your progress. The best time to take your resting pulse is just before getting out of bed in the morning. Have a clock with a second hand visible on awakening so you can take your pulse before moving much more than to put your hand on your carotid artery. Jot it down. This gives you a reliable basis for comparison in future weeks.

Decide on a Method of Exercise

Bicycle riding is the best conditioning exercise for bicycle touring. It is not the only one, but consider some of the advantages of beginning a riding program. Bicycling, since it is a means of transportation, serves a dual purpose when used in an exercise program.

Commuting to work or regular use of the bicycle for daily errand running not only fits easily into your goal of regular exertion, but also contributes to a lifestyle independent of nonrenewable fuel use. Instead of having to set aside a special hour in your day for exercise, make use of normal travel time to and from your job or other daily business. Your bicycle becomes a way of life rather than purely a pleasure machine. Join the thousands who regularly commute by bicycle; you will be doing yourself and your country a service.

If you cannot use your bicycle regularly for transportation, you will have to set aside time to ride purely for exercise. To be fair, we must point out that there are other, quicker ways to obtain physical fitness, but bicycling itself is the best overall preparation for bicycle touring.

The President's Council on Physical Fitness and Sports has rated popular sports on a scale with a higher number indicating the better aerobic exercise. You must refer elsewhere for a complete discussion of the meaning of aerobic exercise (read Dr. Kenneth Cooper's book on aerobics); suffice it to say here that aerobic exercise is that done at a rate and in such a way as to provide maximum benefit to the cardiovascular system. The council's list looks like this:

Jogging — 148	Tennis — 128
Bicycling — 142	Walking — 102
Swimming — 140	Golf — 66
Handball — 140	Bowling — 51

Cross-country skiing was omitted from the list yet many believe it to be the best single conditioning sport. It certainly is an ideal winter activity for those living in areas not conducive to other outdoor activities in winter.

Another indicator of the comparative values of sports is the number of calories required for performance. The council reports the following calorie cost per hour of performance for a 150-pound subject:

Running — 900 (at 10 mph)
Bicycling — 660 (at 13 mph)
Swimming — 300 (at ¼ mph)
Handball — 600
Tennis — 420
Walking — 210 (at 2½ mph)
Walking — 300 (at 3¾ mph)
Golf — 250
Bowling — 270

Any of the above sports, pursued strongly and regularly, will improve your cardiovascular condition, thus aiding your touring potential. Bicycling at 13 mph on an unloaded bicycle is not an excessive pace. A general training ride is in the neighborhood of 15-20 mph. Even so, it is obvious that conditioning on a bicycle is going to take longer than running. A running program, unless you are a dedicated competition runner, will not harm your cycling ability. Neither will other forms of vigorous exercise. Please realize that exercise must be combined with limitation of calorie intake if weight loss is expected to ac-

company conditioning. Exercise alone will not do the job.

But what about muscular conditioning? Obviously, nothing develops your cycling muscles better than cycling. Even if you use another exercise for cardiovascular conditioning, you must spend time on your bicycle to assure development of the muscles you will need on tour. Only miles put in on your bike will do that task.

Begin a Conditioning Program

No matter what method you choose to get into shape, the basic goal is the same — to achieve physical fitness (the capacity of the heart, blood vessels, lungs and muscles to function at optimum efficiency). How do you arrive at that happy state and how do you know when you get there? Will a walk around the block twice a week do it? Or perhaps three half-hour sessions of fast handball a week? Will a bike ride a day lead to a conditioned body? No method will work unless your pulse rate consistently gets high enough to matter.

You must exercise hard enough to reach the "training effect." That is the level at which the heart and lungs are stressed enough to improve in performance. With regular exercise a healthy heart pumps more blood per beat and recovers faster to a normal rate after exercise. It is also the prime factor in determining the point at which glucose is broken down into carbon dioxide and water for release to the body as energy. To exercise adequately you must determine the point at which the training effect takes place for your own heart, then you must stress it at that point long enough to cause improvement over a period of time. Without reaching the training effect, you could "exercise" daily for hours, yet never improve your physical condition beyond your initial level.

There is a simple means of determining the approximate point where the training effect takes place for you. First, find your "maximum heart rate" by subtracting your age from 220. This is the pulse rate you should take care not to exceed during exercise. Now, subtract your resting pulse rate from the maximum heart rate and multiply the difference by .75. Add this result to your resting pulse rate to obtain your optimum training-effect rate.

Example: (for a 38-year-old with a resting pulse of 58)

$$220 - 38 = 182 - 58 = 124 \times .75 =$$
$$93 + 58 = 151$$

Recent studies suggest a similar formula but without using the resting pulse rate. This gives a somewhat lower training-effect rate; we suggest using this if you have not exercised at all in the last year and need to begin gradually. There is wide controversy over the training-effect rate in general but most studies support the generalization that the heart rate must be at least 140 to produce a training effect.

Once you know your training rate, regulate your exercise to reach that point and hold it for the required amount of time (see below). Do not attempt to exercise at the training rate immediately if you are just beginning. Your heart rate may elevate dangerously fast. A slow, methodical approach is ultimately faster than an all-out attempt that might only get you into bed or, worse yet, into a hospital room.

Don't expect miracles, even if you pride yourself on the shape you are in. Cardiovascular conditioning has nothing to do with appearance. Glenda slipped from an RI of 92 to one of 68 (excellent to fair) over a period of 10 months when she stopped exercising regularly. She never gained or lost a pound, in fact never knew how badly her conditioning had slipped except for tiring more rapidly in general.

Begin exercising gradually and work up to the point where you can continue to exercise until your heart rate reaches the training rate, then continue at that point long enough for conditioning to take place. How long is that? Research is contradictory, but it is generally believed that the period of training-rate stress must continue for at least 12 minutes. Other studies show that in order to obtain the full benefit, which includes the reduction of serum cholesterol level in the blood, the training-stress period must continue for 30 to 45 minutes. These time periods do not include warm-up and cool-down, nor do they include the time it takes for your heart to reach the training rate. It is time spent at or beyond the training rate only.

You must, of course, monitor your heart rate in order to know when it reaches the training rate and to insure that you don't push it beyond your maximum heart rate (your age subtracted from 220). Stop for 15-second intervals to take your carotid pulse, then multiply by four as you resume exercise to determine your heart rate. This is not totally accurate but until we can all afford the digital watches that read out pulse rate as we exercise it is about the best we can do.

If you are at or beyond your maximum rate, slack off just enough to drop below it yet stay above the training rate. As you exercise regularly and become familiar with your pulse rate during exercise you will be able to monitor your heart through familiarity with your whole system rather than having to take your pulse all the time.

The period of exercise at the training rate must be continuous; if you take a break you must begin again and subtract the time it took to reach the training rate once more. As you develop and your body becomes accustomed to vigorous exercise, you will not feel the need for a break, in fact your inclination will be to go beyond whatever time you have set for yourself. Physical exercise is addictive but it is positive.

Frequency is as important as length. Studies vary but it is generally believed that you must exercise for a minimum of 12 minutes at the training rate five days a week to improve your physical condition and only three times a week to maintain it. Do not make the mistake of lengthening your period of exercise, while limiting it to the weekend, thinking that it is the total amount of time that counts. Not so. To obtain the proper effect, exercise must be a consistent activity with no more than two or three days between sessions. If you miss a few sessions you will feel the difference and it will take several additional sessions to regain top condition.

If you are conditioning on your bicycle, you might find it easier to have short, fast workouts of up to 45 minutes (you really have to move along to gain your training rate while pedaling) during the week and then take a long, more leisurely all- or half-day ride on Saturday or Sunday to insure that your muscles hold up for extended touring. Remember, cardiovascular conditioning during short periods is not doing all that is necessary for muscular conditioning. That takes time and miles. Don't try to do it all on the weekends. The weekend athlete leads a dangerous life.

Each period of exercise should include an ample warm-up and cool-down period. This cannot be rushed. Slow bending, twisting and stretching of the major muscle groups go a long way toward prevention of injury and trauma from the stress of all-out exercise. Once you have loosened up you might want

197

to do some basic calisthenics to keep your upper body muscles in shape; they do not benefit much from bicycling or running. The warm-up session should bring you to the point of mild perspiration, then you can begin your primary activity. Rather than pushing off in a high gear on your bike, however, start out with some spinning to accustom your legs to what is ahead.

At the end of your exercise period slow down gradually rather than come to an abrupt halt. Allow your muscles to ease into disuse; let your breathing return to normal as you slow down. Then after you have dismounted, do a few more stretching, twisting and bending motions.

To review the key points in physical conditioning: get a physical exam; choose your means to fitness; determine your present condition with the Harvard Step Test and your resting pulse; determine your particular training heart rate; begin your exercise program slowly and build gradually in both length and intensity; maintain the training heart rate for an unbroken, adequate period each time; be consistent and frequent; and warm-up and cool-down with each exercise period.

Exercising is habit forming and relatively easy. The hard part is beginning each time. Try to think of your exercise period as an integral part of each day, not as something extra to be done if you find time. Develop and maintain a set time, get people around you to think of that time as distinctly yours, not to be interrupted except for an emergency. This is especially important for spouses and parents who have many demands on what little time they have. Think of your exercise period as a gift to one you love, the gift of a healthier, happier and perhaps longer-lived you. The only really valid excuse for skipping a session is illness. But many who maintain a regular exercise program find that periods of illness are few.

After the first several weeks of seeming agony and occasional defeat, you will find that your period of physical strain becomes very important to you and your body. You might even feel general malaise and unease if you miss a session once you really get into it. Much has been written on this addictive aspect of aerobic exertion, much is yet to be discovered about it. But for now, let yourself find the real you, the physically fit, sleek, efficiently running machine that makes up your body and encases your spirit. Do it on a bicycle.

All-Year Cycling

The nicest thing about using a bicycle as your exercise medium is that it is enjoyable. The worst thing is that it takes time. But it would not hurt a lot of us to take more time to do enjoyable things that are also of benefit to our physical fitness and well-being. Even when you are riding hard enough to reach the training effect, you can still appreciate your surroundings, the freedom of self-propelled motion, and the harmony of human and machine working together. This physical relationship is smooth and satisfying without the harsh pounding of joints and bones that occurs in ground-contact sports. Many people who try jogging switch to cycling because of the smaller amount of downtime caused by injury. But most of all, in our unbiased opinion, bicycling is just plain more fun.

What if you live part of your year in severe winter conditions? Cycling is not out because it is so simple to move indoors. Rollers are an answer for winterbound enthusiasts, those who can't always find daylight enough for a ride, and those who wish to stay indoors on cold or rainy days.

Rollers are a series of three parallel revolving tubes, 14 to 18 inches long, held in place on a frame. Two of the rollers are close together to hold the rear wheel of the bike at a right angle, the third tube acts as a base for the front wheel that rolls on top of it. There are many brands available, starting at around $75. Our State Aluminum American Rollers ($96) have seen miles of use, especially during harsh winter months.

With practice and not a little apprehension, you learn to mount your bicycle, balance and pedal as normal, all while staying in one spot. There is definitely a trick to riding rollers, but most experienced riders pick it up quickly. Support racks are available if you feel you need them for balance; they hold

Roller riding indoors is an effective winter exercise alternative.

the bike upright and centered on the rollers, or you can place the rollers near a wall or piece of furniture so you can lean while starting and stopping. When riding rollers you must pay full attention to what you are doing until you get the hang of it. Tim has had more accidents riding in the house than out on the road.

Getting your heart rate up rapidly is easy on rollers, and it can be controlled at a steadier pace than out in the real world of hills, wind and stop signs. Since there is no windchill factor on rollers, you may need to ride in front of an open door or window or point a large fan at yourself, depending on the indoor

199

temperature and the rate of your ride. Some people get so good on rollers that they can read (from a book propped on a music stand), watch television or listen to music.

Riding rollers is a good way to get your cardiovascular conditioning and to some extent your muscular conditioning. But it is only a substitute for roadwork, not its equal. Early one spring following a winter of bad weather and lots of roller riding, Tim set out on a rugged, all-day 75-mile ride. He just about died on that ride; wind, steep hills and rough roads took far more out of him than a winter on rollers had put in. Learn from that if you plan to ride rollers. Use them as an adjunct, not as a replacement.

Total Conditioning

Bicycle riding builds the lower body satisfactorily if enough miles are put in on the road. At first there are usually some sore muscles and stiff joints, especially in the knees and calves. If these problems don't disappear after two weeks of consistent exercise, reread chapter three and check for maladjustments on your bicycle. Look especially at the toe clips and the lateral position of your foot on the pedal. Experimental adjustments in this area will usually solve your problems.

The upper body receives little benefit from cycling. There is some conditioning when pulling up a steep grade with the hands down in the drop position, but this is rarely long enough to be of great benefit. Even then the chest and abdomen are left out.

All that is really needed to keep the upper body in good muscular tone is about 20-30 pushups and sit-ups a day. Work up to this number slowly if you are not already in good condition. We do a series of pushups and sit-ups following warm-up exercises just before a ride. These two exercises stress major muscle groups adequately for conditioning yet require very little time. Glenda uses her regular 12-minute Air Force exercise series as a warm-up period since it incorporates a slow start with buildup to pushups, sit-ups, back and hip conditioners. If you want to carry out a more extensive program, so much the better. The ride then becomes a real reward as well as an exercise in its own right.

Tim has a problem shared by a number of other cyclists; he develops severe pain in the upper back just to the side of one shoulder blade while riding. This might be the result of prior injury or simply the strain of long-distance riding on a particular body structure. Although medical aid can sometimes alleviate the problem (see Dr. Robert E. Bond's articles in the *League of American Wheelmen Bulletin,* March, April and May 1978), some people — Tim included — get relief by strengthening the upper back muscles. Simple calisthenics such as pushups or pull-ups might do the trick; Tim finds relief through pressing a barbell with 40 to 60 pounds of weight behind his neck as part of his normal workout.

Again the fit of the bicycle is important. Tim uses a short-reach, extra-long handlebar stem (SR Custom 60-millimeter reach, 180-millimeter length) that allows placement of the bars farther back and at the same height as the saddle. Some riding efficiency is lost, but he thinks it worth it for comfort considering his back problem. Fit your bicycle properly to your own specified needs; give your body sufficient time to adjust to a new exercise program (at least two weeks); do your supplemental exercises for the upper body; if problems persist, experiment with modifications of your machine.

Conditioning for Touring

If you maintain a consistent fitness program as discussed in this chapter, you will have very little to do to get ready for a long tour. Your normal workouts keep you in cardiovascular condition; muscular conditioning occurs if you supplement your program or do all of your conditioning by bicycle. However, when touring 50-100 miles a day on a loaded touring bike day after day, you are putting your body under a new kind of stress for which there is no preparation other than mile after mile of conditioning, preferably with your touring load.

After you have been out touring several weeks, you will be able to leap tall buildings in a single bound, but it takes some doing to reach that point no matter how good your condition was to begin with. The knees and butt get the brunt of long touring days; many tours are aborted in the first few days because of problems with these two areas. There is no preparation for it other than adequate conditioning through enough miles and time spent on the bike beforehand and a properly equipped and adjusted bicycle. You might be able to run a marathon in under three hours but that will not prepare you to sit on a bicycle seat for eight hours at a time.

When you start out on tour, limit your first few days to minimum mileage. If you plan to average 70 miles a day, do no more than 40-50 miles on your first days out. If you plan 50 miles a day, limit your first two days to about 30 miles each. Your body has enough to do in adjusting to long hours on the bike, different eating patterns and unfamiliar sleeping arrangements.

Do your warm-up routine prior to starting out each morning on tour. Your muscles need that stretching, loosening and warming-up especially when under the strain of long hours on the road. If possible, try not to overexert yourself during the first several miles of the day even if it means walking to the top of a steep grade you would normally ride up. Your body will signal its readiness for full exertion by beginning to perspire a little.

Keep your knees warm, especially in the early morning, on cool days or when making rapid descents. It may seem troublesome to put on long pants or leg warmers for only the first half hour on the road, or to stop to do it during the day. But the knees are very sensitive to cold and tend to be the most injury-prone part of the cyclist's body. A little extra care and forethought can prevent injury that might end your tour.

When touring for more than a week at a time, plan to take a day off your bike every five to seven days. Your body will benefit from the break and you can use the time to catch up on sightseeing, visiting, housekeeping or bike maintenance. On really extensive trips of a month or more, plan a period of up to a week in the middle of the tour during which you do no cycling at all. Long-distance bicycle touring is physically and mentally demanding; even with occasional days off the strain will show. Keep your body healthy and your attitude positive. Take a break now and then and change your activity as much as possible.

Almost two-thirds of the way across the country, our family met the Reichen-bachs, an Indiana farm family who invited us to spend some time seeing what farming was all about and enjoying their hospitality in the form of real beds, home-cooked, homegrown foods and interesting talk of things other than cycling. We spent three days with them and are pretty sure we would have ended our trip sooner had we not enjoyed both the company and the break. We left feeling refreshed and mentally renewed for the last leg of our journey, and our stay with them remains one of the highlights of the trip. Take advantage of such fortune by allowing time in your plans for noncycling breaks.

High-Elevation Touring Hazards

Too many cyclists plan tours through high mountain regions with little thought about the special requirements of physical exertion at high elevations. Even though you are in documented, excellent physical condition, that conditioning does not transfer into adjustment to high elevations. There is no way to condition for high elevations other than spending time at high elevations. If you live at or near sea level, then fly or drive to a point 5,000-6,000 feet above to tour, your body must have time to adjust. Allow a minimum of three days to do little or no cycling. Adjustment is a physiological matter. Once you begin touring, take it slow and don't attempt any rapid elevation gains right off.

Charles S. Houston, in an excellent article called "High Altitude Sickness" (*BACKPACKER,* no. 27), stresses that no amount of conditioning, training or medication will prevent high-altitude sickness. Your only choice is to increase your elevation at a moderate

Fully loaded cycle tourists with adequate clothing protection, riding in high mountain environment.

rate. Dr. Houston recommends no more than a 1,000-foot gain per day for the hiker; so what about the cyclist who might be climbing 3,000 or more feet in a single day? Obviously, there is risk involved. Aside from a gradual approach to higher elevations, your only defense is a knowledge of the warning signs of illness and the first aid necessary should they appear.

The most common and least dangerous form of high-altitude sickness is acute mountain sickness. Many people are troubled with this no matter how slowly they arrive at higher elevation. It occurs at lower elevations but is more common above 7,000 feet. The most frequent symptom is headache possibly accompanied by nausea, shortness of breath and vomiting. The only real remedy is to go no higher until the symptoms disappear, take aspirin with plenty of liquids and rest.

High-altitude pulmonary edema is more serious than acute mountain sickness as it involves the accumulation of fluid in the lungs with a resulting limitation of the amount of oxygen a victim can absorb. This illness rarely occurs below 10,000 feet, so would more likely be a problem for cyclists aspiring to alpine touring. Basic symptoms are general weakness, shortness of breath and a cough beginning 12-48 hours after a rapid ascent above 10,000 feet. Cyclists arriving at high elevations abruptly, then ascending passes above 10,000 feet should be aware of the danger presented by this illness. It is quite serious and can be fatal; the best treatment is to descend to a lower elevation as quickly as possible and get medical aid.

Cerebral edema is the most serious and most rare of high-altitude illnesses. Instead of fluid collecting in the lungs, this occurs in the brain. Symptoms are severe throbbing headache, weakness, uncoordination, double vision and possibly hallucinations. All or most of these occur 24-60 hours after a too-rapid ascent, usually above the 12,000-foot level. As in high-altitude pulmonary edema, cerebral edema victims must be taken to a lower elevation immediately and given expert medical treatment.

Let us stress again that good physical conditioning does not provide protection against these illnesses. Your only protection is gradual acclimation to altitude and an awareness that these things can occur in elevations traversed by touring cyclists. Keep symptoms in mind. The illnesses can progress from any one to any other, but there are overriding symptoms peculiar to each as mentioned above. Dr. Houston believes that no fewer than 100 thousand people develop some form of high-altitude sickness each year and as many as 20 thousand have to descend to lower elevations for recovery. The problem is not rare; with the increasing number of cyclists touring in mountainous regions it is something to be aware of and prepared for. As in any other activity there are risks, but you can do a lot to circumvent them through preparedness and knowledge.

Hypothermia

Hypothermia, sometimes known as exposure, is the reduction in temperature of the central core of the body to a point (below 95°F.) where the body is unable to recover warmth by itself and death can occur. It is brought on by fatigue, lack of sufficient food, wetness, exposure to wind and lack of proper clothing. Although usually associated with higher elevations, it can occur anywhere and at temperatures as high as 40°F. Wetness and windchill seem to be the primary factors; touring cyclists particularly need to be aware that this combination can lead to unbelievably rapid death.

The most startling aspect of hypothermia is that victims can do little to save themselves once the illness has progressed to the danger point. Victims have been found lying near food, shelter and warm sleeping bags; hypothermia overtook their senses before they could help themselves. The best protection besides adequate food, clothing and shelter is sound judgment in the use of those items, and an awareness of the symptoms and hazards of hypothermia so evasive action can be taken in time.

Danger signs are chill with uncontrolled shivering, loss of coordination, inability to think rationally and hallucinations, difficulty in speech (slurring or hesitation), and dilated pupils. Hypothermia is an individual thing and each person responds differently.

The only effective treatment is to immediately bring the victim's body temperature up to normal. In touring conditions, this means you should (1) immediately place the victim in a sheltered area out of the wind (preferably a tent); (2) remove all damp and wet clothing, replacing with dry if available (especially on the head); or put the naked victim inside a dry sleeping bag with a healthy member of the party, also naked, who will use body heat to warm the victim. (The sleeping bag alone is of no value since the victim is producing no warmth. There must be an external source of warmth to the victim.) (3) give the victim hot, sweet drinks (nonalcoholic) and food (warm if possible) to aid in internal warmth generation. Time is critical. Don't wait for all danger signs before beginning treatment. Be aware of symptoms so preventive measures can be taken before curative measures are needed. For additional information, consult Dr. Theodore G. Lathrop's excellent booklet, "Hypothermia: Killer of the Unprepared," available at most backpacking and outdoor stores for $1.

Hypothermia kills more "weekend sport" participants than members of high-altitude mountaineering expeditions. It occurs at relatively low elevations in summer months when rapid changes take place in the weather and people are caught unprepared. Cyclists are particularly vulnerable due to windchill generated by the very nature of the sport, fatigue on long rides and light clothing inappropriate to changes in the weather. Never assume you can outride bad weather or that good weather will be constant. Your body only produces so much warmth at a fixed rate; if the warmth is lost faster than it is produced, you are heading for hypothermia.

Heat Illness

Illness brought on by exposure to heat coupled with lack of fluid replacement is more common among cyclists than hypothermia, perhaps because a majority of cycling activity occurs during summer months at low elevations. Heat cramps, heat exhaustion and heat stroke are the three main illnesses threatening the hot-weather cyclist. Dehydration with salt imbalance is the primary cause of them all, but first let's look at each one so you will be familiar with symptoms and treatment.

Most common and least dangerous is heat cramping, brought on by exercising vigorously without proper attention to salt intake. Salt deficiency is the primary cause. Symptoms are severe cramping of the large muscles, especially in the legs but not limited to them. The treatment is to replace salt, usually with salt tablets but a 3 percent salt-water solution is preferable. Rest until the cramping subsides. Some people are more prone to this problem than others; if you find yourself susceptible, increase your table salt consumption a day or two before and during a long, hot ride. Do not bolt down salt tablets; it is unnecessary and dangerous as too much salt in your system draws water from your tissues to your stomach in an effort to neutralize the salt intake, causing dehydration complications you do not need. Simply increase your fluid intake and salt your food more than normal. A little salt goes a long way.

Heat exhaustion is more serious than heat cramping, but seldom fatal and easily treated. It is caused by vigorous exercise in hot — especially humid

— weather without sufficient fluid replacement and salt intake. It is a progressive illness and may take several days to manifest itself. It can occur more rapidly during overexertion with people in poor physical condition or with people not acclimatized to the heat. Symptoms include mild headache, drowsiness, fatigue, loss of appetite — possibly with vomiting, muscle cramps, confusion and light-headedness. In the final stage the victim is pale and sweats profusely.

Prompt, adequate treatment is necessary due to the seriousness of heat exhaustion and the danger of progression to heat stroke. Make the victim lie down immediately (if conscious) in a cool, shady place and administer salted fluids (about 3 percent solution). *Do not give plain water.* Plain water will compound the illness by removing even more salt from the body. In mild cases, salt tablets can be given but with generous amounts of water. Severe cases (unconscious) require intravenous salt solution and medical aid. Although almost miraculous recovery results from administration of salt solution, it is important that the victim rest for several days to insure adequate rehydration and restoration of electrolytes. Until the deficit is made up, recurrence is likely.

Heat stroke is fatal unless treated, then it is still fatal in one out of three cases. Correct treatment must be immediate. Symptoms are similar to those of heat exhaustion except in the terminal stage when the skin is red and dry (there is no sweating). This lack of sweat is the danger sign indicating the need for immediate action. The victim is literally burning up and the body is no longer able to help itself cool down. Body temperature must be brought down quickly; this is done with the application of cold water or by packing the victim in ice before transportation to a medical facility. Time is critical. If the victim is conscious, administer cool, salty water. *Do not give plain water* or allow medical personnel to give glucose intravenously. Athletes have been killed by the administration of plain water and sugar solutions before their electrolyte level had been raised. Do not assume that medical personnel know this.

The best treatment for heat stroke is prevention. It should never happen. Do not allow yourself or those cycling with you to become dehydrated. Eat proper foods to insure correct chemical balance (salt, potassium, and so on). Do not attempt strenuous activity without being in good condition, and allow your body to acclimatize to heat and humidity through mild physical activity in those conditions for about five to ten days. Do not assume you can perform physically in heat and humidity at the same level you do in cooler conditions. Even if you live in a hot climate, your body may not be acclimatized if you live and work with air conditioning. Approach hot-weather cycling gradually to allow maximum acclimation. In other words, don't do all of your riding on rollers in an air-conditioned room, then attempt 60 miles a day in the heat and humidity of the real world.

Another step toward prevention is to avoid antihistamines, belladonna products, alcohol or any other drug that inhibits the body's sweat mechanism. Illness accompanied by vomiting and diarrhea can seriously dehydrate your body; do not attempt to cycle in hot or humid conditions until fully recovered. At the least, carefully monitor your body's reactions so you can take preventive steps if necessary.

Dehydration

Dehydration is a primary causal factor in heat illnesses, and is the key to both serious and minor physical irritations experienced by long-distance cycle tourists. First, however, you must understand the function of fluids in vigorous exercise.

Your body cools itself during heavy exercise almost 100 percent through evaporation. It is totally dependent on its ability to sweat during exercise to keep its heat level within acceptable limits. Given favorable external conditions, available fluid is the prime requisite of your body's evaporative cooling system. Drinking enough fluids is the key factor in maintaining adequate fluid levels during exercise, especially in hot weather.

Do not let the temperature dictate your concern about fluid replacement. Many people assume there is nothing to

worry about until the thermometer reads above 90°F. Not so. Humidity is a much more positive indicator than temperature. Adequate fluid intake and possible heat illness should be of concern to you at any time the temperature is above 70°F. and the humidity is above 50 percent. Cooling can take place only if the sweat is able to evaporate from your skin. If your body or clothing is so saturated with sweat or the humidity is so high that the evaporation process is blocked, you are overloading your body's cooling mechanism and risking heat illness.

A positive feature of bicycle touring is that wind created by movement is usually sufficient to evaporate and cool the body. In tropical areas, however, or even in many areas of the United States where high humidity couples with high temperatures, danger exists even for the cyclist. The same conditions are created when you are cycling the same speed as your tail wind, creating a negative windchill factor in which the body is not cooled sufficiently.

You can't make assumptions about climate conditions because of this humidity factor. While cycling in the Mojave Desert, we experienced days when the temperature exceeded 110°F., yet due to low humidity and the evaporative breezes we generated by cycling, all we had to do was maintain adequate fluid levels for protection and even a degree of comfort. In the very high humidity but lower temperatures of the Midwest and East, however, we developed fatigue and symptoms of heat illness due to the lack of adequate evaporative cooling.

As temperature is not an accurate indicator of heat, thirst is not an accurate indicator of need for fluid. Studies have shown that by the time your body signals to replace fluid, you can already have a significant fluid deficit that cannot be made up while continuing exercise. So while exercising vigorously in hot weather you must drink before you become thirsty, at the rate of about 1 cup of fluid every 15 minutes. The body can lose as much as 1½ quarts (6 cups) of sweat in 1 hour, yet the body is capable of absorbing only about half that amount from the stomach in the same amount of time. If you are cycling vigorously in warm conditions over a long period of time, you can see how chronic dehydration develops.

When touring you must constantly replace fluid even if you are not thirsty. When touring in the western deserts of the United States during summer months, we find it necessary at times to rest more frequently than our usual one day out of six or seven. A day off every two or three days during extreme heat allows the body to recover enough fluid to insure against dehydration. During the rest periods and at the end of every cycling day, we drink fluids copiously and regularly to offset deficiencies while cycling. Not only does this reduce the potential for heat illness, but it also helps to overcome physical and mental fatigue, making for a much more enjoyable tour.

Some cyclists question desert touring in the first place, treating it as something to be avoided or performed at utmost speed. The desert is our favorite touring environment, offering open space, scenery and empty roads enough to last a lifetime. There is nothing like an early-morning ride in the desert to sharpen your senses and soothe your spirit. Fear of the unknown robs many riders of this joy. If you take the necessary safeguards to keep both your physical and mental processes in good condition through diet and fluid replacement, the desert can be yours to enjoy on your bicycle.

What is the best fluid to keep your body's reservoir filled to an adequate level? One fluid is far superior to all the rest — water. Nothing is as quickly absorbed from the stomach. Other fluids offer advantages such as electrolytes in athletic drinks and natural sugars in fruit juices, but water is best for the simple prevention of dehydration. The higher the amount of sugar in a particular drink (glucose, sucrose or fructose), the slower that liquid passes out of the stomach. Sugar is found in large amounts in carbonated drinks and should be avoided when rapid fluid replacement is necessary. In addition, carbonation can upset your stomach when exercising hard. Commercial electrolyte replacement drinks like Gatorade, ERG and Body Punch serve a purpose in replacing salts and giving energy through sugar, but at the risk of slow absorption and stomach upset.

Touring in a desert environment. The cyclist in long pants and long-sleeved shirt on the right is protected from the sun; the others risk sunburn.

Some people can drink gallons of commercial athletic drinks, others can't. Some can only tolerate them following heavy exercise, not during. If you use these drinks, use them to supplement your intake of water, not to replace it.

Avoid milk products entirely while exercising. Milk is very slow to pass out of the stomach and in the meantime blocks absorption of other liquids. Do not drink it while cycling under strenuous, hot conditions.

Our favorite touring drink besides water, is a weak orange-juice solution. We buy a small (6 oz.) can of frozen, unsweetened concentrate to mix in two water bottles, weaker than directions on the can suggest. If we are consuming more than a gallon of water a day, then we add just a pinch of salt (not enough to taste) to the orange juice. This makes a refreshing adjunct to our predominantly water intake and has the advantage of containing high amounts of potassium, which is necessary for the utilization of salt (sodium chloride) in

209

the body. It also contains fructose, a natural sugar that enters the blood at a slower rate than glucose. Fructose causes a steady, longer-lasting rise in blood sugar that does not trigger production of insulin, which causes a sugar crash as in drinks containing glucose. The weaker solution helps aid absorption by the body, but we do not use this instead of water, only in addition to it.

Salt is the subject of many myths passed around the athletic community. A lot of people firmly believe that salt tablets should be taken frequently during strenuous exercise in hot and humid weather. Our own reading, research and experience in this matter indicates that such is not the case. In fact, many times salt tablets are not only ineffective, but downright harmful.

Americans have an extremely high intake of salt, somewhere between 6-18 grams of sodium (salt is 40 percent sodium) per day according to *Dietary Goals for the United States.* This government study places the average normal requirement for sodium at about ¼ gram per day. This amount of sodium is supplied in an adequate diet with no addition of salt to food whatsoever.

What about the touring cyclist who is sweating profusely over a long period of time? Opinions differ widely. Some research indicates that no additional salt is needed if the diet is adequate in potassium (found in bananas, whole grains, nuts, oranges, dried fruit), which allows proper use of sodium by the body. Others say that additional salt is needed in the form of salt tablets by the exercising athlete. *Dietary Goals* quotes a passage from *Recommended Dietary Allowances* produced by the National Academy of Sciences:

Whenever more than a 4-liter intake of water is required to replace sweat loss, extra sodium chloride (salt) should be provided. The need will vary with sweating in the proportion of 2 grams sodium chloride (salt) per liter of extra water loss, and on the order of an extra 7 grams/day for persons doing heavy work under hot conditions. . . . In unadapted individuals, the need for additional water and salt may be somewhat higher than in fully acclimated persons.

The study points out the important balance between sodium and potassium and recommends that about 2½ grams of potassium should be provided in the diet each day. The recommended 7 grams of sodium chloride per day for persons doing heavy work under hot conditions is equal to only about 1½ teaspoons of salt, and that is only when about a gallon of water has been consumed.

People vary in their needs and capacities no less so when it comes to salt and potassium. Whether or not you take additional salt and potassium should be decided upon according to your own body's need for and tolerance of these substances; by the amount of salt normally provided in your diet; by the amount of salt you add to food; by the temperature and humidity during your exercise; by the amount you sweat; and by the amount and kind of fluids you consume.

Personally, we do not take salt tablets unless we are drinking more than a gallon of liquids per day or when we begin to feel unusually tired or lightheaded after a period of hard touring during hot and especially humid conditions.

Dr. Creig Hoyt, medical editor of *Bike World* magazine and one of the most experienced endurance bike riders in the United States, feels that salt replacement is necessary when engaged in really vigorous exercise extending over long periods of time (See "Beyond All Reasonable Limits" in the January 1976 issue of *Bike World*.) Dr. Hoyt has written a number of excellent articles on various medical and dietary aspects of cycling. If you are interested in these subjects look through issues from the last three or four years of *Bike World* to see what he has to say. Not only does he thoroughly research his topics, he experiences them as well.

If you decide to take additional salt, you can either add it to your food, drink athletic drinks that contain sodium, add a pinch of salt to your orange juice or take salt tablets. Salt tablets should be the type that have potassium added and a paraffin coating that slows the break-down in the stomach and small intestines, thereby lessening the chance for stomach upset. Whenever you take a salt tablet, drink plenty of water along with it. Otherwise the increased concentration of salt in the digestive tract will draw water from the blood to help dissolve it, cutting into the supply available for cooling the body and defeating your purpose. Drink at least one pint of water with each tablet, more if you can.

Adequate fluid and salt intake, proper rest, good diet and attention to protecting the body from exposure to the sun lessen your chances of developing heat illness. If you are traveling with a group, be aware of others' actions. Know when someone is overheated and acting confused or weak. By being aware of what can happen, you are helping to protect yourself and others from it actually happening.

Our detailed coverage of various health hazards associated with bicycle touring should not be taken as indicating that it is a dangerous activity. To the contrary, the very nature of touring makes it one of the most healthful things you can do for your body and your mind. There are dangers, of course, as there are dangers in crossing a street or taking a bath. Preparation, common sense and awareness of what is going on greatly disarm potential danger. You do not have to dwell on the hazards; rather be aware of their causes, circumvent those conditions whenever possible and know what to do if illness strikes so as to minimize its effect on you or those around you.

One of the great joys of bicycle touring is the self-reliance it fosters. Knowledge of and preparation for health hazards are part of the package. Don't leave your health up to fate more than is absolutely necessary. Take control and become an even more competent bicycle tourist.

Chapter Thirteen
Food for Touring

Unlike backpacking, bicycle touring does not require special, lightweight foods. Except for one compact emergency meal that should always be carried, food can be purchased fresh each day. The later in the day you buy it, the less you will have to be concerned about carrying it.

We didn't give much thought to food at the start of our touring career. Most people don't unless it's something they think about a lot anyway. The only change bicycle touring made in our eating habits was to increase our appetites as we exercised more. We always considered ourselves fairly up to date nutritionwise; Glenda spent as much time as our busy student lives and, later, our professions allowed trying to improve our eating habits and general levels of health.

Then our tours increased in length,

taking in hot summer deserts and strenuous, high mountain passes. We wondered why we were not performing physically at the level we thought ourselves capable of, but usually wrote it off to "not being in any hurry." Our bicycles were in top condition, well fitted with good equipment, and our physical conditioning was good by most standards. Yet we felt there was something missing, something holding us back from our full potential.

On the cross-country trip we enjoyed excellent health and well-being until just after lunch most days, then we were frequently wiped out by the mid-afternoon blahs that we attributed to heat, late hours the night before, too many hours on the road, any excuse we could think of except the right one — we weren't eating right.

On our return Tim found a copy of

Food for Fitness published by World Publications. It is a book about various aspects of health and diet especially for the athlete or the athletic. We don't consider ourselves athletes by any stretch of the imagination, but much of the information in the book is directed to anyone who feels that the average American diet isn't the answer to total health. Some chapters seemed pretty far-out to us at the time, some still do, but as a single source of information on getting control over your food intake it was a turning point for us.

We began to make some basic changes in our eating habits, not only while bicycle touring but in our everyday life. Over the years we have experimented with many popular notions that have since been forgotten and we incorporated others into our eating style that now seem so basic we can't remember eating any differently. The conclusion we have come to is that there is no such thing in our family as a touring diet. We eat on the road as we eat at home; the secret is that we have totally revamped our previous normal Ameri-

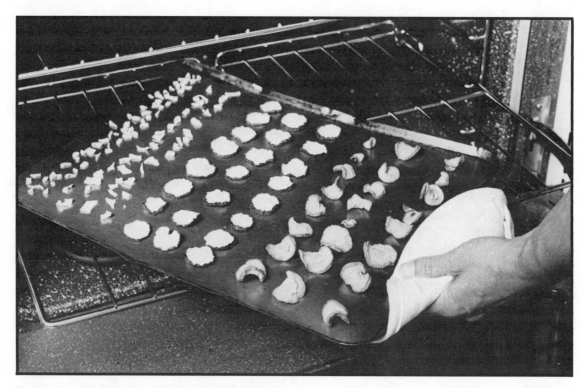

Drying food in advance is becoming an increasingly popular way for cyclists to have a dependable supply of nutritious, lightweight food in any environment.

can diet at home so that we should say instead that we eat at home as we eat on the road.

Changing Habits

What have been the outstanding changes? We have almost completely stopped eating white-flour products, substituting whole wheat commercial products or homemade breads and pastries when our life is conducive to Glenda spending the necessary time in the kitchen. She enjoys making much of her own food — bread, yogurt, noodles, cereals and sprouts — but we have not always had a kitchen or the time and tools needed to do it on a regular basis. But we are careful about the ingredients contained in commercial products.

We also make concerted efforts to cut our sugar consumption — not just white sugar but all sugars except those occurring in fruits and foods naturally. With a teenager in the house that is sometimes a desperate battle and we don't always do so well ourselves, but it is something we are constantly aware of and working toward.

Our protein consumption has dropped tremendously, especially meats and dairy products, and most of the latter are low-fat or nonfat milk products when we do have them. We are now working on cutting salt intake — we have a long way to go there but the battle lines are drawn. Cutting fat intake was fairly easy as we have never been

much for fat consumption. Our children have been raised on nonfat milk (for economic reasons before we knew otherwise) and now we find delightful the variety of foods available with low or unsaturated fats.

Moderation

The one thing that has kept us in the game this long is moderation. As we watch and worry we see generalized trends constantly emerging in a wide variety of studies by many differing organizations and individuals. When we decide that something needs changing, as when we decided to do away with white flour, we begin gradually and work through it over a long period — as much as a year or two. We find this necessary with children especially; you might be able to "cold turkey" some forbidden food if you are alone or not responsible for anyone else's eating habits, but a sure way to turn a perfectly normal child into an unrecognizable monster is to suddenly and without warning take away the sugar bowl, Twinkies, Captain Crunch and Pop Tarts (which are anything but tart). It can be done gradually so that as the supply dwindles so does the appetite for it. If fruit and yogurt are waiting in the refrigerator after school, there is hardly a glance in the cookie jar.

It takes time to develop new habits in food purchasing and preparation. Take it from Tim that a good way to seriously strain a marriage is to suddenly require a totally new look on the dining table. Go easy once you decide what changes to incorporate into your diet, especially if those changes affect others as preparers or partakers. A long bicycle tour is no place to make radical changes in your diet.

Why Bother?

Two of the most important sources for our personal approach to nutrition have been the excellent but all-too-few articles by Dr. Creig Hoyt, medical editor of *Bike World* magazine, and *Dietary Goals for the United States,* a study done by the U.S. Senate Select Committee on Nutrition and Human Needs. This study, issued in early 1977, was compiled by Senators Percy, Dole, Kennedy, Humphrey, Schweiker, McGovern and Zorinsky. The original edition urged people to eat considerably less meat, eggs and dairy products but came under such intense lobbying from the food industry that the senators were forced to publish a second, revised edition in late 1977. That one is available as *Dietary Goals for the United States — Second Edition,* Stock No. 052-070-04376-8 (83 pp.) for $2.30 from the U.S. Government Printing Office, Cap Street, Washington, DC 20401. Considering the amount of research, time and expense that went into it coupled with the whole business of politics, lobbying and compromise that modified it, the result is truly a moderate approach. Not some reactionary appeal or far-out health-food proposal, it is a middle-of-the-road approach to a very controversial subject. Yet, taken in the context of American eating habits, its findings seem truly radical. Let it speak for itself:

Too much fat, too much sugar, or salt, can be and are linked directly to heart disease, cancer, obesity, and stroke, among other killer diseases. In all, six of the ten leading causes of death in the United States have been linked to our diet.

Last year every man, woman and child in the United States consumed 125 pounds of fat, and 100 pounds of sugar. . . . In 1975, we drank on the average of 295 12-ounce cans of soda.

In the early 1900s almost 40 percent of our caloric intake came from fruit, vegetables and grain products. Today only a little more than 20 percent of calories comes from these sources.

With increasing affluence, we have also increased our body weights. Obesity is probably the most common and one of the most serious nutritional problems affecting the American public today. . . . Over 30 percent of all men between 50-59 are 20 percent overweight, and 60 percent are over 10 percent overweight. One-third of the population is overweight to a degree which has been shown to diminish life expectancy.

One in three men in the United States can be expected to die of heart disease or stroke before age 60 and one in six women. It is estimated that 25 million suffer from high blood pressure and that about 5 million are afflicted by diabetes mellitus.

Deaths from colon and breast cancer are uncommon in countries with diets low in animal and dairy fats.

Groups whose diets are low in fat and high in dietary fiber have much lower rates of cancer of the colon, rectum, breast, and uterus than comparable groups of Americans who consume more fat and less dietary fiber.

Compared with persons of normal weight, obese people have a higher risk of developing cancer, especially cancer of the uterus, breast, and gallbladder.

In the United States the number of cancer cases a year that appear to be related to diet are estimated to be 40 percent of the total incidence for males and about 60 percent of the total incidence for females.

Fat, sugar, salt, and white flour, all are present in far greater amounts than is necessary, desirable or reasonable in our diets. Anything affecting the national health to so great an extent could certainly affect your personal health and your ability to enjoy and benefit from bicycle touring. You can slip off a normally good diet while touring, either because of unavailability of proper foods or the convenience of what is available, and still get by OK. But you cannot make up for a lifetime of poor eating by eating properly while you are bicycle touring. That is why we are dealing here with your regular diet rather than your dietary needs for a few days or months while you are on tour.

A primary problem in changing dietary habits are those who control our diets and profit by that control. Wait, you say, only I decide what I eat. Maybe, but then maybe not. You learned eating habits as a child from your parents, from your peers, and from television or radio. By the extensive use of mass advertising on almost unlimited budgets coupled with the philosophy of "give them what they want only after the desire has been created," the food processing and distributing industries are in control of the vast majority of Americans' diets. When was the last time you heard a TV commercial for fresh vegetables, fruits or whole grains? *Dietary Goals* puts it this way:

Food production and processing is America's number one industry and medical care ranks number three. Nutrition is the common link between the two. Nutrition is a spectrum which runs from food production at one end to health at the other. . . . Demand for better nutrition could bring a halt to the expansion and/or use of less nutritious or so-called "empty calorie" or "junk" foods in the American diet, as well as make nutrition the rallying point of public demands for *better* health, as opposed to *more* medical care.

The question to be asked, therefore, is not why should we change our diet but why not? What are the risks associated with eating less meat, less fat, less saturated fat, less cholesterol, less sugar, less salt, and more fruits, vegetables, unsaturated fat and cereal products — especially whole-grain cereals. There are none that can be identified and important benefits can be expected. . . . Heart disease, cancer, diabetes and hypertension are the diseases that kill us. They are epidemic in our population. We cannot afford to temporize. We have an obligation to inform the public of the current state of knowledge and to assist the public in making the correct food choices. To do less is to avoid our responsibility.

Recommended Goals

So what are the "correct food choices" we, the public, should be informed about? Here is the abbreviated list of dietary goals recommended by the U.S. Senate Select Committee with our comments in parentheses.

U.S. Dietary Goals

1. To avoid overweight consume only as much energy (calories) as expended; if overweight, decrease energy intake and increase energy expenditure. (Bicycle touring will take care of that for you while increased consumption of unprocessed fruits, vegetables and whole grains will help curtail your initial caloric intake.)

2. Increase the consumption of complex carbohydrates and "naturally occurring" sugars from about 28 percent of energy intake to about 48 percent of energy intake. (When possible do not use sugars or processed food that is high in sugar such as barbecue coatings, catsup, relishes and processed cereals. Honey is better but not if used excessively.

3. Reduce the consumption of refined and processed sugars by about 45 percent to account for about 10 percent of total energy intake. (No carbonated soda whatsoever. This alone would bring about half the recommended reduction in sugar for the average American. Unsugared breakfast cereal would bring another substantial reduction.)

4. Reduce overall fat consumption from approximately 40 percent to about 30 percent of energy intake. (This is still a rather high-fat diet, but better than the American average.)

5. Reduce saturated-fat consumption to account for about 10 percent of total energy intake, and balance that with polyunsaturated and monounsaturated fats, which should account for about 10 percent

of energy intake each. (Substitute poultry and fish for red meat and pork and eat only low-fat or nonfat dairy products.)

6. Reduce cholesterol consumption to about 300 milligrams a day. (One egg has 250 mg., 3 oz. cooked shrimp have 130 mg., 3 oz. cooked liver have 370 mg. and 3 oz. brains have 1,700 mg.)

7. Limit the intake of sodium by reducing the intake of salt to about 5 grams a day. (One-quarter gr. per day is all that is needed for health and this is easily acquired through the most rigid nonsalt diet. One tablespoon of catsup and ten salted french fries equal about 25 percent of the suggested 5 gr.)

Think about your own diet and how it compares with these seven modest proposals. These are the recommendations of a Senate select committee; nothing radical or politically damaging ever came out of a Senate committee. All of these recommendations are compromises and should be taken, not with a grain of salt, but as a starting point for a good nutrition program.

In addition to the government's proposals, we suggest these as well:

1. Reduce protein consumption, especially red meats. The average American eats approximately 100 grams of protein a day. Protein is necessary for good health but more and more evidence is coming in that an oversupply of protein is having a serious deroga-tory effect on the health of the few developed nations that can indulge in this luxury. The body simply doesn't need enormous amounts of protein.

One cup of whole cow's milk contains 9 grams of protein, a cup of cottage cheese has 33 grams. Three ounces of ground beef have 21 grams, three ounces of chicken contain 20 grams and one cup of lima beans has 16 grams. Obviously, it doesn't take much to make up your daily allotment. Americans who consume meat three times a day with several glasses of milk and eggs for breakfast are getting vastly beyond the normal daily requirement for protein. Not only is that unhealthy, but in a world where two-thirds of the population is undernourished, it is also a crime.

2. As much as possible, eliminate consumption of white flour. Processed white flour (including so-called "unbleached" flour) acts like glue in your digestive system and some nutritionists think it actually retards the absorption of needed nutrients by thickly lining the walls of the intestinal tract. It is linked with the high percentage of lower-digestive-tract cancer in our society.

Although bran is popular today, the best way to get bran is as it grows on the wheat kernel, coupled with wheat germ from that same kernel. White-flour processing removes both bran and wheat germ. Why add them separately in your diet when it all comes together in whole wheat products? In addition to whole wheat breads, you can now buy many whole wheat products from muffins to pasta. Pie and pizza crusts are easy to make with whole wheat flour, or if you use package mixes, add bran and wheat germ to make up for what the manufacturer took out. This is one time when buying bran and wheat germ separately makes sense.

Read the ingredients on all flour products you buy and switch to those that use whole wheat. Let the store manager know your preference. Many products add whole wheat but the primary ingredient is white flour. Wheat flour and unbleached flour are still white flour; it must say whole wheat or graham flour to be the real thing.

3. Instead of reducing sugar consumption by 45 percent as the Senate committee recommends, we suggest working toward total restriction of processed sugar from your diet. As you restrict your sugar intake your taste and craving for sugar decreases, not in a week or even a month perhaps, but over a year or so. Americans are started on sugar from the first drink of infant formula. Just now we are beginning to cut sugar from baby foods (commercial), admitting it was put there for the mother's taste, not the baby's.

As you restrict your intake of sugar you will be shocked at the immensity of the task. Unsugared cereal is relatively easy to get used to with fresh fruit mixed into the cereal, but just try finding unsugared fruit juices, catsup, salad dressing or canned fruits or even some canned vegetables. When we banned white sugar from the house, we substi-

tuted brown sugar with a glorious feeling of nobility. Then we found that, instead of one step less in processing, brown sugar had one more with molasses added to the finished white sugar. We now know that sugar itself is the enemy in any form — even honey if used in excess. Honey is a good substitute in that it is easily digested and is sweeter tasting than a comparable amount of white sugar so you can use less. But try training your taste buds to relish the sweetness of a fresh carrot or a tree-ripened apple instead.

If you must eat out frequently or rely on convenience foods, at least don't add sugar (or salt) at the table. It offers nothing but empty calories and, like salt, is an acquired taste. Sugar has been linked to a number of our modern diseases, including hypoglycemia and hyperactivity in children.

4. Eat plain, unprocessed, fresh foods whenever possible. Simplify your eating habits; cut down on multicourse meals. The time spent on washing, peeling (when necessary) and cutting fresh fruits and vegetables is time saved from cooking them. Most people (including children) prefer vegetables raw to cooked if given a choice. Keep fresh fruits and vegetables ready to eat in your refrigerator. Soon you and your family will develop the habit of looking there first for quick, refreshing snacks.

Soups and salads have replaced the standard high-protein, high-starch meat/potato/bread meals we were raised on. Our personal preference for Mexican foods, especially homemade refried beans on corn tortillas topped with tomatoes, sprouts, guacamole (avocado) and yogurt dressing fits well into our primarily nonmeat, fresh and raw foods diet. Homemade breads or breadsticks make any simple soup and salad meal into something special.

The only way you can completely control the foods you eat is to grow and prepare everything yourself. Although many people have returned to that lifestyle, it is not possible or even desirable for many others. In a complex society where we work at one task full time in order to pay someone else to do other tasks for us, there simply is no possibility of control over primary sources. But you can develop new habits and control your consumption through educated beliefs and a lot of label reading. The food-processing industry makes billions of dollars at the expense of our health and pocketbook, with popular compliance and encouragement we might add. Even our rebellions are tempered; look at the "natural cereals" now available. Many contain as much as 50 percent sugar (usually brown sugar and honey), and we even hear the claim that sugar itself is OK because it is a natural product. Sawdust is natural too, but that doesn't mean it belongs in our food.

We are proposing that you add to your health for all activities, bicycle touring especially, through an educated, knowledgeable approach to eliminating from your diet foods that are known to be harmful to health — white flour, sugar, salt, excessive fat and excessive protein. It is difficult to talk about such changes without sounding fanatical, but for many of us such changes are radical and touch the very basics of our lives. You can make these changes without ever entering a "health food" store or reading a book on health foods. If you want more information, read *Food for Fitness, Dietary Goals for the United States* and *The Complete Book of Food and Nutrition* by J. I. Rodale. Your own interests and need for information will take you from there.

Eating on Tour

How does all this actually relate to bicycle touring? As with physical conditioning, if you have developed good habits before you ever roll out your front door, you will have few changes to make or worries about conditioning (or eating) on tour. But there is a little more to eating during an extended bicycle trip than maintaining your already excellent (we hope) food practices. Bicycle touring, since it relies on roadways, rarely takes you beyond access to a grocery store. Your only limitations to food preparation and consumption are how much of a kitchen you wish to carry and how you feel at the end of a day. Whereas fresh, raw foods are impractical or impossible on an extended backpack trip, you can tour for months with little or no change from your normal home diet.

When touring for any length of time keep your diet as simple and easy to digest as possible. You must have enough calories and nutrients to maintain a balanced diet and meet your energy requirements. The biggest difficulty is in eating enough. When exercising continually over long periods of time, you feel perpetual hunger. You are burning up a tremendous number of calories, yet dare not load your stomach to the point where the mere task of digestion robs your body of its ability to convert calories to muscular energy.

Rather than eating three heavy meals a day, give your body a steady, moderate supply of food that is easily digested and quickly converted to the task at hand. What foods are best? Carbohydrates (sugars and starches) provide almost all of the energy supplied to the body when exercising. They are converted and stored primarily in the liver in the form of glycogen. Glycogen is rapidly and efficiently burned by the body but must be continually replaced as a full supply can be used up in 50 miles of strenuous riding depending on the individual and the circumstances. When glycogen is depleted, a condition known as "hitting the wall" occurs at which point the person is simply unable to continue without rest and refueling.

Carbohydrates are a cheap, quick source of energy. They pass quickly through the digestive tract and continual "nibbling" will carry you to and beyond the 50-mile limit without stress (although you are unlikely to "hit the wall" at a leisurely touring pace). Foods high in carbohydrates should make up the bulk of your daily bicycling diet.

Fruits, nuts, whole wheat products — the list is endless and as varied as your imagination and appetite.

Some of the most avid cyclists we know are people who have a really profound love of eating, yet not one of them is fat. Of course taking in more than you put out adds pounds, but those who love riding as much as eating seem to find a happy, slim, healthy balance that lets them load their plates without calorie counting. Keep a supply of your favorite carbohydrates handy all day while you ride and eat at regular, brief intervals.

Fats can be converted to body energy, but the process is much slower than with carbohydrates. You can live off the "fat of the land" (body fat) to some extent but not enough to keep exercising comfortably. If you want to lose weight, limit your intake of calories and increase your amount of exercise, but recognize that it is rapid digestion of carbohydrates that keeps you going. As fat takes time to accumulate, so it takes time to dissolve; an extended bicycle tour is no time to go on a starvation diet.

Fat consumption should be severely limited while exercising due to the amount of time it takes to pass through the digestive tract. Fruit passes out of the stomach in as little as 30 minutes while a piece of meat can take up to four hours. Your body has better things to do than spend energy digesting a high-fat meal while you are trying to bicycle up a hill. Fatty foods like french fries and a hamburger at noon when your glycogen supply is depleted only insure an afternoon of the "blahs" as your body does battle with the fat when it should be easily digesting a load of carbohydrates for immediate use.

Protein (needed in small amounts to build and repair tissue) provides vitamins and regulates water and salt balance, but is of little value in the production of quick energy. Of greater concern to the touring cyclist is that most foods high in protein are either hard to digest (meat) or block the rapid absorption of fluids (dairy products). On long, hot days it is all too tempting to stop for cool, "refreshing" treats like ice cream, frozen yogurt or malts. We learned the hard way that such habits only bring on a down-and-out afternoon slump. We are not saying never indulge in such things, just don't make a habit of it.

What does all this mean in terms of actual foods? Go for high-carbohydrate foods and keep snacking steadily through your cycling day. Eat a moderate breakfast high in carbohydrates like cereals, fruit and breads. Resist the temptation to have a three-egg omelet with sausage or ham on the side. Snack on fruits throughout the day — never very hard to do on tour — but supplement them with nuts, seeds, and whole wheat or other grain crackers, breads or muffins.

If you must eat lunch, make it merely a sit-down version with the above snack foods. Most people are so used to big lunches of cheese, meat and egg products that it takes some doing to restrict noon intake to mostly carbohydrates, but the result is well worth the effort. Keep in mind, however, that even with the right foods eating too much has a sluggish effect on your afternoon energy level.

After your cycling day ends indulge your cravings; stuff yourself with protein and as many calories as you desire if you must. Concentrate on those proteins (vegetable over animal) that are more easily digested so your body can make maximum use of the time until you hit the road again, but if you have been seeing visions of hamburgers all day, or — for us — tortillas, beans and cheese, go ahead and indulge. Eat only enough protein to meet your daily needs; use high-carbohydrate foods to fill the vacant space in your middle.

If you are touring in hot and humid weather, be conscious of those foods that slow down absorption of liquids in the stomach. The evening is your most important reservoir-stocking time; don't sabotage your fluid replenishment efforts by loading up on high-fat foods or dairy products. Before dinner, drink several glasses of water or other fluids (nonalcoholic), which will pass into your system before a heavy meal. Clear soup as an appetizer is a good choice (see chapter twelve for types of fluids good for rehydration).

Avoid coffee. Even if you are a typical American coffee addict, try to cut down on consumption while bicycle touring. Aside from the many dubious aspects of coffee consumption, it is a diuretic that removes more fluid from your system than it puts in. If you must have some, save it for nighttime rather than morning to give yourself time to re-

build your fluid supply before getting back on your bicycle. Herb tea is good if you must have a hot drink in the morning; once on the road pedaling hard, however, you wake up pretty fast.

We hesitate to get involved in the

Sample Menu

(no cooking)	(some cooking)	(more cooking)

Breakfast

(no cooking)	(some cooking)	(more cooking)
Raw oat cereal w/almonds or Dry whole-grain cereal	Cooked whole-grain cereal w/raisins	Hash brown potatoes or Wh/wh pancakes w/honey or fruit
Nonfat or 2% milk	Nonfat or 2% milk	Poached egg
Bananas	Seasonal fruits	Cantaloupe or grapefruit
Wh/wh bread w/butter or w/peanut butter & honey	Bran muffins	V-8 juice
Orange juice	Grapefruit juice	Herb tea or Postum
	Herb tea	

During the Day

(no cooking)	(some cooking)	(more cooking)
Bananas, oranges, apples	Pineapple	Hot soup
Seasonal fruits	Melons	Hot cereals
Nuts, seeds (sunflower, chia, sesame)	Wh/wh crackers	Canned beans
Fruit juices (unsweetened)	Rice cakes w/honey	Sandwiches:
Dried fruit, nut & seed mixes	Applesauce (unsweetened)	avocado w/sprouts tomato w/cheese slices peanut butter/banana
Granola bars		

Dinner

(no cooking)	(some cooking)	(more cooking)
Reconstituted frozen juices (unsweetened)	Reconstituted frozen juices (unsweetened)	Hot soup
Raw vegetables and canned beans, drained	Green salad	Wh/wh pasta w/spaghetti sauce
Cold cuts & cottage cheese	Raw vegetables	Cooked vegetables
Wh/wh bread w/butter	Wh/wh macaroni & cheese	Raw vegetables/salad
Applesauce (unsweetened)	Yogurt w/fruit	Hot, garlic wh/wh muffins
Seasonal fruits or yogurt	Muffins, crackers or bread	Seasonal fruit or yogurt

224

vitamin controversy, but we personally take supplemental vitamins B and C because we have found them useful during our cross-country tour. In *Bike World* magazine, Dr. Creig Hoyt mentions the advantages of these vitamins in protecting against lip and mouth sores and in the possible alleviation of the mental strain he and his colleague experienced in the 750-mile Paris-Brest-Paris race. On long-distance tours the body undergoes considerable stress; we believe vitamins B and C help to minimize the negative effects of physical and mental strain.

Somewhere in most discussions of athletic diets the topic of carbohydrate loading comes up. This is a technique used by racers to increase the amount of stored glycogen in the liver so that "hitting the wall" (glycogen depletion) does not occur during highly strenuous, relatively short races (under three hours). Since bicycle tourists cycle for longer periods and at a more leisurely pace and are able to resupply carbohydrates while exercising, we feel carbohydrate loading is of no real value to the tourer. In fact, there are distinct hazards for some (see Dr. David L. Smith's excellent article "Carbohydrate Loading" in the April 1978 issue of *Bicycling* magazine).

Food preferences are such a highly individual matter that we hesitate to inject our own here other than as generalized recommendations for reduction of sugar, white flour, salt, protein and fats. But if you are still at a loss for ideas, following are three menus we use on tour, listed according to their degree of difficulty in preparation. You may find, as we sometimes do, that sugar intake increases while touring. We deal with this by spreading the sugar intake over a long period of time. We nibble from our "gorp" bags (peanuts, raisins and sunflower seeds) small amounts every hour rather than dumping a lot of sugar into our systems at once.

The main idea is to be flexible — whether it is in the expected amount of mileage for the day or in diet. Take what you can get, use what you have and most of all, enjoy every minute.

Chapter Fourteen
Maintenance for the Tourist

Self-sufficiency and independence are real pleasures of bicycle touring. You are free to travel almost without restriction and independent of our overly developed industrial complex. If you are camping as well, the only limitations are those you place on yourself coupled with your ability to take care of both yourself and your machine.

Many cyclists find the bicycle itself is the biggest stumbling block to total self-sufficiency. Although it is easy to ride, they feel inadequate in the maintenance and repair of their trusty steed. We won't say — as many writers do — that bicycle maintenance is a snap. It isn't, but we do believe that anyone with the time and motivation can master basic repair procedures and preventive maintenance.

The bicycle is a "simple" machine, but that is a relative statement. It is simple compared with automobiles and motorcycles, but is certainly more complicated than a rowboat or canoe. Its components are manufactured with close tolerances for minimum weight and efficiency of form. Precise adjustments are required. So the design is simple but adjustments must be exact.

Time is a key element in learning about and working on bikes. We are always surprised at how long it takes to perform the most basic repair and maintenance procedures. This might partially explain why there are so few really good bicycle shops in this country; to do the job right would price shops right out of business. Only those shops with highly skilled and fast repair personnel can give first-rate service at an affordable price. The majority of shops must perform mediocre repairs within the price structure or charge exorbitant rates for a time-consuming job.

This is where you come in with knowledge and skill in maintenance. You take the time to do the job right because it is your own bicycle. It seems a truism that the more dedicated the cyclists, the higher the maintenance level of their machines and the greater the likelihood that they do their own work.

OK. But you're all thumbs and don't have any desire to take up wrench and screwdriver? You are not alone. There are many serious riders who never get seriously involved in maintenance. But there is also a price paid in downtime while the bike is at a shop and in pocketbook trauma when retrieving it. It is possible to tour long distances without knowing how to fix a flat tire, but you are then of necessity dependent on others to transport you and your bike to a repair facility. Although it can mean long, expensive delays many tourers are willing to pay the price for the privilege of cycling without tools or the know-how to use them.

But why limit yourself? Anyone can master the emergency repairs we discuss in this chapter given the desire to do so, the patience to read for understanding and a bicycle for hands-on practice. If you wish more than an elementary understanding of repairs to get you back on the road, there are a number of excellent books available (see Bibliography). We cannot possibly and do not want to make this chapter a comprehensive repair manual. We do want you to come through it with good, basic skills in repairing problems that develop on the road and in preventing many of these problems from happening through adequate and knowledgeable preventive maintenance.

Get Acquainted with Your Bike

There is no substitute for intimate knowledge of your bicycle's parts and how they function. Basic to any educational process is mastery of vocabulary; this is no different in bicycle repair. Learn the name of each part of your bicycle so you recognize it and understand its use in repair terminology. Learn to call things by their correct name so you can talk with and listen to others without confusion. You should have picked up a great deal of "bike talk" by now through the various chapters of this book. If you want to refresh your memory, sit down in front of your bicycle with this book open to the parts diagram on page 9. Find each part, study it, and learn its name.

As you identify each component, study it to understand how it works. What really happens as you squeeze the brake levers? What holds the forks to the rest of the frame? What keeps the chain from going too far and falling off the chainwheel when you shift? Ask yourself questions, then find the answers even if they are not obvious at first. Use other books if necessary to help you understand the working of your bicycle, or get an interested friend to help you with this process. Get several friends together and go over your bicycles using the proper terminology. At some point you will come to understand how your bicycle propels you and your gear down the road, climbs hills and stops at stopping places. There are no shortcuts, but you should only have to do it once.

Keeping your bicycle clean is a great help in this learning process. Not only does it give you pride of ownership, but it prolongs the life of your bicycle and requires you to look closely at and handle each of the various components. As you gain experience, you will recognize when something isn't quite right. A frayed brake cable, a bent derailleur, or a worn brake pad cannot be ignored when you periodically go over your bike with the cleaning rag. You can then correct the problem before serious malfunction brings you to a halt somewhere out on the road. Many potential emergency road repairs are found and corrected in the comfort of a touring cyclist's garage or living room because of a regular, cleaning reconnaissance.

The amount of maintenance you actually perform is up to you. Many riders do just enough to get by, leaving major repairs and overhauls to the bike shop. Others are not happy unless they personally perform every normal and many intricate repairs. Where you fit in this spectrum depends on your access to tools and work space, and on your desire for self-reliance, but most of all it depends on whether you enjoy working on your bike.

The best way to master your machine for total confidence on tour is to completely dismantle and put it back together again. Yes, we mean the whole thing. With a good repair manual at your side, strip the frame of all components, take the crankset apart, remove the cluster from the rear wheel, dismantle the brakes, derailleurs, freewheel and everything else until it lies in an organized, but extensive panorama before you. With time, patience, your trusty manual, and perhaps some coaching from a friendly bike shop, you should be able to get it all back together. In the process you should have gained a thorough understanding of your bicycle.

Tim has done this at least once to each of our bikes and he does it prior to any really extensive tour. Glenda is going to do it this winter with our daughter, Kirsten, so they will feel confident when touring alone or away from the family bike mechanic (Tim).

Dismantling your bike requires a modest expenditure on tools but once you have the right ones, future maintenance and repair expenses will involve only replacement parts. If you are serious about biking, your investment in tools will be far cheaper in the long run than having maintenance done for you.

Preventive Maintenance and Safety Checks

Few problems on bicycles are due to simple, spontaneous component failure. Damage through accident, improper handling or neglect is the usual cause of parts' breaking or wearing out. Many repairs are avoided simply by treating the bicycle with care and respect. It is a fragile machine that takes incredible punishment while in operation but will cave in to neglect or careless handling when stopped, stored or transported.

Derailleurs get most of the stationary damage. Never lay a bicycle down on the derailleur side. If you don't use a kickstand, lean your bike against buildings or large, solid objects on the same side as the derailleur, so that if the bike falls that mechanism will not be damaged. When transporting your bike on its side inside a car, keep the derailleur side up. If two or more bikes are stacked on top of one another, put a piece of cardboard or other padding between them. Always shift the derailleurs to the inside (low gear) position so they are as protected as possible. Transporting bikes on rear-mounted car racks or inside vehicles takes a major toll on bike finish, derailleurs, cables and brakes. Always pack your bike carefully. The more you work on it, the more you will handle it gently.

Give your bike a safety check whenever you transport it and before every ride. Even if it is sequestered in your garage, things can happen to it. Small children have busy, curious hands and can do the oddest things to your bike — like flipping the quick-releases on your wheels. You can live a long time without surprises like that on a ride. A good garage storage method is to hang the bikes by one or both wheels from J hooks on the rafters, well out of harm's way.

A preride safety check does not have to be an elaborate, preflight shakedown. Once the habit is formed, it takes a minute or less. You are simply trying to find out if the vehicle is safe to ride. At first this check-over will require careful thought; you might even post a check list or keep one in your handlebar pack on a three-by-five-inch card. After a while, it becomes automatic and you are able to set off on a ride feeling confident about of your bicycle and its condition. A simple, quick routine check can prevent an accident or breakdown by revealing a problem area.

- Preride safety check:
- Press the tires with your thumb or use a gauge to check proper inflation.

229

- Squeeze the brake levers for adequate leverage and see if the brake-release mechanism is closed.
- Look at the brake blocks to insure that they meet the rim and are aligned. They should be evenly spaced from the rim when the lever is released.
- Check the front and rear wheel quick-releases to make sure they are tight and see that the wheels are centered in the frame.
- Spin each wheel to insure that nothing is catching in the spokes and that the tire casings are in good condition.

- Additional daily checks when touring:
- Squeeze each spoke using two hands around each wheel to squeeze two spokes at a time for uniform spoke tension and to be sure none are broken.
- Spin the wheels and sight between the brake blocks and the rims to make sure they do not wobble (out of true).
- Check racks for tightness.
- Make sure panniers and baggage are secure with no loose straps, cords, springs, or pieces of equipment that might become entangled in the wheel or chain.

Another preventive step is to listen to your bike while underway. Your bike usually indicates that things are going wrong by making unusual sounds. Be sure you know what your bike sounds like when it is working normally; when an uncommon sound appears, it is time to investigate. Sometime when you are near a well-traveled bike trail sit down beside it to listen for a few minutes. You will hear a variety of sounds from the well-tuned clicking of a freewheel to the clamor of bent derailleurs rubbing on chains, pedals hitting kickstands, chains squeaking for lack of oil, and various other sounds of undetermined but likely soon-to-be-discovered (by the owner) origin. Know how your bike sounds when in its best condition, then you have an edge on sounds that can mean trouble.

When an unusual sound occurs, try to isolate its origin. Does it stop when you stop pedaling? Then it is probably in the running gear — chain, crankset, cluster or pedals. Does it stop when you move the derailleurs slightly? It may have been only an offsetting of the derailleur when you shifted, or it could be a problem with the derailleur itself or the cable. Shift your weight around on the saddle or pull back hard on the handlebars to see if it is in the seatpost or handlebar stem. If the sound is steady, check your wheels for rubbing stays, rack bolts, fenders or other add-ons.

Once you have located the origin of the sound, you can do something about it if you feel confident in that aspect of repair, or you can take it to a qualified bike mechanic. You will be able to save his or her time, thus your money, by pointing out the area of the problem. Unusual sounds, especially in the running gear, frequently indicate a need for lubrication or overhaul of the complaining component. Don't put off the problem; small ones tend to grow into big ones that cause irreparable damage to costly parts. A little prevention goes a long way toward avoiding the need for massive cure.

Tools

The bicycle is a highly specialized machine requiring its own assortment of tools. Many general tools you already have or can easily get meet some requirements, tools such as adjustable wrenches, screwdrivers and pliers. For the most part, however, certain jobs can only be performed with certain tools. Tools are expensive, but cheaper in the long run than paying someone else to do the job for you. Many jobs can be done with a bare minimum of tools, but the more specialized your tools the faster and easier a particular task usually is. It seems one never has enough tools. Just ask Glenda! For every specialized tool in his workroom, Tim laments over two others he doesn't have.

It is no savings to purchase tools that are cheap or of poor quality. For safety's sake and in the interest of long-term economy, when you invest in a tool make it the best you can buy. Price is usually a good indicator if you have a difficult time recognizing quality. Most generalized tools are available at hard-ware and department stores, but special bicycle tools are found only in bike shops or mail-order houses that advertise in cycling publications. The Third Hand mail-order firm is the best single source of all types of bicycle tools. The address is in Appendix C. Their catalog leads you gently and long into the world of bicycle tools.

Don't purchase a preassembled tool kit if you are serious about doing your own repairs. See what you need as you go along to insure that the tool you buy is appropriate for the job at hand. The tool must fit the component on your bicycle; anything else is a total waste of money. Many bicycles use components of many other brands that require their own specialized tools. Always check the component carefully to make sure you are getting the right tool; take it to the shop with you if necessary. A complete tool list is found in Appendix B.

Flat Tires

Fixing flat tires is the most common road repair made by touring cyclists. Contrary to popular opinion, flats do not occur as punishment for deeply hidden sins. If you look at the conditions over which we run our light and tiny bicycle tires, it is surprising that there are not many more flats than there are. The curse of the American road is the broken, nonreturnable bottle, but we bring tire problems on ourselves with poor riding habits, lack of attention to the road surface, poor judgment when buying tires and neglect in keeping them properly inflated. If you continually have flat tires, look on the probable causes as a message to change your ways.

Some of the better bicycle tires have a potential for 3,000-5,000 miles or more. The Schwinn Le Tour tires we used on our cross-country tour were finally replaced after 5,000 miles. On the trip itself, using normal tubes, none of the Le Tours flattened. Our daughter crossed the country on a set of 24-inch wheels with Michelin Fifties tires that lasted 2,000 miles; she had two flats until we temporarily put in thorn-resistant tubes in Kansas, none thereafter.

Good tires (Schrader valve, clincher tires) make the difference when it comes to downtime for flats, longevity and good handling qualities on a loaded touring bicycle; many cycle tourists are undershod. For standard, paved roads we recommend 27 × 1¼-inch Schwinn Le Tours or Michelin High Speeds; Michelin Sports for heavy-duty wear and dirt or gravel roads; on excellent road surfaces with lighter loads you can get by on Specialized Bicycle Imports Touring Tires and Michelin Fifties among others.

Try to do without thorn-resistant tubes due to the deadening effect that their almost doubled weight has on wheel resilience. When necessary, don't hesitate to use them. Don't add one of those liquid solutions to the tube, either as a patch or as flat prevention. Some of these products work, at least on small holes, but the stuff will not hold

when a patch does become necessary. They also gum up a good tire gauge pretty fast if any gets inside.

Regularly check the pressure in your tires. High-pressure bicycle tires lose air naturally and rapidly compared with larger-volume automobile tires. Get into the habit of checking them every other day or so at home, every day on tour. This also alerts you to slow leaks. If there is a more than normal loss of pressure (a slow leak), check the valve core first (the spring-loaded device inside the valve stem that allows air to be inserted without loss). The valve core screws into the stem and sometimes works itself loose or malfunctions, allowing air to leak out.

Check your valve core by putting some spit on top of the stem. If a bubble appears or the spit is moved around, you have a leaky valve. Tighten the valve core with a valve core remover. If that doesn't stop the leak, replace it. Valve cores are available at bike shops, tire stores or gas stations. Always check the valve core first when you have a seemingly mysterious leak to save yourself the frustration of needlessly removing the entire tire.

If the valve core is not at fault, check the tire itself. Turn the wheel slowly looking for nails, pieces of glass, thorns, worn spots or torn casings that expose the tube. If you find something, don't remove it until you mark the spot with a pen, pencil or chalk. At this point you must decide whether you want to patch the tube by pulling it out from the

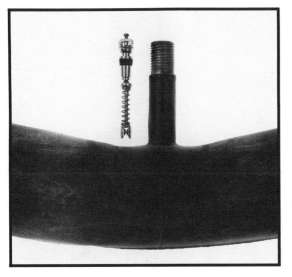

Schrader valve stem with core removed.

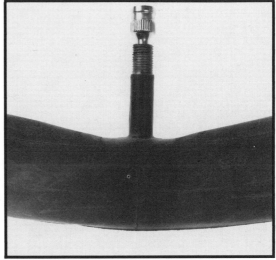

Valve core remover in place on the valve core.

rim at that point only with the wheel left on the bike, or whether you want to remove the wheel to take the tire and tube completely off the rim. We usually do the latter out of habit and because it lets us check the condition of the tire, tube, rim strip, rim and interior spoke ends. Practice both ways so you will have a real choice. Get your bike and perform the following procedure even if you don't have a flat. To do a partial removal, modify the steps accordingly.

When you can't find the source of the puncture or leak you must remove the entire wheel, tire and tube to search for it. Since an inflated tire is wider than the rim and the opening between the brake pads, first release the brakes to get the wheel and tire off. Locate and loosen the brake-release mechanism (found on most higher-priced bikes) ei-

ther on the brake lever itself, on the brake-cable hanger, or on the brake arms. This loosens the brake cable so that the brake blocks move apart to let the wheel out. If the tire is completely flat, or you wish to flatten it, you need not release the brakes; but don't pump the tire up when you replace the wheel.

To remove the wheel, release the quick-release levers or loosen the axle nuts. This lets you drop the front wheel away from the forks and proceed with the repair. The rear wheel is a little more complicated. First make sure the chain is on the smallest cog, then grasp the main body of the rear derailleur, pulling it back out of the way, so the wheel can fall from the dropouts. Once the wheel (either front or rear) is free, support the bike so it will not fall, or gently lay it out of the field of action. Do not lay the de-

233

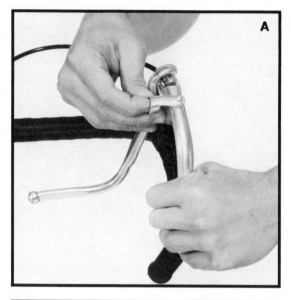

Three types of brake-release mechanisms: brake lever (A), cable hanger (B), and brake arms (C).

railleur, chain or crankset in the dirt.

You need tire irons to remove the tire from the wheel rim. These come in sets of two or three (under $2) and are made of steel or aluminum. They are inserted between the rim and tire to lift or pry the bead (lower edge of the tire) up and over the rim. When you buy a set, remove any rough or sharp edges left by the manufacturing process with a fine file or sandpaper. Don't use screwdrivers or other tools to remove tires; it is hard enough to keep from pinching holes in tubes using tire irons, let alone using anything not specifically designed for the task.

Expel all air from the tube, then pinch the tire with your fingers around the entire wheel so that it drops down into the deeper center section of the rim — this allows more slack for working with the tire. Insert one tire iron under one side of the tire, opposite from the

Quick-release lever on front wheel.

Solid axle and nut on front wheel.

valve stem, and lift the edge of the tire above and over the rim. You must put pressure on the iron to accomplish this, but once done the tire iron can be hooked to a spoke to hold it in place. There is a small groove at the end of the tire iron to hook onto the spoke. Place the second tire iron under the tire bead about four to six inches from the first, pulling it over the rim; then hook that iron to a spoke also. Now slide the first tire iron — after unhooking it — away from the second, prying the bead over the rim as you go. In most cases the bead will pop over the rim all the way around. If not, you will have to use a third iron as you did the first two, then move it around until the one side of the tire pops off.

Once one side of the tire is off the rim, the other side can usually be rolled

To facilitate removal of the rear wheel, pull rear derailleur back out of the way.

off with the hands. Be sure to start removing the tire on the side opposite the valve stem so it doesn't get bent or cut

235

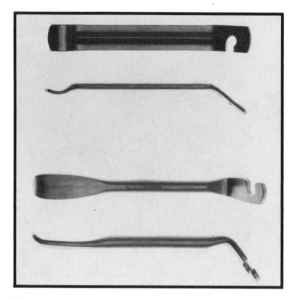

Two types of common tire irons (full and side views).

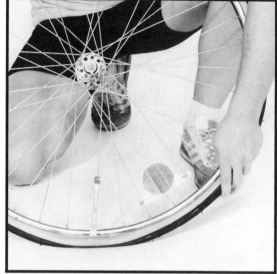

Removing a tire from the rim: Put the first tire iron in place under the bead of the tire and hook on a spoke (opposite valve stem).

in the removal process. If you can't force the second side off with your hands, use a tire iron to get it started. Be careful not to pinch the tube with the tire iron or you will have one more patch job to perform.

Push the valve stem through the hole in the rim being careful not to tear the rim strip (ribbonlike strip of material covering the spoke ends around the rim). You now have a tire/tube combination and can lay the wheel aside out of the dirt. If you marked the puncture, find that spot and remove the tube to expose the hole, marking it also. If not, inflate the tube slightly larger than life size, then pass it through your hands near your face and ear so you can hear or feel a leak. If this doesn't locate the

Put the second tire iron in place four to six inches from the first while using first to slide around the rim lifting the tire over rim.

leak, immerse the tube in a puddle or pan of water. As you rotate the tube watch for a rising string of bubbles coming from the puncture. Once you find the hole, mark it so you don't lose it. Check around the entire tube near the puncture; whatever punctured it might have gone through both layers, puncturing more than once. This might save considerable frustration later.

You are now ready to patch. Patch kits come in a wide variety of shapes and sizes; most will do the job. We like the German-made Tip-Top. It comes in two sizes, a smaller one for optimists, a larger one with more glue and patches for pessimists. The patches are very thin, sized just right for bike tubes, and have easily removed protective backings. The kit has a useless steel scraping device that you should replace with a piece of emery cloth or sandpaper, and the directions are in German. But one reads the directions only when all else fails anyway.

With your patch kit close by sit down with the tube wrapped around your knee and foot so there is slight tension on the portion of the tube over your knee with the hole centered and facing up. With your sandpaper gently scrape an area around the puncture a little larger than the patch will be. Don't touch the sanded area with your fingers; you sanded it to remove all traces of dirt and oil and to roughen the surface. Carefully get the backing started off the patch (don't remove it yet) being

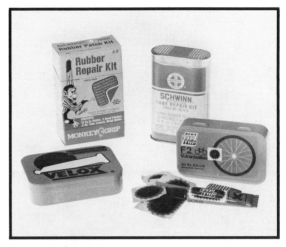

A variety of tire patch kits.

sure not to touch the face of it. Puncture the tip of your glue tube if it is a new one; at this point you might discover that your tube of glue has mysteriously lost its contents; this can happen even with new tubes. The tiniest hole allows the highly unstable glue to evaporate. We always carry a spare tube, sometimes two, available at better bike stores. Keep them inside the patch kit for maximum protection.

Place a dab of glue on the sanded area, smearing it evenly with the tip of your finger. Here is where the road forks; some cyclists allow the first coat to dry completely, add a second coat, then peel the backing off the patch and apply it (they are usually the ones with the larger patch kit too). Others put on a single coat of glue, allow it to almost dry (it gets an even, dull color), then apply the patch to the puncture area. Either

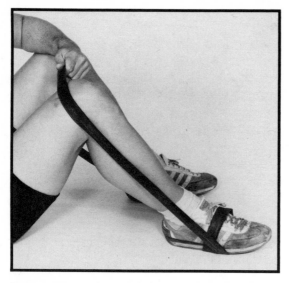

To maintain tension while patching a tube, sit on the ground with the inner tube wrapped around your foot and over the kneecap where the patch will be placed on the tube.

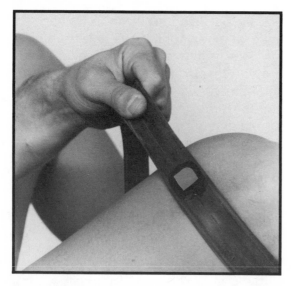

Here the patch is attached to the tube. A small area of glue should be visible around the entire edge of the patch. If you use too much glue as in the photograph, cover the area with talc.

way, there should be a little extra glue showing all the way around the edge of the patch.

Once the patch is on, rub hard with a smooth section of your tire iron or other tool to remove any air bubbles and insure good adhesion. Tip-Top patches have a transparent, plastic-skin covering the back of the patch. This can be removed but we leave it to act as a shield between exposed glue and the tire casing. If you remove it or are using another type of patch, dust any exposed glue with road dust or talc (baby powder useful for patches, seating tires and tiring seats carried in a 35 mm film canister). This keeps the new patch from sticking to the inner casing of the tire so the next time you remove the tube, the patch will stay on the tube rather than come off with the tire.

A patch should set up in a minute or two, depending on the weather; then you can unwind yourself from the tube. We usually wait three to five minutes more before putting everything back together to make sure the patch has set. Take the time to make sure as it will save you trouble in the long run.

While you are waiting for the patch to set up, check over your rim for sharp edges — especially where it is pieced together opposite the valve stem hole. (Do this as you practice at home — new rims can have surprisingly sharp protrusions.) Look also for protruding or nearly protruding spokes. During wheel truing spokes might be drawn up to the point where the end extends beyond the nipple head, spelling trouble for your tube unless corrected. On tour we carry a four-inch extra-slim tapered file (available at Sears) for filing spoke ends and rough edges that develop along the way.

Check the condition of the rim strip; make a note to buy a new one if it seems very worn. This strip protects your tube from spoke ends and nipple holes in box-design rims. Made of rubber or cloth tape, it can be replaced in an emergency with adhesive tape from your first-aid kit or even your handlebar tape.

After checking the rim, look over the tire to see if you can find what caused the puncture if you don't already know. Spread the tire sides and check the inner surface for protrusions or damage. Remove anything obvious, then run a rag around the inside of the tire to insure that you didn't miss anything; this will catch on small slivers of glass or nearly invisible thorns that you cannot see. You can do this with your fingers but make sure the first-aid kit is handy.

By now the patch should be dry. Pump up the tube just enough to give it some shape; don't blow it up big to "see if the patch will hold." It won't. Without the pressure of the tire on it, it will most likely peel off as the tube stretches beyond normal bounds. Put the tube in the tire and work the valve stem through the hole in the rim. Just start it through, making sure it has a straight shot. Don't tug on it. Put one side of the tire onto

View of a rim with rim strip removed showing a spoke extending through the nipple that needs filing down.

the rim, working around both sides beginning at the valve stem. Do the same for the second side. If you have trouble with this, put a little talc around the bead of the tire prior to slipping it over the rim. A bar of soap rubbed on the bead will do the same thing. Try to roll the tire on using the palms of your hands and a firm grip. If you can't possibly get it on, you will have to use a tire iron. Be careful not to pinch the tube between the iron and the rim. Some tires are difficult to fit on their rims; take your time, get tough and you'll make it.

Once the tire is on the rim, make sure the valve stem is straight in its hole before pumping to full inflation. Don't pull on it; as long as it is straight it will seat right. Inflate the tire to about 30 pounds, using a gauge until experience tells you how much air that is. Take off

Use the palms of your hands to roll the last section of the tire over the rim.

Two tires: the one on the right has a molded-in protrusion that guides the placement of the tire on the rim for correct alignment; the left tire does not have the molded-in guide. Without this, be careful to align tire properly on rim.

the pump and carefully sight around the edge of the tire on both sides next to the rim. Many tires have a rubber protrusion indicating where the tire should seat on the rim. Others might be sighted in by using a reference point on the tire. The object is to make sure the tire settles evenly into the rim on both sides. With only 30 pounds of pressure you can still work the tire with your hands if it is off at any point, using your thumbs and palms to even it up. Some tires pop right into place, others are difficult the first few times, others are damn hard every time. When you know everything is going properly, finish inflating the tire to its correct pressure.

Check the seating again. Some tires only seat under high pressure; if it

didn't at 30 pounds, it might as maximum pressure is reached. If it still doesn't seat at full pressure, let the air out, apply talc around the entire bead on both sides and try again. If you know ahead of time that your tires are difficult to seat, put the talc on to start with. If after all of this it still doesn't seat, your only choice is to ride slowly until you get to an air hose. Usually short, quick (careful!) blasts from a high-pressure hose will pop the bead into place.

Dealing with the front wheel is simply a matter of aligning the axle in the dropouts on the fork and tightening the

Wheel in rear triangle, chain on small cog, derailleur pulled back out of the way, and ready to place axle into dropouts.

Spring-loaded alignment (adjustment) screws on rear derailleur allow proper positioning.

quick-release or axle nut. On the rear wheel you have to contend with the chain and derailleur. Place the wheel in the rear triangle and put the chain on the outside (small) cog. Pull the derailleur out of the way to the rear and slip the axle into the dropouts. Make sure the tire fits between the brake blocks (released to allow the inflated tire through). If your bike has spring-loaded alignment screws in the dropouts, pull the wheel back until the axle bottoms out on the screws. If you don't have these, pull the wheel back until it reaches the end of the dropouts. With the wheel in place the bike will support itself (if you have a kickstand) but you aren't finished yet.

You must be sure the wheel, front or rear, is centered. First, turn the adjuster nut (on the opposite end of the quick-release) until you feel pressure on it with the quick-release open all the way. You want to be able to close the quick-release lever without feeling pressure until it is about two-thirds closed. When you have the proper adjustment on the adjuster nut and before closing the quick-release all the way, center the wheel in the forks (front) or between the chainstays (rear). Pull back firmly on the rear wheel, or pull up firmly on the front wheel to make sure you are in the dropouts all the way. Eye the wheel for centering before tightening the nut or the quick-release mechanism. For an exact fit, measure the distance between each

241

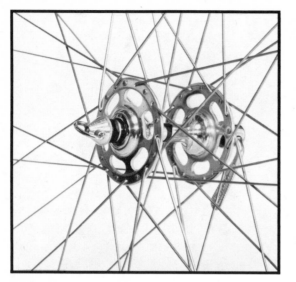

Adjuster nut on skewer, opposite quick-release lever on front wheel.

Practice it in the privacy of your home rather than having to do it for the first time under road conditions. Take your time, read the directions step by step, and practice until you can do it without the book. It is the only way you will gain mastery and have confidence when the inevitable happens out there on your tour.

You can save yourself half the hassle and time if you carry a spare tube and leave the patching until later. A spare tube also saves your day if your tube develops irreparable damage. Make sure, however, that you check both the rim and the tire for the cause of the original puncture before inserting your spare tube.

side of the rim and the fork blades or chainstays with a small ruler, turning the adjuster nut until you have it right. Then grab the fork or chainstay with your fingertips to close the quick-release the rest of the way, using the palm of your hands on the lever. Once closed, the position of the lever is not critical, but most cyclists have a preference. We like the lever parallel with the front fork or, in the rear, pointing up between the seatstay and the rack strut for as protected a position as possible. Experiment to see where you prefer yours.

Finally, tighten the brake release or you might be in for a real thrill on the next hill. There now, wasn't that easy? Murder to read about, even worse to write up, the actual process is quite simple once you have done it yourself.

Spoke Failure

Spoke breakage is second only to flats in frequency and is just as disabling to the touring cyclist. You might not break a spoke in thousands of miles of recreational riding but, under the stress of gear loaded on your bike for a tour, spokes are likely to protest by breaking. Replacing a broken spoke is not difficult if you take the time to learn the fundamentals before you have to do it cold turkey somewhere out on the road. Your best insurance is to remove a spoke from your bike according to the following directions, take it to a bike shop for some identical spares, then replace the spoke and always carry the spares with you on your bike. Once you have done this at home under ideal conditions, it no longer will be an insurmountable problem if you break a spoke on tour.

No matter how good the quality, spokes do not last forever. Their varied life spans depend on original quality, the precision used in lacing them onto the rim, the load carried on the bicycle, the riding skill of the cyclist, and the care taken to keep the wheel true through maintaining proper tension on the spokes. The latter is your best assurance of long life in your spokes, especially on factory wheels, which are marginal at best.

Wheel building is as much an art as it is a science. It takes a special knack and desire to do a good job. Don't trust your wheels to just anyone who says they can true or build them. If your wheels have been on your bike for several years, or if you regularly break spokes, it would be a good idea to have a new set built up before an extended tour. Never cut corners where your wheels are concerned. Find an experienced builder and use top-quality spokes and rims (see chapter two). Especially with new wheels, put some miles on with the load you plan to carry on your bike before starting out on tour.

Always have extra spokes on hand for emergencies whenever you ride. Tape them to your rear rack strut or somewhere on the frame out of the way. Even though we haven't broken a spoke since Tim has been building our wheels, we always carry at least five extras. Crossing the country Tim broke about a dozen spokes on his bike alone riding on factory-built wheels. After that we always have extras on hand even though we don't need them now.

You sometimes hear a sharp, metallic twang when a spoke breaks. You may notice a decided wobble in your wheel or find a broken spoke in your periodic safety check as you squeeze them together. If you do find one, do not continue to ride. You will pull the wheel farther and farther out of true, possibly ruining the whole wheel. Stop and replace the broken spoke immediately.

If the broken spoke is on the front wheel or on the noncluster side of the rear wheel, you needn't remove the wheel to replace the spoke. However, if it is on the cluster side of the rear wheel, the process is more complicated. Let's deal with the easy ones first. If you have the right length of spoke with identical nipple threads (this is why you need identical spares) you don't have to remove the tire. If the spoke threads are rusted into the nipple, the nipple threads are stripped, the nipple is rounded off so it won't accept the spoke wrench, or the replacement spoke is too long the tire, tube and rim strip must be removed to perform the repair. A spoke that is too long has to be clipped off and filed down where it protrudes through the rim so it won't damage the tube.

Most spokes break at the curved "head" near the hub flange. To remove a broken spoke loosen the nipple with a

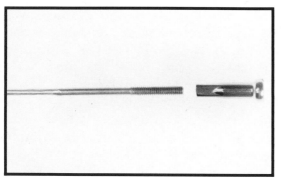

Spoke lying flat with nipple almost touching threaded end. Spare spoke thread must match threading of your wheel nipple for easy replacement.

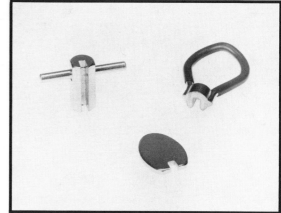

A variety of spoke wrenches.

clockwise motion (it seems backward but isn't). If this is impossible by hand, hold the spoke with pliers while loosening the nipple with the spoke wrench. Spoke wrenches come in many shapes and sizes so be sure you have the proper wrench before you need it. Most 10-speeds use Japanese or European spokes; the Japanese type requires a slightly larger wrench. Some wrenches work on both but you run the risk of rounding off the nipples with an ill-fitting wrench. Prices run from 50¢ to $3.50; the more expensive Park model is the best of the lot. Keep away from combination types unless you have many different kinds of spoked vehicles and need one tool to fit all.

The head of the broken spoke (in the hub flange) will probably have dropped out; if not, pull it out. Note which side of the flange the head is on. If it is missing you can determine this by

the neighboring spokes. They are staggered with heads on alternating sides. Put the new spoke into the flange hole on the correct side. This is tricky and may require bending the spoke a little. Don't worry, bending it a little won't hurt.

Once the spoke is in the hub, lace it in a corresponding pattern to the nipple in the rim. You can determine the pattern by looking closely at the other spokes. Each spoke crosses another either three or four times on the trip from the hub to the rim. On the final crossing the spoke is usually laced just the opposite of the previous crossings; for example, if the spoke passes under the first two or three spokes, it will pass over the last spoke. If you are not checking this as you read, look at the spoke pattern on your wheel now to make sure that you understand what we are saying.

When you reach the rim, catch the

244

Hub showing staggered pattern of spoke heads.

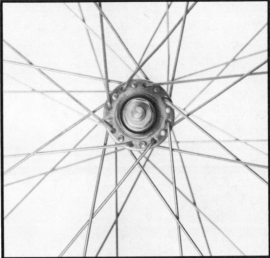

Spokes crossing one another on trip from hub to rim.

new spoke in the nipple turning it counterclockwise to tighten. Start the tightening with your fingers, then increase the tension with your spoke wrench. Continue tightening until it feels similar to neighboring spokes. Squeeze pairs of spokes with your fingers to determine the correct tension.

Quick! Before you lose sight of the one you replaced, mark the sidewall of your tire by it with a pen or pencil so you can find it later — even after 20 dirty miles. You need to keep checking for wheel trueness and spoke tension, more easily done if you know which spoke is the new one.

When you have the right tension, spin the wheel while sighting between the rim and the brake blocks to see what happens when the new spoke

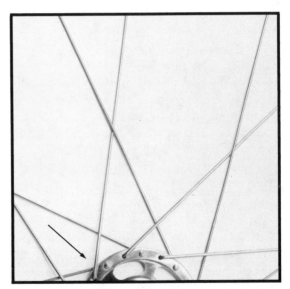

Arrow indicates first spoke crossing. Note that this spoke crosses over the other spoke and also crosses over the next spoke, but crosses under the third spoke on trip from hub to rim.

245

passes through. Does the rim stay in the same position relative to the blocks? If so, you are in good shape. If your wheel was originally in true and you did not ride on it after breaking the spoke, your wheel will likely remain true if you put equal tension on the new spoke.

On the other hand, if your rim jumps to one side as it passes through the blocks you have some adjusting to do. It's important here not to get in a rush. You might end up doing more harm than good. Spokes must be worked in pairs. The wheel is in a state of balanced tension held true by the pull of opposing spokes. Tightening or loosening the spokes on only one side of the wheel interferes with that balance. If you want to move the rim to the right, loosen the spokes to the left of the affected area, then tighten the spokes on the right by the same amount. Work cautiously and slowly; generally a quarter- to a half-turn on the nipple is enough to produce results. To monitor your progress sight on the rim between the brake pads and spin the wheel as you perform each adjustment. You should at least be able to bring the wheel close enough to true that you can ride it to a bike shop for final adjustment. This type of adjustment is only necessary when your wheel has moved out of true for some reason; it is not usually necessary for a simple on-the-road spoke replacement.

Once you have replaced a spoke you will see that it is not particularly difficult. But we have been talking only

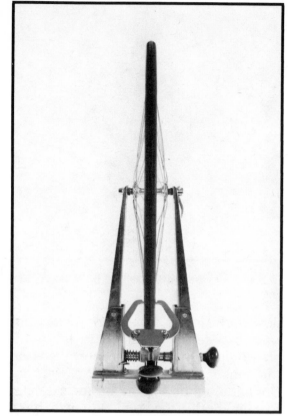

Truing stand helps considerably, but is not necessary for minimum wheel truing.

about broken spokes on the front wheel or on the noncluster side of the rear wheel. If you want to shake up touring cyclists, just tell them they broke a spoke on the cluster side of the rear wheel. Actually, fixing the spoke is as easy as we have described; the difficulty is in getting to it.

Look at your rear wheel where the spokes meet the hub flange on the cluster side. The rear cogs (cluster) extend beyond the flange, preventing the lac-

You cannot replace a spoke on the cluster side of the rear wheel without removing cluster from hub.

A variety of freewheel-remover tools.

ing of a spoke through the hub without removing the cluster first. Therein lies the problem. As you pedal the chain exerts constant pull on the cluster, tightening the freewheel onto the rear hub. Because of this, removing the freewheel with the attached cluster takes a good deal of leverage, more than is possible with tools normally carried by a cyclist.

But you can be sure that someday you will break a spoke on the cluster side, so practice the repair now and get rid of the fear that always accompanies the unknown. First, you need a freewheel-remover tool. Be sure you have the right one since each brand of freewheel has its own special tool. Prices are reasonable ($1.25-$5.00) and the tool is small enough to carry in your kit. The difficulty is in how to grip the freewheel-remover tool so you can exert the leverage needed to turn it. Your choices are a small hand tool light enough to carry on tour, a 12-inch or larger adjustable wrench, or a bench vise. These last two are too big to carry on tour but are available at most gas stations or farms. We made do with these sources until recently. Now we carry a Bendix 7/8-inch cone adjustment tool, which Tim enlarged (23 mm) to fit the Sun Tour (Maeda 888) freewheel-remover tool. Other freewheels require other tools but the Phil Wood Atom-style remover takes the 7/8-inch Bendix without modification. The Bendix is relatively short and light enough to be packed along; in most instances it readily removes the freewheel, although sometimes a rock used as a hammer on the Bendix handle is needed to break things loose at the start. The Bendix is an emergency tool; we opt for a 12-inch wrench or vise when available.

To remove your freewheel, first re-

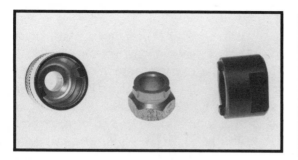

Notched-type freewheel removers.

Notched-type freewheel remover being held against freewheel with quick-release mechanism.

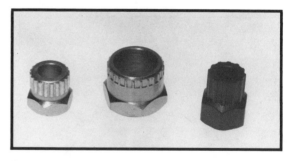

Splined-type freewheel removers do not require use of quick-release to hold in place.

move the rear wheel as explained in the section on flat tires. At the same time remove the quick-release skewer if you have one. For the notched-type of free-wheel-remover tool (Sun Tour, Old Regina, Cyclo, Simplex, Maillard and others), insert the quick-release skewer back through the axle, position the free-wheel-remover tool on the freewheel, then put the adjusting nut on the skewer. Turn the nut snug against the freewheel tool but not tight. This holds the tool in the notches of the freewheel. If you have the splined-type of free-wheel (Shimano, Atom, Zeus, Schwinn Approved, Normandy and others), you won't need to use the quick-release to hold the freewheel tool.

Put the flat sides of the freewheel tool with your attached wheel into a vise or grab the wheel with an adjustable wrench or your modified Bendix tool. If you are using a vise, twist the tire and rim counterclockwise. If you are using a wrench or the Bendix tool carefully turn counterclockwise, being sure to keep the wrench parallel to the wheel as you apply pressure. Don't give up, you will

be amazed at how much pressure it takes to break things loose. This is especially true if the manufacturer or bike shop that originally assembled your bike did not grease the freewheel and hub threads.

As soon as the freewheel breaks loose, STOP. You must remove the quick-release if you have one. Loosen the adjusting nut or just remove the skewer so the freewheel can be spun off the hub. Now the cluster is out of the way and you have clear access to the spoke holes on the cluster side of the rear hub.

This procedure is only necessary if you break a spoke on the cluster side, but unfortunately many breaks occur there due to the almost 40 percent greater tension on the spokes because of the wheel dish (offsetting of the hub on the rear wheel to make room for the freewheel yet allowing the tire to run centered in the frame). Your best preparations are to have done a cluster-side spoke replacement at least once and to grease your freewheel and hub threads to ease future removals.

An alternative method for replacing spokes on the cluster side without removal of the freewheel is to remove each cog from the cluster. Ian Hibbel, the world's greatest cycle tourer, carries a brass punch that he uses with a rock to loosen the cogs to unscrew them from the freewheel. Another variation is to carry six to eight inches of chain and a small pair of Vise-Grip pliers (a commercial chain-type cog remover is available but is too large and heavy for touring); you wrap the chain around the cog and pull with the Vise-Grips to twist the cog off. You may only have to unscrew the first two cogs, the rest may slip off depending on the make of freewheel. Some require unscrewing of all five. Both methods require that the

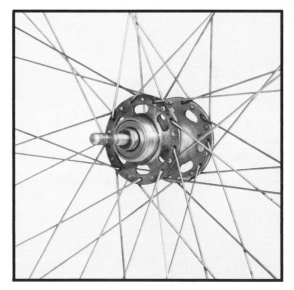

Rear hub with cluster removed allowing access to spokes.

wheel be left on the bicycle and a crankarm strapped securely to the seat tube with a toe strap until the cogs are broken loose. If you meet this emergency in Upper Volta and the nearest freewheel remover is in Egypt, Hibbel's trick would come in handy. There is no harm in knowing the various methods and even trying them — it can only boost your confidence.

As a last-ditch effort, the broken spoke could be replaced with a hybrid. Using an extra-long spoke, cut off the head, then bend that same end to form a J hook. Hook this through the spoke hole in the hub flange, lace to the rim in the proper pattern, and proceed on your way. This is suitable only in an emergency; it is better to do the job

249

right in the first place so you can get on with enjoying your tour.

Brakes

Although their efficiency leaves something to be desired, especially when wet, brakes on a bike seldom fail spontaneously. They are a reliable component if given regular preventive maintenance.

Caliper-brake stopping power on a loaded touring bike is marginal at best so anything you can do to increase it is extremely important. Think about a 150-pound tourist riding a 30-pound bicycle with 30 pounds of gear; that is 210 pounds going 25 mph or more downhill. Now look at the little brake pads and thin cables that make up your braking system. When the time comes, especially in a panic situation, you had better be sure those brakes are in top working order and excellent condition.

Although brake design has some effect on your ability to put maximum force on the brake pads, the most critical aspect is the amount of lever travel. If your brake pads are farther from the rim than they should be, you are losing stopping power. If the pads are worn, dirty and imbedded with foreign material, you are losing stopping power. If the pads are out of adjustment so that only part of their surface area makes contact with the rim, you are losing stopping power. Can you afford it?

Check the condition of your brake pads. Are they worn past the grooves (not all pads have grooves, be sure yours did before you panic)? Press hard into the edge of the pad with your fingernail. Does it sink in slightly or does it feel as though you are pressing on wood? Most brake pads need replacement due to old age rather than actual wear. As the pad ages, especially when exposed to sunshine, it hardens so much that it loses much of its frictional quality. To keep your pads in good condition, clean them occasionally with a toothbrush dipped in alcohol or other mild cleaning agent.

When your pads need to be replaced, you will discover a wide variety to choose from at most bike shops. We haven't had the opportunity to test many of them, so cannot speak authoritatively on their individual merits. Of the newer, exotic pads available there are many manufacturer's claims but the only one we have heard fairly consistent positive reports about is the Mathauser brake block. At around $15 per set we haven't felt the necessity to switch, but if you have braking problems or use caliper brakes on a tandem, you might try them out. Our personal choice through the years is Weinmann Vainqueur, a pad with four large segments on the face. A full set (four) can be had for about $3 — a good price for a good product.

You need certain tools to replace your brake pads. A 6-inch adjustable (crescent) wrench is the most all-around bicycle tool. There is a trend toward more allen head bolts (bolts with a small hole for insertion of an allen wrench); check your bike for nuts and bolts versus allen bolts to see if you should invest in a high-quality, 6-inch adjustable wrench ($4-$7). If you plan to take full charge of your brake maintenance, get a set of brake wrenches. These come in sets of two, usually a 10-millimeter open end/8-millimeter box end and a 9-millimeter box end/10-millimeter box end. The best set we know is the Dia-Compe, which is a joy to use around brake bolts and frame members due to its bent ends ($6 and up).

When replacing brake blocks or pads, make absolutely sure that the enclosed metal portion that holds the pad in place is to the front of the bike. Some brake blocks have one end uncovered for ease in replacing the pad; never put that uncovered end forward or you might see your brake pad preceding your bike downhill the first time you put on the brakes hard.

To replace the pads, remove the brake blocks from the yoke arms by undoing the retainer nut, then push out the old pads and put in the new. Much easier and what we recommend is to replace the whole block. When you put the brake blocks back in the yokes, make sure they are aligned so the pads are of equal distance from the rims. To do this, loosen the nut that holds the entire brake unit on the frame just enough so that you can pivot the brake system until it's aligned. Another way to do this is to first make sure the nut holding the brake on the frame is snug — using a

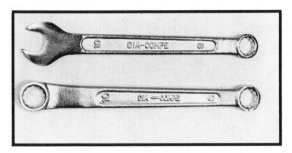

Specialized brake-adjusting tool.

Brake blocks showing open and closed ends on shoes.

$\frac{3}{16}$-inch solid line punch (or a long $\frac{3}{16}$- or $\frac{1}{4}$-inch bolt) against the steel spring on each side of the brake — tap it until the brake system shifts to a centered position over the rim. Don't put the punch against the brake yokes as this will scar them. Centerpull brakes can be centered using the punch against the springs or by using a 4- to 6-inch piece of wooden dowel against the yokes themselves without damage. Sidepull brakes must be centered with a punch on the springs; some sidepulls have a narrow slot near the main bolt attachment where you can straighten them

Top view of brake pads close to and with equal distance between pads and rim.

When adjusting brakes with 3/16-inch solid line punch, make sure the punch is against the steel spring, rather than against the alloy portion of the brake.

with a narrow, 10-millimeter open-end wrench.

When the brake is centered so there is equal space between the pads and the rim adjust the pads vertically to sit on the rim properly. To do this, squeeze the brake lever so the pad is firmly on the rim. It should be just down (1/32-1/16 inch) from the top edge of the rim. If not, loosen the nut that holds the block in the yoke and move the block to the right position. While squeezing the brake lever, tighten the nut by hand. Then release the lever, grip the brake block carefully (don't move it) with your adjustable wrench and firmly tighten the nut with a 10-millimeter wrench.

Once the pads are perfectly aligned both laterally and vertically, take up any slack in the brake cable so the brake shoes are as close to the rim as the trueness of the wheel will allow. If your wheels are out of true by more than 1/8 inch you should true your wheels or have it done before you adjust the brake cable.

A friend will do but a third hand tool makes adjusting the brake cable much easier. This inexpensive spring-steel tool compresses the pads to the rims allowing you to use both hands to take up the cable. Third hand tools for home use cost $1.50-$2.50. Using the tool or someone's hands compress the pads against the rims; check to see that your brake-release mechanism is closed, then look for the cable-tension adjuster either on the yoke of sidepulls, on the

A properly adjusted brake block has a pad $\frac{1}{32}$-$\frac{1}{16}$ inch down from the top of rim.

While tightening the brake block nut with a ten-millimeter brake wrench, hold the brake shoe (metal part) with a six-inch adjustable wrench.

cable hanger assembly of centerpulls, or on the brake lever housing of some models. If the cable is only slightly loose, take up the slack by unscrewing (raising) the adjuster. If the adjuster is not already screwed to its maximum po-

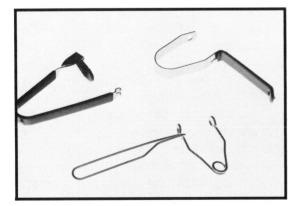

A variety of third hand tools.

sition, thus lengthening the cable housing that in turn puts more tension on the cable, you have some room to maneuver here. The adjuster sometimes has a small barrel nut to lock the adjuster nut in place; be sure to run it all the way down after making your cable housing adjustment.

If the brake cable is slack with the adjuster nut or nuts at maximum, prepare to work on the cable itself — but first put the adjuster nut at its lowest position so it can be used for minor adjustments in the future. With either your adjustable wrench or your brake tools, loosen the nut on the pinch bolt that holds the cable in place on the brake itself (sidepulls) or above the brake (centerpulls). Loosen this nut until the

Cable-tension adjusters found on: brake lever (Mafac type) (A), cable hanger assembly on centerpulls (B), brake arm of sidepulls (C).

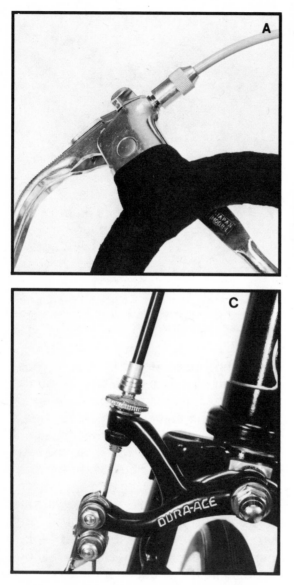

nut. Pliers are useful for pulling on the cable while tightening the nut, but not necessary. If you have done all this right, when you release the brake pads they should rest as close to the rim as possible — without touching — as the wheel turns. If they are touching the rims you will have to loosen the cable a fraction, but this is unlikely. Don't be discouraged if it takes you several trys to get it right; once accomplished, exact brake adjustment is yours for the doing.

Periodic brake maintenance includes oiling of the pivot points. If you ride with fenders and keep your bike clean, you should oil your brakes every three or four months. Dirty, dusty conditions and bad weather dictate more frequent lubrication.

cable can be pulled through the hole in the pinch bolt to tighten it. When you have pulled the slack out of the cable (remember to hold the brake pads firmly against the rims), tighten the pinch-bolt

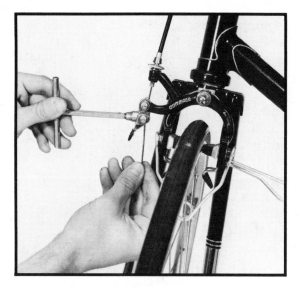

Third hand tool in place, cable-tension adjuster screwed down, brake wrench on pinch nut, and other hand pulling cable to adjust length.

When your wheels are off your bike (now if you are following our advice for hands-on practice), squeeze the brake arms together with your hand then release them. Observe and feel how they open and close. The movement should be smooth and precise; if not, several drops of oil in the pivot point of the yoke arms should solve the problem. First, clean the area to be oiled with a rag, then drop the oil in carefully. Wipe off excess oil.

When in doubt, the tendency is to spray everything with some sort of fine oil spray. This is not the way to oil a bicycle. Oil does more harm than good if sprayed indiscriminately; it attracts dirt. Most fine sprays like WD-40 are not thick enough to lubricate adequately.

They penetrate and loosen stuck mechanisms but leave no long-lasting residue. A general rule is to oil only at the point of friction. Use an oil with adequate holding properties.

The type of oil is up to you. On brakes and derailleurs, any medium-weight or lightweight oil is fine; 20-weight engine oil, LPS-3 (not LPS-1 or WD-40), special bicycle oil, Sturmey-Archer or other oil of a petroleum base. Vegetable oils tend to gum things up. Tri-Flon is also excellent if not sprayed. Dri-Slide manufactures a small, plastic applicator with a needlelike tip that is a great boon in bicycle maintenance. It puts the oil (one of the above or Dri-Slide) only where you need it one drop at a time. There is no overspray, no mess, no fumbling to fit large applicators in tight spots. Ask for an applicator at the shop where Dri-Slide products are handled. This is the best method of carrying oil on tour we have found yet. It is compact, light and does not leak (under $2). A light spray like WD-40 or LPS-1 is good for squeaky brake levers if you want to loosen the action without leaving a mess. Squirt a short spray inside the lever near the pivot bolt.

Once every six months to a year, depending on the type and amount of cycling you do, lubricate your brake cables unless you have Teflon-lined housings, which should not be lubricated. Loosen the nut on the pinch bolt to free the cable end, then strip it out of its housing. Clean the cable with a rag, then lubricate with grease, paraffin, oil

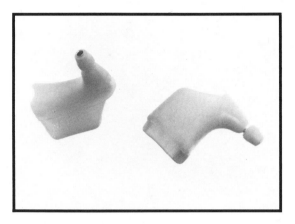

Gum-rubber brake hoods.

eventually tear apart if not cared for. Intense sun and heavy air pollution also take their toll. The best protection is a product called Armor-All. Spray a little on a rag and work it into the brake hoods every month or so. It is good also for the gum sidewalls of your tires but be careful to keep it off the rims.

Drive Line Maintenance

or one of the special bicycle-lubrication products. If you use a spray, squirt into the housing also.

Brake (and derailleur) cables need replacing every two years or so depending on where you ride and how much. Look for broken wire strands and other signs of wear around the pinch bolts and where the cable enters and exits the housing. When you replace cables buy the best you can. Campagnolo, Elephant Brand, Wescon, Rixe, Schwinn and Sun Tour are some of the best. Don't try to save a few cents with cheap, thin cables. Get thicker cables with a woven pattern instead of a simple twisting of wire strands. Near the ocean, stainless steel cables are a wise investment for protection from corrosion.

One last area of brake maintenance is caring for the gum-rubber brake hoods (covers) on your brake levers. You can add these yourself; they are stock on some bikes. These tend to get hard and stiff like your brake pads and

As a touring cyclist you should be competent in maintaining and repairing those areas where the chain has contact: chainwheels, cogs, jockey (idler) wheels on the rear derailleur, and the chain itself. Keep the entire drive line as clean as possible to increase efficiency and prolong the life of the various components. The chain must be lubricated enough to keep friction to a minimum but not so much as to attract dirt.

Some cyclists go for months without needing to lubricate their chains, others touring or riding 50-100 miles a day should lubricate their chains weekly. You know your chain needs attention when it talks back to you. If you hear even one squeak in one link, get out the oil. Riding in the rain assures the need for a lube job; as you gain experience you will know when to oil by the sound of the chain.

The right lubricating medium for chains is a topic of much interest and controversy in cycling circles. Every-

256

thing from yak fat to paraffin and hot motor oil has its proponent. Until several years ago we used various spray chain-lube products developed for both bicycles and motorcycles, finally settling on LPS-3. They all did the job but picked up plenty of dust and dirt from the road. The whole idea is for the outside of the chain to be as clean and dry as possible while the inside rolling surfaces are lubricated enough to resist friction and wear.

We now use Dri-Slide, one of the wet-solution propellants that dries on contact leaving a film of molybdenum disulfide (graphite-like), highly resistant to friction and water penetration. There is no exterior coating to attract dirt. It is available in both squirt cans and aerosol sprays; spraying is easier but some prefer to apply it drop by drop to each link of chain.

A variety of chain tools.

To keep your chain in top condition periodically remove, clean and lubricate it. You can do it now even if your bike is brand-new both for practice and to get started right. You will need a chain tool ($3-$7). On a derailleur bicycle there is no master link as on single-speed or 3-speed bikes. Use your chain tool to break apart any link. The Shimano Uniglide chain requires a special tool of its own. With your chain tool press any rivet until the chain can be separated at that point. Do not press it all the way through or you will be sorry when you must link it back together again. Let it stay in the chain link's outer plate as the inner pulls free. Your chain tool directions may specify how many turns it takes to perform this job; at any rate, practice so you know how far you can go. Press the rivet just far enough to barely hold the links together, then twist the links for final separation. If you are taking your chain off for the first time, make a drawing of how the chain laces through the jockey wheels in the rear derailleur. You'll be glad you did.

Once the chain is off the bike, soak it in a clean solution of solvent. Once available in any amount at most gas stations, solvent now is hard to find in less than five-gallon cans. You can use paint thinner, some recommend kerosene (we find it leaves a greasy film), or — only as a last resort — white gas or automobile gasoline does the job. Be careful with gas; use it outside and away from any flame (including pilot lights on gas water heaters). If you can,

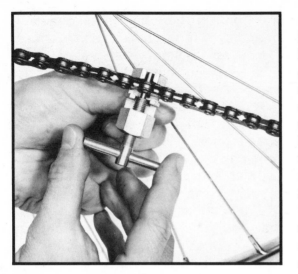

Chain tool in action with rivet almost driven out.

put the chain in a small can with a cover and shake it around. As the solvent gets black, dump out the old, clean the can, and put in some fresh. Usually one change of solvent is enough, but repeat the process if necessary until the final rinse comes out clean. New chains require a good soaking to remove grease packed into them. When the chain is completely clean, take it out and hang it to dry. Vigorous shaking speeds up this process.

As you wait for your chain to dry, clean all the components over which it passes. It doesn't do any good to put a clean chain on dirty components. With a rag pinch the encrusted grease and dirt from the sprockets on the jockey wheels, chainwheels and cogs. This takes time but is an alternative to taking each of these components off for individual soaking in solvent.

This is a good time to check the lubrication in your freewheel. Spin it. Does it sound gritty and sticky? How about the cogs? Are they reasonably clean or deeply encrusted with grease and dirt between them? If yes, you should service your freewheel as well but only if you are sure it needs it. To do this, remove it from the hub as outlined in the spoke failure section on page 242. Scrape off as much dirt as possible, then immerse it in a can of clean solvent. Use a small brush and a rag to clean between each cog. Change the solvent in the can when the worst of the dirt is off. Keep cleaning with new solvent until the entire cluster is sparkling. When it is spotless, soak it once more in clean solvent to remove any fine, inner grit from the freewheel. Spin it on your finger and listen for gritty sounds. Slosh it around in solvent until it spins smoothly without any telltale signs of grit. Remove it from the solvent for the last time, shake it and lay it down flat to dry, changing sides periodically.

When the freewheel is completely dry it can be lubricated. Any medium-weight oil will do or you can use Dri-Slide. Spin the freewheel on your finger observing where the inner portion separates from the outer on both sides. Squirt oil in that separation while turning the freewheel until it begins to run out the other side. Wipe it off and spin again. Do the same on the other side. When finished, wipe it all again and grease the threads on the freewheel and hub with ordinary bicycle grease before screwing it back onto the wheel.

The arrow shows point at which oil is inserted into freewheel (front side).

Chain properly run through jockey wheel of rear derailleur and chain tool pushing rivet back into place.

Freewheels commonly are a neglected part of the bicycle; apply oil whenever you have the wheel off or at least every 1,000 miles to insure long life. You should be able to oil the freewheel without an extensive cleaning procedure unless there is a problem with the spin (grit inside). You don't have to take the freewheel off the hub just to clean and oil it; only when it is too dirty to clean with rag and brush.

By now your chain is dry and ready to lubricate. Hold the chain by one end and slowly spray down the top side; turn it over and repeat. With a clean rag, wipe all excess spray from the side plates leaving lubricant only on the inside between the bushings, rollers and rivets.

At this point your entire drive line is free of grease and dirt. Thread the

You can lubricate chain with spray (Dri-Slide) while it's still on bike, but you need some help. One person should hold the bike and turn the crankarm slowly backward. The other should spray the chain and hold newspaper against the wheel to protect against spraying the rims.

chain back on the bike and assemble the links. Remove the chain tool when the rivet is pushed in so that an equal amount shows on each side. Check the link for flexibility; if it is stiff, hold the chain on either side of the sticky link and twist back and forth to loosen it.

With the drive line clean and free of excess oil we believe you will go many carefree miles before you need tend to it again. Periodic lubrication can be done with the chain on the bicycle. Have a friend hold the bike up while turning the crankarm slowly backward. You should insert a newspaper between the chain and the rear wheel to keep oil away from the rims. Spray a continuous stream of chain lube as the chain makes one revolution. Let it dry for a minute or two, then wipe excess oil from the outside of the chain. Make doubly sure there is no lubricant on the tire or its rim. If there is, do not wipe it with the same rag you used on the chain. The rim must be cleaned with solvent. This shouldn't be necessary if you're careful.

Part of a periodic maintenance is cleaning off the jockey wheels and brushing dirt out of the cluster with a small, stiff bristle brush used for this sole purpose. Thanks to products like Dri-Slide the days of sticky, dirty chains are over.

Derailleurs

Derailleurs seldom break down by themselves, nor are they particularly dif-ficult to adjust once properly set. Most derailleur problems are traceable to one of three situations: neglect, abuse or improper installation. We can't go into derailleur installation and adjustment here; our purpose is to keep you on the road, not in your garage. Many books adequately cover this subject if you find yourself in need of more information along this line. *Glenn's Complete Bicycle Manual* is probably the best single source.

If your derailleurs function properly to begin with, you are careful with them, and no accident befalls them on tour they should keep right on functioning well. But in the sometimes-not-so-ideal world of bicycle touring, small adjustments are occasionally needed. You should know what is necessary and how to do it. Because of the many derailleur types and designs, it is impossible to be specific. Spend some time observing your particular derailleurs. See how they function in action either with the bike on a bike stand or hanging by a rope from your garage rafters or a tree so the rear wheel is off the ground. Check them out as you read the following, then, if you still have trouble, look in one of the many repair books available.

Rear Derailleur Cable Adjustment

If the derailleur cable is too loose — if it can be pulled away from the frame a full inch or so with little pressure while the shift lever is fully forward

Rear derailleur cable adjustment: Place wrench on rear derailleur pinch bolt and pull cable tight with pliers. (The chain should be on smallest cog.)

To align rear derailleur with sprocket, adjust screw in or out until center line of the jockey wheel lines up with the center line of the smallest cog.

and the chain is on the smallest (high gear) cog — the cable tension must be adjusted. First, try screwing out the cable-adjusting barrel if your derailleur has one. If that does not correct the slack, screw the cable-adjusting barrel all the way in, loosen the nut that pinches the cable, and pull the cable tight with a pair of pliers. Pull firmly (but not too tight) then tighten the nut.

To Align Rear Derailleur with Sprockets

Put the chain on the smallest cog and largest chainwheel (high gear). Be sure to rotate the crank when shifting gears. If the derailleur is not marked with the letters H and L (high- and low-

End view of rear derailleur jockey wheels (directly under the small cog).

gear screws), look inside the derailleur mechanism to see which adjustment screw is touching or nearly touching its stop. This will be the high-gear adjustment screw. Adjust the screw (in or out) until the center line of the jockey wheels lines up with the center line of the smallest cog. It is best to align the pulleys slightly inboard (toward the spokes), then adjust the screw while turning the crank to revolve the wheel, so the chain will jump onto the smallest sprocket from the next largest.

Next, shift or put the chain on the largest cog and smallest chainwheel (low gear). Adjust the low-gear screw as before until the center line of the jockey wheels lines up with the center line of the large cog. Align the pulleys slightly

outboard (away from the spokes), then gradually adjust the screw so the chain will just jump onto the largest sprocket from the next largest as the wheel turns.

Front Derailleur Cable Adjustment

If the cable can be pulled away from the frame an inch or more with little effort while the cable is in its slack position, it must be tightened. Loosen the nut or screw that locks the cable in place. Pull the cable firmly with pliers (but not too tight); retighten the nut or screw.

To align front derailleur with chainwheels, place the wrench on front derailleur pinch bolt while pulling cable firmly with pliers.

Top view of inner side of front derailleur cage (1/16 inch from chain) with chain on smallest chainwheel.

Top view of outer side of front derailleur cage (¹/₁₆ inch from chain) with chain on largest chainwheel.

To Align Front Derailleur with Chainwheels

Place the chain on the large rear cog and the smallest chainwheel (low gear). Make sure the shifter lever is fully forward or back, whichever determines low gear on your particular derailleur. Turn the low-gear adjusting screw until the inner side of the derailleur chain guide (cage) clears the inner side of the chain by ¹/₁₆ inch and the chain does not rub when rotating the pedals.

Next, shift or put the chain on the largest chainwheel and the smallest cog (high gear). Turn the high-gear adjusting screw until the outer side of the front derailleur cage clears the outer side of the chain by ¹/₁₆ inch and the chain does not rub when rotating the pedals.

Emergency Repairs

No matter how excellent your preparation, there are going to be some emergency repairs that will tax your skills and certainly your tool kit. If you are caught without the proper tool or spare part, there are a few tricks that you might use to keep yourself on the road.

Broken Chain

With your chain tool, remove the defective link(s) and rejoin the chain. Do not use your large chainwheel and cogs until you check to see if the rear derailleur will handle the shortened chain. If not, ride in higher (smaller) gears until you can get spare links. Better yet, carry some with you.

Broken Rear Derailleur

Manually put the chain on a mid-range cog and shift only the front derailleur when needed. If the rear derailleur is totally mangled so that the jockey wheels won't take up the slack, take the chain off the rear derailleur completely, put it on a middle cog, then shorten the chain until it is tight. You now have a 1-speed to get you to a repair shop.

Broken Front Derailleur

Manually put the chain on the

263

smaller chainwheel (unless you can handle the higher gears on relatively flat terrain). You now have a 5-speed using the rear derailleur alone.

Broken Brake Cable

This repair will work only if the break occurs near the lever and you have at least three inches of cable left beyond the pinch bolt at the other end for just such an emergency. Release the pinch bolt, pull the cable partway out and lace it through the shifter or brake lever. Tie a knot or two in the end, pull the cable back and tighten the pinch bolt. Better yet, always carry a spare — the longest cable that you might need.

Broken Critical Bolts

Spare bolts for your chainwheels or derailleurs can sometimes be found in your racks or fender dropout eyelets. Bits of wire picked up along the road can be used in these less-critical connections. On long tours carry spare, hard-to-find nuts and bolts. This is especially important for bar-end shifter parts since few shops stock spares for those. In some cases, you might end up having to buy an entire shifter set for the want of a simple nut or bolt. A 35 mm film can filled with carefully thought-out spare parts is invaluable on long tours.

Damaged Tire

The best remedy is carrying tire-casing booting in your repair kit. This is a cloth, sometimes rubberized, that is glued inside the tire to cover damaged areas and to protect the tube. Booting is available at better bike stores and is well worth getting ahead of time. In a pinch, use an old inner tube or a piece of heavy truck inner tube found along the highway. Glue it in with your patch-kit glue.

Foldable spare tires give less-than-perfect results; the one we tried was murder to mount on a 27 × 1¼-inch rim and prone to popping off, disturbing to say the least. A regular spare tire is easily carried folded in a figure eight (tripled) about 11 inches in diameter. We

To protect and carry your clincher tire, fold it into a figure eight and a double circle about 11 inches in diameter.

wrap this with plastic for protection so it looks somewhat like a large donut. It can then be carried wherever convenient in baggage or tied onto the frame or fork with two extra toe straps. This has never damaged the tire and has saved us considerable grief at least once.

Ian Hibbel, the touring cyclist mentioned earlier, has been known to wrap friction tape around the whole tire and rim over the damaged area. In really harsh road conditions, he covers that with a layer of wire to protect the tape. If you must do this, do not apply the brake on the patched wheel.

Ruined Rim Strip

It might be possible to do without one for a short time but it is best to replace it with a spare or a strip of inner tubing, handlebar tape or adhesive tape from your first-aid kit. A spare rim strip doesn't take up much room in your repair kit.

o o o o o o o

When you are able to perform the adjustments and repairs to your touring bike that we have covered so far, you will be qualified to handle about 80 percent of the trouble that can come your way on the road. You are in an excellent position as a touring cyclist if you are able to keep your own machine on the road without assistance.

There are, of course, many other maintenance procedures and repairs beyond what we have covered here. Many are as easy to master as fixing a flat, others require skill, experience and special tools. If you enjoy working on your own bicycle, there is no end to the pleasure it offers you. Tinkering with your bike can overcome weatherbound depression just as waxing your skis seems to make winter hurry along. If you become competent in the basic maintenance and repair procedures in this chapter, we think you will develop the self-confidence to tackle other, more complex areas with the help of manuals on the subject. Meanwhile you can tour long miles and feel confident in your ability to take care of yourself and your bicycle. That is what this book is all about.

Chapter Fifteen
Touring Made Simple

It was slower than normal that Thursday around the shop, but Tim was glad since he had a number of customized touring bikes to build up for the spring touring season. He was working alone at our friend's bike shop and hoping that the walk-in traffic would be slow so he could concentrate on the bikes. As he tells it . . .

I was pulling off the freewheel of a fine touring bicycle to change the cogs and grease the hub when the front door opened. Oh great, I thought, looking up to see who it was. In walked a thin, older man with tough, leathery skin — the kind you get from working outdoors most of your life. It was hard to tell if he was 40 or 65. There was an ageless quality about him, maybe due to his close-cropped hair with that white-side-wall, barber-college look that went well

with his clean-shaven face. His clothes were long out of style and his well-worn dress coat looked out of place on that warm California day. But his clothes were clean and he looked like someone who had seen the good and the bad and given his best in return.

This guy must have the wrong shop, I thought, as he walked back toward the service area. Probably wants some directions, then I can get back to work. I gave the $400 touring machine a pat and said, "Hi, what can I do for you?"

"Do you have those baskets for the front of a bicycle?" he asked timidly.

Thinking it must be a gift for someone, I said, "Sure, the type that fits on the handlebars?"

"That's it," he replied. "The biggest you've got."

With the stepladder I made my way to a high shelf in the corner of the store. I pulled down several of the bigger models. He looked them over carefully and chose the stronger of the two.

"Will there be anything else?" I asked.

He thought a minute, then said, "Yes, I guess I need a pump too."

I showed him six or seven types that we had in stock explaining that only a couple really worked well, then quoted him the prices. Taking my advice he chose a Zefal hp, then asked if I would mind mounting the basket and pump on his bike. Oh no, I thought. He must be one of the retired locals who needs his bike just to get around — it's probably a wreck, he has all the time in the world and I have a hundred things to do today.

"Well, I'm kind of busy today and alone besides." His face fell but recovered with a smile right away when I added, "But I guess I can find the time if you will bring the bike around back. Of course, there is a service charge," I added. He looked like that might make a difference.

It didn't and he soon arrived at the back door. In he came with a new, heavyweight 3-speed of undistinguished lineage with two suitcases, a beat-up flight bag and a gunny sack half full of something all tied to a rather doubtful rear rack. I couldn't believe it. The entire load was tied with baling twine so I decided against unloading it to put it on the repair stand. When I tried to lift the bike I gasped in shock and surprise; no way was I going to get that thing off the ground. The bike itself must have weighed 45 pounds and the load must have been over 50 pounds.

"What on earth do you have in there?" I asked, steadying the bike with both hands.

"Just my things," he shrugged.

"Well, if I am going to work on this you'll have to unload all of this stuff."

As he set to work I returned to the custom touring bike. The new owner would be riding the California coast next month and wanted it ready by that evening so he could start serious training with packs and panniers. We had spent a lot of time talking and the owner was anxious to have the best of everything and everything just right for his trip.

When the old fellow finished unwinding the cord and unloading his gear, he stood quietly waiting for me to get back to him. I finished changing the cogs on the touring bike to a good gear range of 28/96 that would be able to handle 1,000 miles of California coastal cycling. Satisfied, I turned to the 3-speed and was able to lift it onto the repair stand. He watched as I mounted the basket and pump and seemed appreciative when I replaced the standard bolts with heavy-duty ones.

"Did you just get this bike?" I asked.

"Yes, just this morning," he said. "I

bought it at a shop about 30 miles up the coast."

"Oh? Where are you heading?" I said, trying to conceal my surprise at this turn of events.

"Home," he said as he walked out in the store area to look around some more.

He must be going to San Diego, I figured, the next town of any size down the coast. Still, it was 80 miles away and quite a jaunt for this setup. As I finished attaching the pump he put a water bottle down on the counter.

"Do you think you'll need one?" I said. "There are places to get water all the way down the coast from here."

"Oh, I'll need it in the desert for sure," he replied.

"The desert! There isn't any desert from here to San Diego," I told him.

"I'm not going to San Diego and there is plenty of desert between here and North Carolina."

"North Carolina?" I sputtered. "You plan to ride from here to North Carolina?" I didn't add "on this" but I think he caught my meaning.

"Sure, I paid almost $100 for this bike and it has three gears." His smile was disarming.

"Yes, but . . ." I couldn't think of what to say next. "Do you know what you are getting into?"

"Well, I've traveled the country quite a lot and I always thought I would like to cross it on a bicycle. So here I am with time on my hands and a long way from home and, well, it seems like a good way to get there, don't you think?" He looked at me obviously expecting a reply.

"Maybe I had better check it over for you a little," I said and quickly dodged back to the 3-speed.

"Don't bother yourself with it," he argued. "The man at the shop said it was in real good shape."

"Well, I'll just double-check everything for you," I said as I set to work adjusting the brakes and tightening assorted nuts and bolts. I added oil to the rear hub and explained the importance of putting in a couple of drops every two weeks or so. To make sure he would, I gave him a sample can of oil from the last bike show I attended.

"Guess I should have a tire patch kit and maybe a couple of those stretchy cords you've got hanging over there," he said.

I took the cords he indicated from behind a display of cross-country touring panniers. This guy really means it, I thought. He is going to try to pedal that tank 3,000 miles across the country. But then people thought Glenda and I were crazy to try it with our two kids. Who am I to judge? However, we put months of planning into that trip; this guy started preparations this morning and he was leaving today.

"What about water?" I asked. "One bottle won't be enough for the desert."

"Oh, I know. I have two plastic milk cartons there in that gunny sack. That gives me a whole gallon extra. I just liked the size of this little bottle for sipping as I go along. Besides, I will be doing a lot of my desert riding at night. Do you have bike lights?"

A bike light was added to the mounting bill.

"Well, that's about it," he said as he looked around the shop full of the latest and best in touring equipment. "Can't see anything else I need."

The bill came to almost $30. Most people spend that much on a handlebar bag alone, but it seemed pretty high to both of us. I forgot to add the labor charge. He repacked his load, carefully putting the lighter, bulky things up front in his new basket. I grabbed a couple of spare tubes off the shelf and thrust them into his hand.

"A gift," I said at his puzzled look. He asked me to write my name and address for him so he could send me a card when he got home. I wrote them on the tube box. We shook hands and he pedaled rather shakily across the parking lot, adjusting to the new load arrangement as he winced at the glare of the afternoon sun.

Several months later I found a plain postcard in the mailbox. It said, "Thanks again. I made it OK." It was postmarked North Carolina.

Appendix A:
What to Take on Tour

Day Touring
Wear:
- Shirt or cycling jersey
- Cycling shorts
- Undershorts — if riding in unlined shorts
- Shoes
- Socks
- *Handkerchief
- Riding gloves
- Helmet — name and emergency phone number written inside
- Sunglasses with attached rearview mirror
- *Comb
- *Wallet with ID and emergency phone number
- *Key for bike lock
- *Dime

On your bicycle:
- Seat bag and/or handlebar bag

*Optional on body or in handlebar pack.

Tire pump
Water bottle
Halt dog repellent (optional)

In your bag:
- Snack food
- Long pants and light jacket or warm-up suit
- Rain cape or rain jacket (optional)
- Sunscreen lotion
- Lip cream or zinc oxide
- Map
- Bike light (optional)
- Lock and cable
- Repair kit (see Appendix B)

Weekend Motel Touring
Wear:
- Same as for Day Touring

On your bicycle:
- Rear rack
- Stuff bag or small panniers
- Front handlebar bag (optional)
- Tire pump

Water bottle
Halt dog repellent (optional)

In your stuff bag, panniers or handlebar bag:

Spoon, knife, cup, can opener (if buying cold food at markets)
Snack food
Long pants and light jacket or warm-up suit
1 pair of socks
1 pair of undershorts
1 shirt
Rain cape or rain jacket
Shower shoes (optional)
Swim suit (optional)
Toothbrush, paste and case
Shampoo
Lip cream or zinc oxide
Sunscreen lotion
Map
Bike light (optional)
Lock and cable
Repair kit (see Appendix B)

Weekend Camping Touring

Wear:

Same as for Day Touring

On your bicycle:

Rear rack
Panniers
Handlebar bag and/or front panniers
Sleeping bag, stuff bag (plastic lined) and tie-down straps
Sleeping pad
Tent, poles and stakes, ground cloth, brush and bag (optional)
Tire pump
Water bottles
Halt dog repellent (optional)

In your panniers and handlebar bag:

Rain poncho or tarp, stakes, nylon cord, ground cloth
Spoon, cup, knife, can opener, matches in waterproof case
Snack food
Staple foods in bags
Garbage bags
Insect repellent
Toilet paper in plastic bag
Plastic trowel
Clothes bag
Long pants and light jacket or warm-up suit
1 pair of socks
1 pair of undershorts
1 shirt
Rain cape or rain jacket
Shower shoes (optional)
Swim suit (optional)
Toilet kit or bag
Small towel, washcloth in plastic bag
Toothbrush, paste and case
Soap in case
Detergent or biodegradable shampoo for dishes
Lip cream or zinc oxide
Sunscreen lotion
Map
Bike light — battery type
Lock and cable
Repair kit (see Appendix B)

Extended Camping Touring

All of the above plus:

Sigg cook kit with pressure stove containing: plates, pots, skillet, pot scrubber, dishcloth, plastic straw or priming eyedropper, pot

gripper, dish towel, matches (optional)
Extra stove fuel (optional)
Folding 2½-gallon water bag
Thermometer (optional)
First-aid kit
Writing supplies and stamps
Paperback book
Small notebook
Small radio (optional)

Emergency compact meal
1 long-sleeved shirt
1 pair of socks
1 pair of undershorts
Cycling shorts
2 large handkerchiefs
Dental floss with sewing needles
Fingernail clippers
Razor with extra blades (optional)

Appendix B: Bicycle Repair Tools

Day/Weekend Town or Suburban Touring

Tire patch kit — patches, 2 tubes of glue, sandpaper, valve core extractor
Tire irons
6-inch adjustable (crescent) wrench
Small screwdriver
Spoke wrench
Freewheel remover tool
2 spokes (carried on rack or frame)

Rural/Extended Tours Away from Bike Shops

All of the above plus:
8/10-millimeter wrench
9/10-millimeter wrench
Tire-pressure gauge
Allen wrenches for chainwheels, handlebar stem, seatpost, derailleurs, bar-end shifters and so on.
4-inch taper file
Chain rivet extractor
Chain lubricant
5 spokes
1 rear brake cable
1 rear derailleur cable
1 transverse cable — yoke cable (centerpull or cantilever brakes only)
3 chain links
2 brake blocks
Tire booting fabric
1 tube
Extra nuts and bolts (in 35 mm film can)
Powdered hand soap (in 35 mm film can)
Talc (in 35 mm film can)
Rag

Isolated Area and Extended Expedition-Type Touring

All of the above plus:

- Cone wrenches — proper number and size
- Crankset extractor and wrench
- Bottom bracket adjustment wrenches
- Freewheel remover tool "grabber" (Bendix wrench, 6-inch chain and Vise-Grips, or drive punch — depending on your cluster-removing philosophy)
- Oil in Dri-Slide applicator or equivalent
- Grease (35 mm film can)
- 1 additional tube
- 1 spare tire

Tools for Home Use

All of the above plus:

- Bike repair stand
- Third hand brake tool
- 12-inch adjustable wrench
- 12-16 ounce ball peen hammer
- Pliers (use bike shop's cable cutters)
- $3/16$-inch solid line punch
- Wooden punch (dowel)
- Medium-size screwdriver
- Medium-size Phillips head screwdriver
- Tweezer (for handling ball bearings)
- Large can chain-lubricant aerosol
- Bike grease
- Cleaning solvent and can

Appendix C:
Equipment Sources

Bicycle Equipment Suppliers (Mail Order)

Bikecology Bike Shops (catalog $1)
2910 Nebraska Avenue
PO Box 1880
Santa Monica, CA 90406

Bike Warehouse (catalog 50¢)
215 Main Street
Middletown, OH 44442

Cycle Goods Corporation (catalog $4)
2735 Hennepin Avenue South
Minneapolis, MN 55408

Metropolitan New York Council
   American Youth Hostels, Inc.
132 Spring Street
New York, NY 10012

Palo Alto Bicycles
171 University Avenue
PO Box 1276
Palo Alto, CA 94302

Recreational Equipment, Inc. (R.E.I.)
PO Box C-88125
Seattle, WA 98140

The Third Hand (tools)
1259 Siskiyou Boulevard
Ashland, OR 97520

Touring Cyclist Shop
PO Box 4009
Boulder, CO 80306

Pack and Pannier Manufacturers

Cannondale
35 Pulaski Street
Stamford, CT 06902

275

Eclipse
261 Jackson Plaza
PO Box 372
Ann Arbor, MI 48103

Frostline Kits
Frostline Circle
Denver, CO 80241

Kangaroo Baggs
306 East Cota Street
Santa Barbara, CA 93101

Kirtland/Tourpak
PO Box 4059
Boulder, CO 80306

Outdoor Equipment Suppliers (Mail Order)

Eastern Mountain Sports, Inc. (EMS)
Vose Farm Road
Peterborough, NH 03458

Herters, Inc.
Rural Route 1
Waseca, MN 55428

Holubar Mountaineering
1975 30th Street
PO Box 7
Boulder, CO 80302

L.L. Bean, Inc.
Freeport, ME 04033

Moor and Mountain
63 Park Street
Andover, MA 01850

Recreational Equipment, Inc. (R.E.I.)
PO Box C-88125
Seattle, WA 98140

Sierra Designs
4th and Addison Streets
Berkeley, CA 94710

The Ski Hut
1615 University Avenue
Berkeley, CA 94704

Appendix D:
Organized Bike Tours

Name and Address	Destination*	Length of Trip	Experience†	Avg. Range‡	Accommoda-tions	Ages	Sag Wagon	Bike Rental
American Youth Hostels, Inc. National Campus Delaplane, VA 22025	19 U.S.; 12 Europe	2-6 weeks	N, I, A	10-60	youth hostels; camping	all	no	no
Bicycle Tours Northwest 6850 48th NE Seattle, WA 98115	NW Washington; Puget Sound	weekends; 5 days	N, I, A	20-30	country inns	all§	yes	yes
Bikecentennial PO Box 8308 Missoula, MT 59807	8 U.S.; 1 coast-to-coast	12-90 days	I, A	40-50	camping	all	no	no
Bike Dream Tours, Inc. PO Box 20653 Houston, TX 77025	Texas; Colorado; New York; Bavaria; Austria	1 week; 3 weeks	N, I, A	40-60	family motels	all§	yes	no
Bike Tour France PO Box 32815 Charlotte, NC 28232	NW France; W Europe	3 weeks; 43 days	I	15-60	hotels	all	no	yes
Bike Vermont PO Box 75 Grafton, VT 05146	SW Vermont	weekends; 4-5 days	N, I, A	25-40	country inns	all	no	yes

* N-North; S-South; E-East; W-West; NW-Northwest; SW-Southwest; SE-Southeast; NE-Northeast.
† N-Novice; I-Intermediate; A-Advanced.
‡ Calculated in miles per day.
§ Ages under 18 accompanied by adult.

Appendix D

Name and Address	Destination*	Length of Trip	Experi-ence†	Avg. Range‡	Accommoda-tions	Ages	Sag Wagon	Bike Rental
Biking Expedition, Inc. Hall Ave. Henniker, NH 03242	U.S.; Canada; Europe	21-42 days	N, I, A	25-45	camping; hostels	13-17	no	yes
Britain Cycling Suite 95 1050 2nd Ave. New York, NY 10022	England; Scotland	3½ weeks	N, I	25-45	"bread and breakfast" houses; youth hostels	all	no	no
California Bicycle Tours 361 28th St. San Francisco, CA 94131	California: Russian River, Sierras, Glen Ellen, Wine Country, Monterey	weekend—5 days	N, I, A	25-60	country inns, hotels, lodges	all§	yes	yes
The Churchill House Inn RFD 3 Route 73E Brandon, VT 05733	Vermont	3 days—1 week	I, A	30	country inns	all	no	yes
Country Bicycle Center 144 Bedford Rd. Armonk, NY 10504	Israel	16 days	I, A	50-60	hotels	all	yes	no
Country Cycling Tours 410 W. 24th St. New York, NY 10011	Massachusetts Berkshires; S Vermont; Long Island; New Jersey	1 day—1 week	N, I	15-30	country inns	all	yes	yes
Euro-Bike Tours, Inc. 1805 Margaret Lane DeKalb, IL 60115	NW France; Germany, Switzerland; France; England	2 weeks, 3 weeks	N, I, A	35-40	hotels	all§	yes	yes
Gerhard's Bicycle Odysseys 1023 SW Yamhill Portland, OR 97205	Ireland; Amsterdam; Munich; Heidelberg; Salzberg	2 weeks	I	35-40	hotels	all§	yes	yes
Greenwood Travel Center 5650 S. Syracuse Circle Englewood, CO 80110	New Zealand	2 weeks	N, I, A	50	hotels	all	yes	no
The Infinite Odyssey 14 Union Park St. Boston, MA 02118	Coastal Maine; Nova Scotia	12 days; 5 weeks	N, I, A	30-50	camping	all	no	no
Keep Listening Wilderness Trips for Women PO Box 446 Sandy, OR 97055	Canadian gulf islands	1 week	N, I	15-40	camping	women	no	no

278

Organized Bike Tours

Name and Address	Destination*	Length of Trip	Experience†	Avg. Range‡	Accommodations	Ages	Sag Wagon	Bike Rental
Madawaska Valley Bicycle Touring 2 Tuna Court Don Mills, ON M3A 3L1, Canada	S Ontario	daily	N, I, A	30-80	camping; lodges; hostel-style chalet	all§	no	no
Michigan Bicycle Touring 511 Second St. Jackson, MI 49203	N Michigan; Mackinas Island	weekends	N, I, A	10-60	lodges; inns	all§	yes	yes
New England Bicycle Tours PO Box 226 Granby, CT 06035	Rhode Island; Massachusetts; Connecticut	1 day— 1 week	N, I, A	10-60	inns; motels	all§	yes	yes
Outdoor Program Room 23, EMU University of Oregon Eugene, OR 97403	New Zealand	open	A	50	camping	all	no	no
Out-Spokin' PO Box 370 Elkhart, IN 46515	U.S.; coast-to-coast; Canada; Europe	2 days— 2 months	N, I, A	15-80	camping	all	yes	yes
Overland Rolls PO Box 4134 Station A Portland, ME 04101	Maine coastal islands, inland regions	weekends; 1 week	N, I, A	25	country inns	all§	no	yes
Pacific Adventures PO Box 5041 Riverside, CA 92517	California; Hawaii	2 days— 2 weeks	N, I	25-60	camping; hotels	all	no	no
Pacific Sports Products Bicycle Tour Hawaii 110 Aloe St. Hilo, HA 96720	Island of Hawaii	2 weeks	I, A	35	camping; cabins; hotels	all	yes	yes
Rock and Rill Rfd 1 Chester, VT 05143	West Germany	2 weeks	I	35	country inns	adults	yes	no
Rocky Mountain Cycle Tours Box 895 Banff, AL T0L 0C0, Canada	Banff National Park, Alberta; British Columbia	5 days; 1 week	N, A	25-50	lodge; camp	all	yes	yes
Scenic Cycling PO Box 15461A Philadelphia, PA 19149	Pennsylvania: Millersville, Allentown	weekends	I, A	25	college dormitories	all§	no	no

Name and Address	Destination*	Length of Trip	Experi-ence†	Avg. Range‡	Accommoda-tions	Ages	Sag Wagon	Bike Rental
Sierra Club 530 Bush St. San Francisco, CA 94108	Maui, Kauai, Hawaii; SE Minnesota; W Wisconsin; Bay of Fundy area	weekend—28 days	I, A	30-55	camping	all§	no	no
Spaceport Bicycle Tours Bill Billingsley PO Box 357 Rockledge, FL 32955	Florida: Disney World, Sea World, Space Center, Merritt Island	3½ days	N, I	0-30	motels; townhouses	all§	yes	yes
Student Hosteling Program of New England Maple Hill Rochester, VT 05767	NE U.S.; NW U.S.; Canadian Rockies; Europe	2-6 weeks	I	25-40	camping; hostels	13-17	no	yes, some trips
Suwannee River Cycle Tours PO Box 319 White Springs, FL 32096	Florida: Central highlands—Gulf of Mexico	weekends; 1 week	N, I, A	25-65	private homes; older hotels; camping options	all	yes	yes
Tamure Study Groups 14613 E. Whittier Blvd. Whittier, CA 90605	Europe	4 weeks	N, I	20-80	hotels	all	yes	no
Vermont Bicycle Touring RD 2 Bristol, VT 05443	Vermont	weekends—28 days	N, I, A	10-75	country inns	all	yes	yes
Wandering Wheels Taylor University Upland, IN 46989	U.S.: E-W Coast; England; Smoky Moutains	6 days—4 months	A	80-120	camping	16-21	yes	yes
Woodswomen 3716 Fourth Ave. Minneapolis, MN 50409	SE Minnesota; W Wisconsin	weekends—10 days	N, I, A	30-70	camping	all (women)	no	yes

Chart Explanation

Destination: Flights to Europe will originate from international airport nearest to the agency sponsoring the tour.

Length of Trip: A hyphen between two digits means there are a number of tours offered of varying lengths. A semicolon between two digits means there are only two different lengths of time for tours.

Experience: Novice — Good physical condition. Occasional biker who cycles once or twice a month. Terrain will be moderate; flat to rolling hills. Intermediate — Very good physical condition. Accustomed to cycling once a week for up to two hours. Terrain may vary from moderate to strenuous. If average range of miles per day is low on chart, then no doubt there will be some hills to climb. Advanced — Excellent physical condition. A regular biker who has experience riding long distances on all terrains. Usually for the rugged biker who is looking for a challenge. Terrain will either be mountainous or distance will be lengthy, or both.

Average Range Mileage/Day: Usually flexible. In almost every case the tours are leisurely and you can go at your own pace. When the range is broad like 10 to 60 miles, it means there are a number of tours offered to accommodate different levels of experience.

Accommodations: If it reads lodge and camp it could mean both are used on one trip; or you have your choice; or separate trips with separate accommodations.

Ages: All generally means 18 years through adult. Adult means 20 years or older. Some require those under 18 to be accompanied by adult. Some tours include all ages but are popular with students or the middle-aged.

Sag Wagon: Yes means at the very least your baggage will be carried. Sometimes it will mean spare parts, tools and food on board. On some tours the sag wagon will transport you and your bike from town to town and provide a ride for the weary. No may mean sag wagon is not necessary as route makes a circular loop. Or it could mean that you carry all your gear on your bike.

Bike Rental: It's best to take your own bicycle because you are familiar with its operation. However, if you decide to rent, you will most likely get a good 10-speed with a reputable brand name.

Appendix E:
Information Sources

Magazines

Bicycling
(9 issues per year — $10)
33 East Minor Street
Emmaus, PA 18049

Cycletouring
(6 issues per year — $5.50)
69 Meadrow
Godalming, Surrey, GU7 3HS United
  Kingdom

*League of American Wheelmen
  Bulletin*
(12 issues per year)
members only (see below)

Organizations

American Youth Hostels
National Campus
Delaplane, VA 22025

Bikecentennial
PO Box 8308
Missoula, MT 59807
(responsible for Trans-America bike
  trail and others — good source of
  touring information)

Canadian Cycling Association
333 River Road
Vanier, ON K1L 8B9

League of American Wheelmen —
  National Headquarters
PO Box 988
Baltimore, MD 21203
(oldest and largest U.S. cycling
  organization)

Touring Cyclists' Directory
John Mosley
13623 Sylvan
Van Nuys, CA 91401
(List of people willing to provide

cyclists with sleeping or camping space. Must join list to get a copy. Send S.A.S.E. Small contribution appreciated for postage and printing costs.)

Touring Exchange
11150 Sun Valley Drive
Oakland, CA 94605
(a variety of tours submitted by cyclists and available at modest cost)

Glossary

adjusting screws—see alignment screws

alignment screws (adjustment or adjusting screws)—spring-loaded screws that are threaded into the rear drop-outs and control the position of the rear axle.

allen wrench—a six-sided, usually L-shaped wrench that fits the recessed head of allen bolts for tightening and removal.

alpine gearing—gear ratios designed for mountainous touring with lows in the mid-20s to low 30s.

ankling—keeping constant pressure on each pedal throughout the entire 360-degree rotation using a maximum number of muscles in the legs, ankles and feet.

Ashtabula—a brand name of the one-piece crankset.

bar-end shifters—see fingertip shifters

b.b.—see bottom bracket

bead—a steel, nylon or fiberglass wire on the bottom edge of wired-on (clincher) tires that seats in the rim to hold the tire in place.

bottom bracket (b.b.)—the cylinder on bike frames that accommodates the crankset parts. Usually used in reference to the frame cylinder and the axle, fixed cup, adjusting cup, lock-ring and ball bearings.

brake block—the rubber portion of the brake that is pressed against the rim on caliper brakes. Sometimes used to designate the combined brake pad and brake shoe.

brake block holder—see brake shoe

brake boss—a braze-on fitting attached to the fork and seatstay used for holding cantilever brakes.

brake bridge—a short tube between the seatstays to which the rear brake is attached.

brake hanger—a metal bracket that

hangs down from the top of the headset and seatpost binder bolt to hold the brake casing on centerpull and cantilever brakes.

brake pad—the rubber portion of the brake that is pressed against the rim on caliper brakes.

brake quick-release—a mechanism located on the brake lever, brake or brake hanger that allows slack in the brake cable temporarily so the wheel can be removed without the tire binding on the brake pads.

brake shoe (brake block holder)—the metal portion of the brake that holds the brake pad in place.

butted spokes—spokes thicker at one or both ends.

butted tubing—frame tubes thicker at one or both ends although the outside diameter is uniform. Double-butted tubing is thicker on both ends and is usually found only on top and down tubes of better bicycle frames.

cable guides—clamped or brazed fittings on the frame to hold the casing and guide the cables for brakes and derailleurs.

cadence—the rate at which the pedals are turned when riding. Expressed in revolutions per minute (rpm).

cage—the part of the derailleurs through which the chain passes.

caliper brakes—rim brakes with opposing arm construction.

cantilever brakes—rim brakes that mount directly on the fork and seatstays (braze-on boss) and pivot independently but in unison via a transverse (yoke) cable.

casing—the outer covering (housing) through which cables pass. Also the outer covering of the tires.

chainring (chainwheel)—the toothed wheel (sprocket) attached to the crankarm over which the chain passes.

chain rivet—the pin in a chain that holds the link together.

chain rivet extractor—see chain tool

chainstays—two tubes extending from the bottom bracket in the frame to the rear dropouts.

chain tool (chain rivet extractor)—tool used to press the chain rivet out so a chain can be taken apart.

chainwheel—see chainring

cleats—metal, leather or plastic plates attached to the soles of cycling shoes to hold the shoes on the pedals.

clincher tires—an old-style tire. The term is incorrectly but commonly used now to mean wired-on tires.

cluster—the group of cogs arranged together on the freewheel.

cog—the toothed wheel (sprocket) that attaches to the rear wheel and over which the chain passes.

cone wrench—a thin, open-end wrench used to adjust the bearings on hubs.

cottered cranks—a crankset that uses cotter pins to hold the crankarms on the axle.

cotterless cranks—a crankset with a bolt in the end of the axle to hold the crankarms on.

cotter pin—a wedge-shaped pin with a nut on one end to hold the crankarms on the axle of cottered cranks.

crank—see crankarm

crankarm (crank)—the part of the crankset that holds the pedals and attaches to the axle.

crank axle—the axle that passes through the bottom bracket and holds the crankarms.

crank bolt—the bolt that holds the crankarms on the axle in cotterless cranks.

crank extractor (crank tool)—a tool for removing crankarms from the axle in cotterless cranksets.

cross—the number of times a spoke crosses any other spoke on the journey from the hub flange to the rim.

crown—the lug where the fork blades and steering tube are attached at the top of the fork.

cyclometer (odometer)—a gauge used for measuring distance.

derailleur—a device that moves the chain from one chainwheel or cog to another.

dish—the offsetting of the hub on the rear wheel to make room for the freewheel yet allow the tire to run centered in the frame.

down tube—frame member extending from the head tube to the bottom bracket.

dropouts—the slots on the rear wheel axle where the seatstays and chainstays meet. Also commonly used to refer to where the front wheel axle fits into the ends of the fork blades.

dust cap—a screw cap that covers the end of the pedal and cotterless crank axles.

fingertip shifters (bar-end shifters)—

gear-shift levers located at the ends of the handlebars.

flange—that portion of the wheel hub extending away from the axle with holes for the spoke heads.

fork—the part of the frame that holds the front wheel.

fork blades—the two curved tubes attached to the fork crown that hold the front wheel axle.

fork ends (dropouts)—slots on the fork blades that hold the front axle.

fork rake—the amount of bend put into the fork blades during the frame-building process.

fork stem—see steerer tube

freewheel—a mechanism in the rear wheel that lets the wheel travel at a different rate from the chain speed. With the cogs it is called a cluster.

gooseneck—the component that fits into the steering tube and holds the handlebars in place.

gorp—a high-carbohydrate snack food made from nuts, sunflower seeds, raisins, and so on.

handlebar stem—see gooseneck

head—the flat, hooked end of a spoke.

headset—the bearing mechanism that holds the front fork (steering tube) onto the rest of the bicycle frame at the top and bottom of the head tube.

head tube—the frame member to which the top and down tube are attached and through which the steering tube passes.

hub—that portion of the wheel to which the spokes are attached and through which the axle runs.

idler wheels (jockey wheels)—the two small wheels in the rear derailleur over which the chain passes.

jockey wheels—see idler wheels

loft—the height of a sleeping bag when closed and fully fluffed on a flat surface as measured from the surface itself to the top of the bag.

lug—a metal sleeve into which the frame tubes fit at the joints.

master link—a removable link on a chain used on nonderailleur bicycles.

microadjust seatpost—a mechanism that allows the tilt of a saddle to be controlled to a minute degree. Most are attached directly to the seatpost.

miniclips—abbreviated toe clips without toe straps.

mixte frame—a frame with the top tube replaced by two parallel tubes extending from the top of the head tube to the rear dropouts.

odometer—see cyclometer

panniers (saddlebags)—bags for carrying gear that attach to a rack and hang down beside the front or rear wheels.

pedal wrench—a long, thin wrench used to attach and remove pedals from the crankarms.

quick-release—a lever-and-cam mechanism attached to a solid rod (skewer) that passes through a hollow axle on the wheel hub and holds the wheel in the dropouts. Operated by hand, it allows removal of the wheel without using a tool.

randonneur handlebars—drop-style handlebars that do not bend down as far as most and rise up with a bend slightly forward across the top.

rear triangle—the triangle shaped by the seat tube, chainstays and seatstays at the rear of a frame.

rim strip—rubber, plastic or cloth strip around the inside of a clincher rim to protect the inner tube from the nipples and spoke ends.

saddlebags—see panniers

safety levers—a second set of brake levers parallel to the flat, top portion of the handlebars.

sag wagon—a vehicle that accompanies cyclists to carry gear, troubleshoot and perhaps provide mechanical assistance.

seat bolt (seatpost binder bolt)—the bolt at the top of the seat tube that holds the seatpost in place.

seatpost binder bolt—see seat bolt

seatstays—the frame tubes extending from the junction of the top and seat tubes to the rear dropouts.

seat tube—the frame tube extending from the top tube to the bottom bracket under the seat in front of the rear wheel.

sew-up tires (tubular tires)—a tire with a completely enclosed inner tube held onto its rim by glue or double-faced tape.

spindle—see crank axle

spinning—pedaling at a high rpm in a low gear.

sprockets—the teeth on a wheel that engage the chain. Used also to refer to cogs or chainwheels.

steerer tube (fork stem)—the tube extending from the fork crown through the head tube into which the handlebar stem fits.

straight-gauge tubing—frame tubes that have uniformly thick walls throughout.

stuff bag—a bag with drawstring closure used for compact storage of a sleeping bag. Usually made of waterproof nylon.

tandem—a bicycle built to be pedaled by two or more riders, one behind another.

third hand—a brake tool used to compress the brakes against the rims to allow for easy adjustment.

tire booting—cloth or rubberized fabric used to repair a damaged tire by gluing it inside the casing.

tire iron—a set of leverlike tools used to remove clincher tires from their rims.

toe clips—thin, flexible metal strips that attach to the front of a pedal and bend around the toe and over the top of the foot.

toe straps—leather straps that pass through the cage of the pedal, extend around the middle of the foot and pass through the end of the toe clip. Used together with the toe clip, they allow the cyclist to pull up on the pedals during ankling.

top tube—the frame tube that stretches from the top of the seat tube to the top of the head tube.

transverse cable—see yoke cable

tubular tires—see sew-up tires

valve core—the inner, removable portion of the valve stem on Schrader valves.

valve stem—that portion of a tube through which air is pumped.

windchill—the cooling of the body that takes place when wind passes over its surface. Especially effective when the body or clothing is wet.

wired-on tires—see clincher tires

yoke cable (transverse cable)—the cable that attaches the two brake arms (yokes) together on centerpull brakes.

Bibliography

Ballantine, Richard. *Richard's Bicycle Book.* 2d ed. New York: Ballantine Books, 1978.

Beinhorn, George, ed. *Food for Fitness.* Mountain View, Calif.: World Publications, 1975.

Bike World magazine editors. *International Bicycle Touring.* Mountain View, Calif.: World Publications, 1976.

————. *Traveling by Bike.* Mountain View, Calif.: World Publications, 1974.

Bridge, Raymond. *The Bicycle Camping Book.* Harrisburg, Pa.: Stackpole Books, 1974.

Coles, Clarence W., and Glenn, Harold T. *Glenn's Complete Bicycle Manual.* New York: Crown Publishers, 1973.

Cooper, Kenneth. *Aerobics.* New York: Bantam, 1972.

Cuthbertson, Tom. *Bike Tripping.* Berkeley, Calif.: Ten Speed Press, 1972.

DeLong, Fred. *DeLong's Guide to Bicycles & Bicycling.* Radnor, Pa.: Chilton Book Co., 1978.

Fletcher, Colin. *The New Complete Walker.* New York: Alfred A. Knopf, 1977.

Food and Nutrition Board. *Recommended Dietary Allowances.* 8th rev. ed. Washington, D.C.: National Academy of Sciences, 1974.

Gilbert, Kathie and Galen, and Heilman, Gail, eds. *Bikelopedia.* San Rafael,

Calif.: Capital Management Publications, 1976.

Greenhood, David. *Mapping.* rev. ed. Chicago: Univ. of Chicago Press, 1964.

Hawkins, Karen and Gary. *Bicycle Touring in Europe.* New York: Pantheon Books, 1973.

Kossak, Joe. *Bicycle Frames.* Mountain View, Calif.: World Publications, 1975.

McCullagh, James C. *Pedal Power in Work, Leisure and Transportation.* Emmaus, Pa.: Rodale Press, 1977.

————. *Ways to Play.* Emmaus, Pa.: Rodale, 1978.

Murphy, Dervla. *Full Tilt: Ireland to India with a Bicycle.* London: J. Murray, 1975.

National Atlas of the United States. Washington, D.C.: U.S. Dept. of Interior, Geological Survey, 1970.

Rodale, J. I. *The Complete Book of Food and Nutrition.* Rodale, 1961.

Select Committee on Nutrition and Human Needs, United States Senate. *Dietary Goals for the United States.* 2d ed. Washington, D.C.: U.S. Government Printing Office, 1977.

Shaw, Reginald C. *Teach Yourself Cycling.* London: The English Universities Press, Ltd., 1953.

Sloane, Eugene A. *The New Complete Book of Bicycling.* New York: Simon & Schuster, 1974.

United States National Oceanic and Atmospheric Administration. *Climates of the States.* Port Washington, N.Y.: 1974.

Wilhelm, Tim and Glenda. "Four Across America" series. "The Desert" (April 1976); "Rocky Mountain High" (August 1976); "A Change in the Wind" (July 1977); "Catch a Falling Leaf" (October 1977); "Afterwards" (May 1978). *Bicycling* magazine.

Index

C

Z